SOLUTIONS TO SELECTED EXERCISES IN

THE LOGIC BOOK

Third Edition

MERRIE BERGMANN *Smith College*

JAMES MOOR *Dartmouth College*

JACK NELSON *Temple University*

The McGraw-Hill Companies, Inc.
New York St. Louis San Francisco Auckland Bogotá Caracas Lisbon London Madrid Mexico City Milan Montreal New Delhi San Juan Singapore Sydney Tokyo Toronto

McGraw-Hill

*A Division of The **McGraw-Hill** Companies*

Solutions to Selected Exercises in The Logic Book

This book is printed on acid-free paper.

5 6 7 8 9 0 FGR FGR 9 0

P/N 006060-6

PART OF

ISBN 0-07-913083-6

This book was set in Baskerville by York Graphic Services, Inc.
The editors were Sarah Moyers and Jack Maisel;
The production supervisor was Elizabeth J. Strange.
The cover was designed by Carla Bauer.
Project supervision was done by The Total Book.
Quebecor Printing/Fairfield was printer and binder.
Cover Photo: Jaco BAR-Portrait of *Luca Pacioli and an Unknown Man,* Capodimonte Museum, Naples.
Photo SCALA/EPA, Inc.

http://www.mhcollege.com

CONTENTS

SOLUTIONS TO CHAPTER 1 1

SOLUTIONS TO CHAPTER 2 6

SOLUTIONS TO CHAPTER 3 15

SOLUTIONS TO CHAPTER 4 34

SOLUTIONS TO CHAPTER 5 69

SOLUTIONS TO CHAPTER 6 109

SOLUTIONS TO CHAPTER 7 121

SOLUTIONS TO CHAPTER 8 130

SOLUTIONS TO CHAPTER 9 156

SOLUTIONS TO CHAPTER 10 201

SOLUTIONS TO CHAPTER 11 240

SOLUTIONS TO SELECTED EXERCISES

CHAPTER ONE

Section 1.3E

1.a. This sentence does have a truth-value and does fall within the scope of this text. (It is true as long as we mean by 'the United States' the political unit established by the Constitution. The Articles of Confederation, which predate the Constitution, established a loose union of states whose first president was John Hanson.)

c. This is a request or command; as such it is neither true nor false and therefore does not fall within the scope of this text.

e. This sentence does have a truth-value (it is true) and does fall within the scope of this text.

g. This is a salutation or expression of good wishes; as such it is neither true nor false and therefore does not fall within the scope of this text.

i. This is an instruction or bit of advice; it is neither true nor false and therefore does not fall within the scope of this text.

2.a. Sarah, John, Rita, and Bob have all worked hard and all deserve promotion.

The company is having a cash flow problem and is offering those over 55 a $50,000 bonus if they retire at the end of this year.

Sarah, John, and Bob are all over 55 and will take early retirement.

Rita will be promoted.

c. I didn't die yesterday.

I didn't die the day before yesterday.

I didn't die the day before the day before yesterday.

I didn't die any day in the past fifty some years.

I am not going to die today.

e. The given passage can be read as expressing the following argument:

The perceived need for the military security offered by the Soviet Union disappeared with the end of the cold war.

Over 70 years of union produced few economic benefits.

The Soviet Union never successfully addressed the problem how to inspire loyalty to a single state by peoples with vastly different cultures and history.

The Soviet Union disintegrated.

Many historians hold that explanations of historical events, which the given passage purports to be, are not best classified as arguments. Rather, they are accounts of events or factors that make the event to be explained understandable. On this view the given passage is a purported explanation and not an argument.

g. This passage is probably not an argument. Rather it is the recitation of a fanciful series of events. The 'So' of the last sentence has the force of 'And then' or 'After giving up their efforts to reassemble Humpty Dumpty. . . .'

Section 1.4E

1.a. False. Many valid arguments have one or more false premises. Here is an example with two false premises:

All Doberman pinschers are friendly creatures.

All friendly creatures are dogs.

All Doberman pinschers are dogs.

c. True. By definition, a sound argument is a valid argument with true premises.

e. False. A valid argument all of whose premises are true cannot have a false conclusion. But if a valid argument has at least one false premise, it may well have a false conclusion. Here is an example:

Reptiles are mammals.

If reptiles are mammals, then reptiles are warm-blooded.

Reptiles are warm-blooded.

g. False. An argument may have true premises and a true conclusion and not be valid. Here is an example:

Chicago is in Illinois.

Madrid is in Spain.

i. False. A sound argument is, by definition, a valid argument with true premises, and, therefore, a true conclusion.

2.a. If collies are mammals, then collies are warm-blooded.

Collies are mammals.

Collies are warm-blooded.

c. If collies are warm-blooded, then collies are reptiles.

Collies are warm-blooded.

Collies are reptiles.

e. Temple University is in Pennsylvania.

Smith College is in Massachusetts.

Dartmouth College is in New Hampshire.

UCLA is in Utah.

Section 1.5E

1.a. This passage about Sarah, John, Rita, and Bob is best construed as an inductive argument. The plausibility of the conclusion rests on the assumptions, not stated, that those who take early retirement will not be promoted, and that if all four of the named individuals deserve promotion at least one will be promoted. Unless these assumptions are made explicit (the first is reasonable, the second less clearly so), the argument is inductively weak.

c. This old argument is best construed as an inductive argument. It is a reasonably strong argument, but it is also possible that the conclusion is false. And we know that one day the conclusion will be false.

e. This passage is best construed as a purported explanation of why the Soviet Union disintegrated. If one accepts the view that such explanations are arguments, it is best to construe this passage as an inductive argument (it is clearly invalid when construed as a deductive argument). How strong the argument is we leave to historians and political scientists to decide.

g. As noted in the answers to the exercises in Section 1.3E, this passage is probably best construed not as an argument but as the recitation of a fanciful series of events. The 'So' of the last sentence has the force of 'And then' or 'After giving up their efforts to reassemble Humpty Dumpty. . . .' Construed as an argument it is deductively invalid and inductively weak.

Section 1.6E

1.a. {Kansas City is in Missouri, St. Paul is in Minnesota, San Francisco is in California}

c. {Kansas City is in Ohio, St. Paul is in Wisconsin, San Francisco is in Oregon}

2.a. This set is consistent though the first member of the set is false. Both members would be true if, as is possible, the United States moved its capital from Washington to New York.

c. This set is inconsistent. If it is true that Iraq has been a dictatorship since 1979 and true that the United States supported Iraq in the 1980s, then the United States does support dictatorships, which contradicts 'The United States does not support dictatorships.'

e. This set is inconsistent. If all the land in Gaylord is owned by Jones and his relatives, Smith cannot both own land in Gaylord and not be a relative of Smith.

3.a. 'Che sara, sara' is a logically true sentence (of French). It means 'Whatever will be, will be.' This sentence, taken literally, is logically true. (Were it not, there would have to be something that will be and will not be, an impossibility.)

c. 'Eisenhower preceded Kennedy as President' is true and is logically indeterminate. It is true because of facts about the American political system and how the voters voted in 1956 and 1960, not because of any principles of logic.

4.a. Logically indeterminate. 'Passing the bar exam' does not involve, as a matter of logic, having gone to law school. Lincoln passed the bar examination but never went to law school.

c. Logically indeterminate though presumably false. If Bob is in the London we generally think of when the word 'London' is used, he is in England, not in Alabama. But what keeps him from being in both that London and Alabama are facts of geography, not principles of logic. It is a truth of geography, not of logic, that Alabama and England are nonoverlapping areas of the globe.

e. Logically false. If Bob knows everyone in the class and Robin is in the class, it follows that he knows Robin, so if the first part of this claim is true, the last part, which claims Bob doesn't know Robin, must be false.

g. Logically true. Since ocean fish are a kind of fish, it follows from 'Sarah likes all kinds of fish' that she likes ocean fish.

i. Logically true. Although we don't always realize it, the claim that someone loves everyone encompasses the claim that that person loves herself or himself.

Section 1.7E

1.a. True. If a member of a set of sentences is logically false, then that member cannot be true, and hence it cannot be that all the members are true. So the set is logically inconsistent.

c. True. Sentences that are logically equivalent cannot have different truth-values. So if all the premises of an argument are true and one of those premises is equivalent to the conclusion, then the conclusion must also be true. Hence, that argument cannot have true premises and a false conclusion. It is, therefore, deductively valid.

e. True. 'Whatever will be, will be' is logically true. Therefore, any argument that has it as a conclusion cannot have a false conclusion and, hence, cannot have true premises and a false conclusion. Any such argument is, therefore, deductively valid.

g. False. Such arguments are invalid unless the conclusion is logically true.

2.a. No. Such a person obviously has at least one false belief, but her or his mistake is about the facts of geography and/or of the political organization of the United States.

c. Normally logic cannot tell us whether a sentence is true or false. For most of the sentences we normally deal with, truth is a matter of how things are with the world. And, to determine whether or not a valid argument is sound, we do need to determine whether the premises are true. However, in one case logic can tell us that an argument is sound. This is where the argument is valid and all the premises are logical truths.

e. If an argument has a logical falsehood as one of its premises, it is impossible for that premise to be true. If one premise cannot be true, then surely it cannot be that all the premises are true, and it cannot be that all the premises are true and the conclusion false. So the argument must be deductively valid.

g. If an argument has a logical truth for its conclusion, it is impossible for that conclusion to be false. And if the conclusion cannot be false, then it obviously cannot be that the premises are true and the conclusion false. Hence such an argument is deductively valid, no matter what its premises are. But it will be sound only if those premises are true. So some such arguments are sound (those with true premises) and some are unsound (those with at least one false premise).

i. Yes. If the set with a million sentences is consistent, then it is possible for all those sentences to be true. Now consider a set each of whose members is equivalent to at least one member of that first set. Sentences that are equivalent have the same truth-value. Therefore, if all the million members of the first set are true, all the sentences of the second set, each of which is equivalent to a member of the first set, will also be true. Therefore, the second set is also consistent.

Section 2.1E

1a. Both Bob jogs regularly and Carol jogs regularly.

B & C

c. Either Bob jogs regularly or Carol jogs regularly.

B ∨ C

e. It is not the case that either Bob jogs regularly or Carol jogs regularly.

~ (B ∨ C)

[or]

Both it is not the case that Bob jogs regularly and it is not the case that Carol jogs regularly.

~ B & ~ C

g. If it is not the case that Carol jogs regularly then it is not the case that Bob jogs regularly.

~ C ⊃ ~ B

i. Both (either Bob jogs regularly or Albert jogs regularly) and it is not the case that (both Bob jogs regularly and Albert jogs regularly).

(B ∨ A) & ~ (B & A)

k. Both it is not the case that (either Carol jogs regularly or Bob jogs regularly) and it is not the case that Albert jogs regularly.

~ (C ∨ B) & ~ A

m. Either Albert jogs regularly or it is not the case that Albert jogs regularly.

A ∨ ~ A

2a. Albert jogs regularly and so does Bob.
c. Either Albert or Carol jogs regularly.
e. Neither Albert nor Carol jogs regularly.
g. Bob jogs regularly and so does either Albert or Carol.
i. Albert, Carol, and Bob jog regularly.
k. Either Bob or Carol jogs regularly, or neither of them jogs regularly.

3. c and k are true; and a, e, g, and i are false.

4. Paraphrases

a. It is not the case that all joggers are marathon runners.
c. It is not the case that some marathon runners are lazy.
e. It is not the case that somebody is perfect.

Symbolizations

a. Using 'A' for 'All joggers are marathon runners':

$\sim A$

c. Using 'L' for 'Some marathon runners are lazy':

$\sim L$

e. Using 'P' for 'Somebody is perfect':

$\sim P$

5.a. If Bob jogs regularly then it is not the case that Bob is lazy.

$B \supset \sim L$

c. Bob jogs regularly if and only if it is not the case that Bob is lazy.

$B \equiv \sim L$

e. Carol is a marathon runner if and only if Carol jogs regularly.

$M \equiv C$

g. If (both Carol jogs regularly and Bob jogs regularly) then Albert jogs regularly.

$(C \,\&\, B) \supset A$

i. If (either it is not the case that Carol jogs regularly or it is not the case that Bob jogs regularly) then it is not the case that Albert jogs regularly.

$(\sim C \vee \sim B) \supset \sim A$

k. If (both Albert is healthy and it is not the case that Bob is lazy) then (both Albert jogs regularly and Bob jogs regularly).

$(H \,\&\, \sim L) \supset (A \,\&\, B)$

m. If it is not the case that Carol is a marathon runner then [Carol jogs regularly if and only if (both Albert jogs regularly and Bob jogs regularly)].

$\sim M \supset [C \equiv (A \,\&\, B)]$

o. If [both (both Carol is a marathon runner and it is not the case that Bob is lazy) and Albert is healthy] then [both Albert jogs regularly and (both Bob jogs regularly and Carol jogs regularly)].

$[(M \,\&\, \sim L) \,\&\, H] \supset [A \,\&\, (B \,\&\, C)]$

q. If (if Carol jogs regularly then Albert jogs regularly) then (both Albert is healthy and Carol is a marathon runner).

$(C \supset A) \supset (H \,\&\, M)$

s. If [if (either Carol jogs regularly or Bob jogs regularly) then Albert jogs regularly)] then (both Albert is healthy and it is not the case that Bob is lazy).

$[(C \vee B) \supset A] \supset (H \,\&\, \sim L)$

6.a. Either Bob is lazy or he isn't.

c. Albert jogs regularly if and only if he is healthy.

e. Neither Bob nor Carol jogs regularly.

g. If either Albert or Carol does not jog regularly, then Bob does.

i. Carol jogs regularly only if Albert does but Bob doesn't.

k. Carol does and does not jog regularly.

m. If Bob is lazy, then he is; but Bob jogs regularly.

o. If Albert doesn't jog regularly, then Bob doesn't jog regularly only if Carol doesn't.

q. Albert doesn't jog regularly, and Bob jogs regularly if and only if he is not lazy.

7.

$\mathcal{P}$	$\mathcal{Q}$	$(\mathcal{P} \vee \mathcal{Q}) \,\&\, \sim (\mathcal{P} \,\&\, \mathcal{Q})$	$\mathcal{P} \equiv \sim \mathcal{Q})$
T	T	F	F
T	F	T	T
F	T	T	T
F	F	F	F

Section 2.2E

1.a. Either the French team will win at least one gold medal or either the German team will win at least one gold medal or the Danish team will win at least one gold medal.

$F \vee (G \vee D)$

c. Both (either the French team will win at least one gold medal or either the German team will win at least one gold medal or the Danish team will win at least one gold medal) and (either [it is not the case that either the French team will win at least one gold medal or the German team will win at least one gold medal] or [either (it is not the case that either the French team will win at least one gold medal or the Danish team will win at least one gold medal) or (it is not the case that either the German team will win at least one gold medal or the Danish team will win at least one gold medal)]).

$[F \vee (G \vee D)] \,\&\, (\sim (F \vee G) \vee [\sim (F \vee D) \vee \sim (G \vee D)])$

e. Either both the French team will win at least one gold medal and the German team will win at least one gold medal or either both the French team will win at least one gold medal and the Danish team will win at least one gold medal or both the German team will win at least one gold medal and the Danish team will win at least one gold medal.

(F & G) ∨ [(F & D) ∨ (G & D)]

g. Either both both the French team will win at least one gold medal and the German team will win at least one gold medal and it is not the case that the Danish team will win at least one gold medal or either both both the French team will win at least one gold medal and the Danish team will win at least one gold medal and it is not the case that the German team will win at least one gold medal or both both the German team will win at least one gold medal and the Danish team will win at least one gold medal and it is not the case that the French team will win at least one gold medal.

[(F & G) & ~ D] ∨ ([(F & D) & ~ G] ∨ [(G & D) & ~ F])

2.a. None of them will win a gold medal.
c. None of them will win a gold medal.
e. At least one of them will win a gold medal.
g. The French team will win a gold medal and exactly one of the other two teams will win a gold medal.

3.a. If either the French team will win at least one gold medal or either the German team will win at least one gold medal or the Danish team will win at least one gold medal then both the French team will win at least one gold medal and both the German team will win at least one gold medal and the Danish team will win at least one gold medal.

[F ∨ (G ∨ D)] ⊃ [F & (G & D)]

c. If the star German runner is disqualified then if the German team will win at least one gold medal then it is not the case that either the French team will win at least one gold medal or the Danish team will win at least one gold medal.

S ⊃ [G ⊃ ~ (F ∨ D)]

e. The Danish team will win at least one gold medal if and only if both the French team is plagued with injuries and the star German runner is disqualified.

D ≡ (P & S)

g. If the French team is plagued with injuries then if the French team will win at least one gold medal then both it is not the case that either the

Danish team will win at least one gold medal or the German team will win at least one gold medal and it rains during most of the competition.

$P \supset (F \supset [\sim (D \vee G) \,\&\, R])$

4.a. If the German star is disqualified then the German team will not win a gold medal, and the star is disqualified.

c. The German team won't win a gold medal if and only if the Danish as well as the French will win one.

e. If a German team win guarantees a French team win and a French team win guarantees a Danish team win then a German team win guarantees a Danish team win.

g. Either at least one of the three wins a gold medal or else the French team is plagued with injuries or the star German runner is disqualified or it rains during most of the competition.

5.a. If it is not the case that the author of *Robert's Rules of Order* was a politician, then either the author of *Robert's Rules of Order* was an engineer or the author of *Robert's Rules of Order* was a clergyman.

Both the author of *Robert's Rules of Order* was motivated to write the book by an unruly church meeting and it is not the case that the author of *Robert's Rules of Order* was a clergyman.

Both it is not the case that the author of *Robert's Rules of Order* was a politician and the author of *Robert's Rules of Order* could not persuade a publisher that the book would make money forcing him to publish the book himself.

The author of *Robert's Rules of Order* was an engineer.

E: The author of *Robert's Rules of Order* was an engineer.
C: The author of *Robert's Rules of Order* was a clergyman.
P: The author of *Robert's Rules of Order* was a politician.
M: The author of *Robert's Rules of Order* was motivated to write the book by an unruly church meeting.
F: The author of *Robert's Rules of Order* could not persuade a publisher that the book would make money forcing him to publish the book himself.

$\sim P \supset (E \vee C)$

$M \,\&\, \sim C$

$\sim P \,\&\, F$

E

c. Either either the maid committed the murder or the butler committed the murder or the cook committed the murder.

Both (if the cook committed the murder then a knife was the murder weapon) and (if a knife was the murder weapon then it is not the case that either the butler committed the murder or the maid committed the murder).

A knife was the murder weapon.

The cook committed the murder.

M: The maid committed the murder.
B: The butler committed the murder.
C: The cook committed the murder.
K: A knife was the murder weapon.

$(M \vee B) \vee C$

$(C \supset K) \ \& \ (K \supset \sim (B \vee M))$

K

C

e. If the candidate is perceived as conservative then both it is not the case that the candidate will win New York and both the candidate will win California and the candidate will win Texas.

Both if the candidate has an effective advertising campaign then the candidate is perceived as conservative and the candidate has an effective advertising campaign.

Either both the candidate will win California and the candidate will win New York or either (both the candidate will win California and the candidate will win Texas) or (both the candidate will win New York and the candidate will win Texas).

P: The candidate is perceived as conservative.
N: The candidate will win New York.
C: The candidate will win California.
T: The candidate will win Texas.
E: The candidate has an effective advertising campaign.

$P \supset [\sim N \ \& \ (C \ \& \ T)]$

$(E \supset P) \ \& \ E$

$(C \ \& \ N) \vee [(C \ \& \ T) \vee (N \ \& \ T)]$

Section 2.3E

1. Since we do not know how these sentences are being used (e.g., as premises, conclusions, or as isolated claims) it is best to symbolize those that are non-truth-functional compounds as atomic sentences of *SL*.

a. 'It is possible that' does not have a truth-functional sense. Thus the sentence should be treated as a unit and abbreviated by one letter, for example, 'E'. Here 'E' abbreviates not just 'Every family on this continent owns a television set' but the entire original sentence, 'It is possible that every family on this continent owns a television set'.

c. 'Necessarily' has scope over the entire sentence. Abbreviate the entire sentence by one letter such as 'N'.

e. This sentence can be paraphrased as a truth-functional compound:

> Both it is not the case that Tamara will stop by and Tamara promised to phone early in the evening

which can be symbolized as '~ B & E', where 'B' abbreviates 'Tamara will stop by' and 'E' abbreviates 'Tamara promised to phone early in the evening'.

g. 'John believes that' is not a truth-functional connective. Abbreviate the sentence by one letter, for example 'J'.

i. 'Only after' has no truth-functional sense. Therefore abbreviate the entire sentence as 'D'.

2.a. The paraphrase is

> If the maid committed the murder then the maid believed her life was in danger.
>
> If the butler committed the murder then (both the murder was done silently and it is not the case that the body was mutilated).
>
> Both the murder was done silently and it is not the case that the maid's life was in danger.
>
> The butler committed the murder if and only if it is not the case that the maid committed the murder.
>
> ---
>
> The maid committed the murder.

Notice that 'The maid believed her life was in danger' (first premise) and 'The maid's life was in danger' (third premise) make different claims and cannot be treated as the same sentence. Further, since the subjunctive conditional in the original argument is a premise, it can be weakened and paraphrased as a truth-functional compound. Using the abbreviations

M: The maid committed the murder.
D: The maid believed that her life was in danger.
B: The butler committed the murder.
S: The murder was done silently.
W: The body was mutilated.
L: The maid's life was in danger.

the symbolized argument is

$M \supset D$

$B \supset (S \;\&\; {\sim} W)$

$S \;\&\; {\sim} L$

$B \equiv {\sim} M$

M

c. The paraphrase is

If (both Charles Babbage had the theory of the modern computer and Charles Babbage had modern electronic parts) then the modern computer was developed before the beginning of the twentieth century.

Both Charles Babbage lived in the early nineteenth century and Charles Babbage had the theory of the modern computer.

Both it is not the case that Charles Babbage had modern electronic parts and Charles Babbage was forced to construct his computers out of mechanical gears and levers.

If Charles Babbage had had modern electronic parts available to him then the modern computer would have been developed before the beginning of the twentieth century.

In the original argument subjunctive conditionals occur in the first premise and the conclusion. Since it is correct to weaken the premises but not the conclusion, the first premise, but not the conclusion, is given a truth-functional paraphrase. The conclusion will be abbreviated as a single sentence. Using the abbreviations

T: Charles Babbage had the theory of the modern computer.
E: Charles Babbage had modern electronic parts.
C: The modern computer was developed before the beginning of the twentieth century.
L: Charles Babbage lived in the early nineteenth century.
F: Charles Babbage was forced to construct his computers out of mechanical gears and levers.
W: If Charles Babbage had had modern electronic parts available to him then the modern computer would have been developed before the beginning of the twentieth century.

the paraphrase can be symbolized as

(T & E) ⊃ C

L & T

~ E & F

W

Section 2.4E

1.a. True

c. False. The chemical symbol names or designates the metal copper, not the word 'copper'.

e. False. The substance copper is not its own name.

g. False. The name of copper is not a metal.

2.a. The only German word mentioned is 'Deutschland' which has eleven letters.

c. The phrase 'the German name of Germany' here refers to the word 'Deutschland', so 'Deutschland' is mentioned here.

e. The word 'Deutschland' occurs inside single quotation marks in Exercise 2.e, so it is there being mentioned, not used.

3.a. A sentence of *SL*.

c. A sentence of *SL*.

e. A sentence of *SL*.

g. A sentence of *SL*.

i. A sentence of *SL*.

4.a. The main connective is '&'. The immediate sentential components are '~ A' and 'H'. '~ A & H' is a component of itself. Another sentential component is 'A'. The atomic sentential components are 'A' and 'H'.

c. The main connective is '∨'. The immediate sentential components are '~ (S & G)' and 'B'. The other sentential components are '~ (S & G) ∨ B' itself, '(S & G)', 'S', and 'G'. The atomic components are 'B', 'S', and 'G'.

e. The main connective is the first occurrence of '∨'. The immediate sentential components are '(C ≡ K)' and '(~ H ∨ (M & N))'. Additional sentential components are the sentence itself, '~ H', '(M & N)', 'C', 'K', 'H', 'M', and 'N'. The last five sentential components listed are atomic components.

5.a. No. The sentence is a conditional, but not a conditional whose antecedent is a negation.

c. Yes. Here $\mathscr{P}$ is the sentence 'A' and $\mathscr{Q}$ is the sentence '~ B'.

e. No. The sentence is a negation, not a conditional.

g. No. The sentence is a negation, not a conditional.

i. Yes. Here $\mathscr{P}$ is 'A ∨ ~ B' and $\mathscr{Q}$ is '~ (C & ~ D)'.

6.a. ‘H’ can occur neither immediately to the left of ‘~’ nor immediately to the right of ‘A’. As a unary connective, ‘~’ can immediately precede but not immediately follow sentences of *SL*. Both ‘H’ and ‘A’ are sentences of *SL*, and no sentence of *SL* can immediately precede another sentence of *SL*.

c. ‘(’ may not occur immediately to the right of ‘A’, as a sentence of *SL* can be followed only by a right parentheses or by a binary connective. But ‘(’ may occur immediately to the left of ‘~’, as in ‘(~ A & B)’.

e. ‘[’ may not occur immediately to the right of ‘A’ but may occur immediately to the left of ‘~’, as it functions exactly as does ‘(’.

CHAPTER THREE

Section 3.1E

1.a. $2^1 = 2$

c. $2^2 = 4$

2.a.

E	~ ~ (E ↓	&	~ E)
T	F T T	F	F T
F	F T F	F	T F

(The arrow ↓ stands over the first ‘~’.)

c.

A	J	A	≡ ↓	[J	≡	(A	≡	J)]
T	T	T	T	T	T	T	T	T
T	F	T	T	F	T	T	F	F
F	T	F	T	T	F	F	F	T
F	F	F	T	F	F	F	T	F

e.

A	H	J	[~ A	∨	(H	⊃	J)]	⊃ ↓	(A	∨	J)
T	T	T	F T	T	T	T	T	T	T	T	T
T	T	F	F T	F	T	F	F	T	T	T	F
T	F	T	F T	T	F	T	T	T	T	T	T
T	F	F	F T	T	F	T	F	T	T	T	F
F	T	T	T F	T	T	T	T	T	F	T	T
F	T	F	T F	T	T	F	F	F	F	F	F
F	F	T	T F	T	F	T	T	T	F	T	T
F	F	F	T F	T	F	T	F	F	F	F	F

g.

A	B	~	(A	∨	B)	↓ ⊃	(~	A	∨	~	B)
T	T	F	T	T	T	T	F	T	F	F	T
T	F	F	T	T	F	T	F	T	T	T	F
F	T	F	F	T	T	T	T	F	T	F	T
F	F	T	F	F	F	T	T	F	T	T	F

i.

B	E	H	↓ ~	(E	&	[H	⊃	(B	&	E)])
T	T	T	F	T	T	T	T	T	T	T
T	T	F	F	T	T	F	T	T	T	T
T	F	T	T	F	F	T	F	T	F	F
T	F	F	T	F	F	F	T	T	F	F
F	T	T	T	T	F	T	F	F	F	T
F	T	F	F	T	T	F	T	F	F	T
F	F	T	T	F	F	T	F	F	F	F
F	F	F	T	F	F	F	T	F	F	F

k.

D	E	F	~	[D	&	(E	∨	F)]	↓ ≡	[~	D	&	(E	&	F)]
T	T	T	F	T	T	T	T	T	T	F	T	F	T	T	T
T	T	F	F	T	T	T	T	F	T	F	T	F	T	F	F
T	F	T	F	T	T	F	T	T	T	F	T	F	F	F	T
T	F	F	T	T	F	F	F	F	F	F	T	F	F	F	F
F	T	T	T	F	F	T	T	T	T	T	F	T	T	T	T
F	T	F	T	F	F	T	T	F	F	T	F	F	T	F	F
F	F	T	T	F	F	F	T	T	F	T	F	F	F	F	T
F	F	F	T	F	F	F	F	F	F	T	F	F	F	F	F

m.

A	H	J	(A	∨	(~	A	&	(H	⊃	J)))	↓ ⊃	(J	⊃	H)
T	T	T	T	T	F	T	F	T	T	T	T	T	T	T
T	T	F	T	T	F	T	F	T	F	F	T	F	T	T
T	F	T	T	T	F	T	F	F	T	T	F	T	F	F
T	F	F	T	T	F	T	F	F	T	F	T	F	T	F
F	T	T	F	T	T	F	T	T	T	T	T	T	T	T
F	T	F	F	F	T	F	F	T	F	F	T	F	T	T
F	F	T	F	T	T	F	T	F	T	T	F	T	F	F
F	F	F	F	T	T	F	T	F	T	F	T	F	T	F

3. a.

A	B	C	↓ ~	[~	A	∨	(~	C	∨	~	B)]
F	T	T	F	T	F	T	F	T	F	F	T

c.

A	B	C	(A	⊃	B)	↓ ∨	(B	⊃	C)
F	T	T	F	T	T	T	T	T	T

e.

A	B	C	(A	≡	B)	↓ ∨	(B	≡	C)
F	T	T	F	F	T	T	T	T	T

g.

A	B	C	~	[B	⊃	(A	∨	C)]	↓ &	~	~	B
F	T	T	F	T	T	F	T	T	F	T	F	T

i.

A	B	C	~	[~	(A	≡	~	B)	≡	~	A]	↓ ≡	(B	∨	C)
F	T	T	T	F	F	T	F	T	F	T	F	T	T	T	T

4.a.

D	F	G	F	↓ ∨	(G	∨	D)
T	T	T	T	T	T	T	T
T	T	F	T	T	F	T	T
T	F	T	F	T	T	T	T
T	F	F	F	T	F	T	T
F	T	T	T	T	T	T	F
F	T	F	T	T	F	F	F
F	F	T	F	T	T	T	F
F	F	F	F	F	F	F	F

c.

D	F	G	[F	∨	(G	∨	D)]	↓ &	(~	(F	∨	G)	∨	[~	(F	∨	D)	∨	~	(G	∨	D)])
T	T	T	T	T	T	T	T	F	F	T	T	T	F	F	T	T	T	F	F	T	T	T
T	T	F	T	T	F	T	T	F	F	T	T	F	F	F	T	T	T	F	F	F	T	T
T	F	T	F	T	T	T	T	F	F	F	T	T	F	F	F	T	T	F	F	T	T	T
T	F	F	F	T	F	T	T	T	T	F	F	F	T	F	F	T	T	F	F	F	T	T
F	T	T	T	T	T	T	F	F	F	T	T	T	F	F	T	T	F	F	F	T	T	F
F	T	F	T	T	F	F	F	T	F	T	T	F	T	F	T	T	F	T	T	F	F	F
F	F	T	F	T	T	T	F	T	F	F	T	T	T	T	F	F	F	T	F	T	T	F
F	F	F	F	F	F	F	F	F	T	F	F	F	T	T	F	F	F	T	T	F	F	F

e.

D	F	G	(F	&	G)	↓ ∨	[(F	&	D)	∨	(G	&	D)]
T	T	T	T	T	T	T	T	T	T	T	T	T	T
T	T	F	T	F	F	T	T	T	T	T	F	F	T
T	F	T	F	F	T	T	F	F	T	T	T	T	T
T	F	F	F	F	F	F	F	F	T	F	F	F	T
F	T	T	T	T	T	T	T	F	F	F	T	F	F
F	T	F	T	F	F	F	T	F	F	F	F	F	F
F	F	T	F	F	T	F	F	F	F	F	T	F	F
F	F	F	F	F	F	F	F	F	F	F	F	F	F

g.

D	F	G	[(F	&	G)	&	~	D]	↓ ∨	([(F	&	D)	&	~	G]	∨	[(G	&	D)	&	~	F])
T	T	T	T	T	T	F	F	T	F	T	T	T	F	F	T	F	T	T	T	F	F	T
T	T	F	T	F	F	F	F	T	T	T	T	T	T	T	F	T	F	F	T	F	F	T
T	F	T	F	F	T	F	F	T	T	F	F	T	F	F	T	T	T	T	T	T	T	F
T	F	F	F	F	F	F	F	T	F	F	F	T	F	T	F	F	F	F	T	F	T	F
F	T	T	T	T	T	T	T	F	T	T	F	F	F	F	T	F	T	F	F	F	F	T
F	T	F	T	F	F	F	T	F	F	T	F	F	F	T	F	F	F	F	F	F	F	T
F	F	T	F	F	T	F	T	F	F	F	F	F	F	F	T	F	T	F	F	F	T	F
F	F	F	F	F	F	F	T	F	F	F	F	F	F	T	F	F	F	F	F	F	T	F

5.a.

D	F	G	[F	∨	(G	∨	D)]	↓ ⊃	[F	&	(G	&	D)]
T	T	T	T	T	T	T	T	T	T	T	T	T	T
T	T	F	T	T	F	T	T	F	T	F	F	F	T
T	F	T	F	T	T	T	T	F	F	F	T	T	T
T	F	F	F	T	F	T	T	F	F	F	F	F	T
F	T	T	T	T	T	T	F	F	T	F	T	F	F
F	T	F	T	T	F	F	F	F	T	F	F	F	F
F	F	T	F	T	T	T	F	F	F	F	T	F	F
F	F	F	F	F	F	F	F	T	F	F	F	F	F

c.

D	F	G	S	S	↓ ⊃	[G	⊃	~	(F	∨	D)]
T	T	T	T	T	F	T	F	F	T	T	T
T	T	T	F	F	T	T	F	F	T	T	T
T	T	F	T	T	T	F	T	F	T	T	T
T	T	F	F	F	T	F	T	F	T	T	T
T	F	T	T	T	F	T	F	F	F	T	T
T	F	T	F	F	T	T	F	F	F	T	T
T	F	F	T	T	T	F	T	F	F	T	T
T	F	F	F	F	T	F	T	F	F	T	T
F	T	T	T	T	F	T	F	F	T	T	F
F	T	T	F	F	T	T	F	F	T	T	F
F	T	F	T	T	T	F	T	F	T	T	F
F	T	F	F	F	T	F	T	F	T	T	F
F	F	T	T	T	T	T	T	T	F	F	F
F	F	T	F	F	T	T	T	T	F	F	F
F	F	F	T	T	T	F	T	T	F	F	F
F	F	F	F	F	T	F	T	T	F	F	F

e.

D	P	S	D	≡ ↓	(P	&	S)
T	T	T	T	T	T	T	T
T	T	F	T	F	T	F	F
T	F	T	T	F	F	F	T
T	F	F	T	F	F	F	F
F	T	T	F	F	T	T	T
F	T	F	F	T	T	F	F
F	F	T	F	T	F	F	T
F	F	F	F	T	F	F	F

g.

D	F	G	P	R	P	⊃ ↓	(F	⊃	[~	(D	∨	G)	&	R])
T	T	T	T	T	T	F	T	F	F	T	T	T	F	T
T	T	T	T	F	T	F	T	F	F	T	T	T	F	F
T	T	T	F	T	F	T	T	F	F	T	T	T	F	T
T	T	T	F	F	F	T	T	F	F	T	T	T	F	F
T	T	F	T	T	T	F	T	F	F	T	T	F	F	T
T	T	F	T	F	T	F	T	F	F	T	T	F	F	F
T	T	F	F	T	F	T	T	F	F	T	T	F	F	T
T	T	F	F	F	F	T	T	F	F	T	T	F	F	F
T	F	T	T	T	T	T	F	T	F	T	T	T	F	T
T	F	T	T	F	T	T	F	T	F	T	T	T	F	F
T	F	T	F	T	F	T	F	T	F	T	T	T	F	T
T	F	T	F	F	F	T	F	T	F	T	T	T	F	F
T	F	F	T	T	T	T	F	T	F	T	T	F	F	T
T	F	F	T	F	T	T	F	T	F	T	T	F	F	F
T	F	F	F	T	F	T	F	T	F	T	T	F	F	T
T	F	F	F	F	F	T	F	T	F	T	T	F	F	F
F	T	T	T	T	T	F	T	F	F	F	T	T	F	T
F	T	T	T	F	T	F	T	F	F	F	T	T	F	F
F	T	T	F	T	F	T	T	F	F	F	T	T	F	T
F	T	T	F	F	F	T	T	F	F	F	T	T	F	F
F	T	F	T	T	T	T	T	T	T	F	F	F	T	T
F	T	F	T	F	T	F	T	F	T	F	F	F	F	F
F	T	F	F	T	F	T	T	T	T	F	F	F	T	T
F	T	F	F	F	F	T	T	F	T	F	F	F	F	F
F	F	T	T	T	T	T	F	T	F	F	T	T	F	T
F	F	T	T	F	T	T	F	T	F	F	T	T	F	F
F	F	T	F	T	F	T	F	T	F	F	T	T	F	T
F	F	T	F	F	F	T	F	T	F	F	T	T	F	F
F	F	F	T	T	T	T	F	T	T	F	F	F	T	T
F	F	F	T	F	T	T	F	T	T	F	F	F	F	F
F	F	F	F	T	F	T	F	T	T	F	F	F	T	T
F	F	F	F	F	F	T	F	T	T	F	F	F	F	F

Section 3.2E

1.a. Truth-functionally indeterminate

A	~ A	↓ ⊃	A
T	F T	T	T
F	T F	F	F

c. Truth-functionally true

A	(A	≡	~ A)	↓ ⊃	~ (A	≡	~ A)
T	T	F	F T	T	T T	F	F T
F	F	F	T F	T	T F	F	T F

e. Truth-functionally indeterminate

B	D	(~ B	&	~ D)	↓ ∨	~ (B	∨	D)
T	T	F T	F	F T	F	F T	T	T
T	F	F T	F	T F	F	F T	T	F
F	T	T F	F	F T	F	F F	T	T
F	F	T F	T	T F	T	T F	F	F

g. Truth-functionally indeterminate

A	B	C	[(A	∨	B)	&	(A	∨	C)]	↓ ⊃	~ (B	&	C)
T	T	T	T	T	T	T	T	T	T	F	F T	T	T
T	T	F	T	T	T	T	T	T	F	T	T T	F	F
T	F	T	T	T	F	T	T	T	T	T	T F	F	T
T	F	F	T	T	F	T	T	T	F	T	T F	F	F
F	T	T	F	T	T	T	F	T	T	F	F T	T	T
F	T	F	F	T	T	F	F	F	F	T	T T	F	F
F	F	T	F	F	F	F	F	T	T	T	T F	F	T
F	F	F	F	F	F	F	F	F	F	T	T F	F	F

i. Truth-functionally true

J	K	(J	∨	~ K)	↓ ≡	~ ~ (K	⊃	J)
T	T	T	T	F T	T	T F T	T	T
T	F	T	T	T F	T	T F F	T	T
F	T	F	F	F T	T	F T T	F	F
F	F	F	T	T F	T	T F F	T	F

k. Truth-functionally true

A	D	[(A	∨	~D)	&	~(A	&	D)]	↓ ⊃	~D
T	**T**	**T**	**T**	**F T**	**F**	**F T**	**T**	**T**	**T**	**F T**
T	**F**	**T**	**T**	**T F**	**T**	**T T**	**F**	**F**	**T**	**T F**
F	**T**	**F**	**F**	**F T**	**F**	**T F**	**F**	**T**	**T**	**F T**
F	**F**	**F**	**T**	**T F**	**T**	**T F**	**F**	**F**	**T**	**T F**

2.a. Not truth-functionally true

F	H	(F	∨	H)	↓ ∨	(~F	≡	H)
F	**F**	**F**	**F**	**F**	**F**	**T F**	**F**	**F**

c. Truth-functionally true

A	B	C	~A	↓ ⊃	[(B	&	A)	⊃	C]
T	**T**	**T**	**F T**	**T**	**T**	**T**	**T**	**T**	**T**
T	**T**	**F**	**F T**	**T**	**T**	**T**	**T**	**F**	**F**
T	**F**	**T**	**F T**	**T**	**F**	**F**	**T**	**T**	**T**
T	**F**	**F**	**F T**	**T**	**F**	**F**	**T**	**T**	**F**
F	**T**	**T**	**T F**	**T**	**T**	**F**	**F**	**T**	**T**
F	**T**	**F**	**T F**	**T**	**T**	**F**	**F**	**T**	**F**
F	**F**	**T**	**T F**	**T**	**F**	**F**	**F**	**T**	**T**
F	**F**	**F**	**T F**	**T**	**F**	**F**	**F**	**T**	**F**

e. Truth-functionally true

C	[(C	∨	~C)	⊃	C]	↓ ⊃	C
T	**T**	**T**	**F T**	**T**	**T**	**T**	**T**
F	**F**	**T**	**T F**	**F**	**F**	**T**	**F**

3.a. Truth-functionally false

B	D	(B	≡	D)	↓ &	(B	≡	~D)
T	**T**	**T**	**T**	**T**	**F**	**T**	**F**	**F T**
T	**F**	**T**	**F**	**F**	**F**	**T**	**T**	**T F**
F	**T**	**F**	**F**	**T**	**F**	**F**	**T**	**F T**
F	**F**	**F**	**T**	**F**	**F**	**F**	**F**	**T F**

c. Not truth-functionally false

A	B	A	↓ ≡	(B	≡	A)
T	**T**	**T**	**T**	**T**	**T**	**T**

e. Not truth-functionally false

C	D	[(C	∨	D)	≡	C]	↓ ⊃	~ C
F	**T**	**F**	**T**	**T**	**F**	**F**	**T**	**TF**

4.a. False. For example, while '(A ⊃ A)' is truth-functionally true, '(A ⊃ A) & A' is not.

c. True. There cannot be any truth-value assignment on which the antecedent is true and the consequent false because there is no truth-value assignment on which the consequent is false.

e. False. For example, although '(A & ~ A)' is truth-functionally false, 'C ∨ (A & ~ A)' is not.

g. True. Since a sentence ~ $\mathscr{P}$ is false on a truth-value assignment if and only if $\mathscr{P}$ is true on the truth-value assignment, $\mathscr{P}$ is truth-functionally true if and only if ~ $\mathscr{P}$ is truth-functionally false.

i. False. For example, '(A ∨ ~ A)' is truth-functionally true, but '(A ∨ ~ A) ⊃ B' is truth-functionally indeterminate.

5.a. On every truth-value assignment, $\mathscr{P}$ is true and $\mathscr{Q}$ is false. Hence $\mathscr{P} \equiv \mathscr{Q}$ is false on every truth-value assignment. Therefore $\mathscr{P} \equiv \mathscr{Q}$ is truth-functionally false.

c. No. Both 'A' and '~ A' are truth-functionally indeterminate, but 'A ∨ ~ A' is truth-functionally true.

Section 3.3E

1.a. Not truth-functionally equivalent

A	B	↓ ~ (A	&	B)	~ (A	∨	B)
T	**T**	**F T**	**T**	**T**	**F T**	**T**	**T**
T	**F**	**T T**	**F**	**F**	**F T**	**T**	**F**
F	**T**	**T F**	**F**	**T**	**F F**	**T**	**T**
F	**F**	**T F**	**F**	**F**	**T F**	**F**	**F**

c. Truth-functionally equivalent

H	K	K	↓ ≡	H	~ K	↓ ≡	~ H
T	**T**	**T**	**T**	**T**	**F T**	**T**	**F T**
T	**F**	**F**	**F**	**T**	**T F**	**F**	**F T**
F	**T**	**T**	**F**	**F**	**F T**	**F**	**T F**
F	**F**	**F**	**T**	**F**	**T F**	**T**	**T F**

e. Truth-functionally equivalent

F	G	(G	⊃	F)	↓ ⊃	(F	⊃	G)	(G	≡	F)	↓ ∨	(~	F	∨	G)
T	T	T	T	T	T	T	T	T	T	T	T	T	F	T	T	T
T	F	F	T	T	F	T	F	F	F	F	T	F	F	T	F	F
F	T	T	F	F	T	F	T	T	T	F	F	T	T	F	T	T
F	F	F	T	F	T	F	T	F	F	T	F	T	T	F	T	F

g. Not truth-functionally equivalent

H	J	K	~	(H	&	J)	↓ ≡	(J	≡	~	K)	(H	&	J)	↓ ⊃	~	K
T	T	T	F	T	T	T	T	T	F	F	T	T	T	T	F	F	T
T	T	F	F	T	T	T	F	T	T	T	F	T	T	T	T	T	F
T	F	T	T	T	F	F	T	F	T	F	T	T	F	F	T	F	T
T	F	F	T	T	F	F	F	F	F	T	F	T	F	F	T	T	F
F	T	T	T	F	F	T	F	T	F	F	T	F	F	T	T	F	T
F	T	F	T	F	F	T	T	T	T	T	F	F	F	T	T	T	F
F	F	T	T	F	F	F	T	F	T	F	T	F	F	F	T	F	T
F	F	F	T	F	F	F	F	F	F	T	F	F	F	F	T	T	F

i. Not truth-functionally equivalent

A	C	D	[A	∨	~	(D	&	C)]	↓ ⊃	~	D	[D	∨	~	(A	&	C)]	↓ ⊃	~	A
T	T	T	T	T	F	T	T	T	F	F	T	T	T	F	T	T	T	F	F	T
T	T	F	T	T	T	F	F	T	T	T	F	F	F	F	T	T	T	T	F	T
T	F	T	T	T	T	T	F	F	F	F	T	T	T	T	T	F	F	F	F	T
T	F	F	T	T	T	F	F	F	T	T	F	F	T	T	T	F	F	F	F	T
F	T	T	F	F	F	T	T	T	T	F	T	T	T	T	F	F	T	T	T	F
F	T	F	F	T	T	F	F	T	T	T	F	F	T	T	F	F	T	T	T	F
F	F	T	F	T	T	T	F	F	F	F	T	T	T	T	F	F	F	T	T	F
F	F	F	F	T	T	F	F	F	T	T	F	F	T	T	F	F	F	T	T	F

k. Not truth-functionally equivalent

F	G	H	F	↓ ∨	~	(G	∨	~	H)	(H	≡	~	F)	↓ ∨	G
T	T	T	T	T	F	T	T	F	T	T	F	F	T	T	T
T	T	F	T	T	F	T	T	T	F	F	T	F	T	T	T
T	F	T	T	T	T	F	F	F	T	T	F	F	T	F	F
T	F	F	T	T	F	F	T	T	F	F	T	F	T	T	F
F	T	T	F	F	F	T	T	F	T	T	T	T	F	T	T
F	T	F	F	F	F	T	T	T	F	F	F	T	F	T	T
F	F	T	F	T	T	F	F	F	T	T	T	T	F	T	F
F	F	F	F	F	F	F	T	T	F	F	F	T	F	F	F

2.a. Truth-functionally equivalent

			↓			↓	
G	H	G	∨	H	~ G	⊃	H
T	T	T	T	T	F T	T	T
T	F	T	T	F	F T	T	F
F	T	F	T	T	T F	T	T
F	F	F	F	F	T F	F	F

c. Truth-functionally equivalent

					↓			↓	
A	D	(D	≡	A)	&	D	D	&	A
T	T	T	T	T	T	T	T	T	T
T	F	F	F	T	F	F	F	F	T
F	T	T	F	F	F	T	T	F	F
F	F	F	T	F	F	F	F	F	F

e. Not truth-functionally equivalent

		↓				↓			
A	A	≡	(~ A	≡	A)	~	(A	⊃	~ A)
T	T	F	F T	F	T	T	T	F	F T

3.a. Not truth-functionally equivalent

C: The sky clouds over.
N: The night will be clear.
M: The moon will shine brightly.

				↓					↓			
C	M	N	C	∨	(N	&	M)	M	≡	(N	&	~ C)
T	T	T	T	T	T	T	T	T	F	T	F	F T
T	T	F	T	T	F	F	T	T	F	F	F	F T
T	F	T	T	T	T	F	F	F	T	T	F	F T
T	F	F	T	T	F	F	F	F	T	F	F	F T
F	T	T	F	T	T	T	T	T	T	T	T	T F
F	T	F	F	F	F	F	T	T	F	F	F	T F
F	F	T	F	F	T	F	F	F	F	T	T	T F
F	F	F	F	F	F	F	F	F	T	F	F	T F

c. Truth-functionally equivalent

D: The *Daily Herald* reports on our antics.
A: Our antics are effective.

A	D	D	↓ ⊃	A	~ A	↓ ⊃	~ D
T	**T**	**T**	**T**	**T**	**F T**	**T**	**F T**
T	**F**	**F**	**T**	**T**	**F T**	**T**	**T F**
F	**T**	**T**	**F**	**F**	**T F**	**F**	**F T**
F	**F**	**F**	**T**	**F**	**T F**	**T**	**T F**

e. Not truth-functionally equivalent

M: Mary met Tom.
L: Mary liked Tom.
G: Mary asked George to the movies.

G	L	M	(M	&	L)	↓ ⊃	~ G	(M	&	~ L)	↓ ⊃	G
T	**T**	**T**	**T**	**T**	**T**	**F**	**F T**	**T**	**F**	**F T**	**T**	**T**
T	**T**	**F**	**F**	**F**	**T**	**T**	**F T**	**F**	**F**	**F T**	**T**	**T**
T	**F**	**T**	**T**	**F**	**F**	**T**	**F T**	**T**	**T**	**T F**	**T**	**T**
T	**F**	**F**	**F**	**F**	**F**	**T**	**F T**	**F**	**F**	**T F**	**T**	**T**
F	**T**	**T**	**T**	**T**	**T**	**T**	**T F**	**T**	**F**	**F T**	**T**	**F**
F	**T**	**F**	**F**	**F**	**T**	**T**	**T F**	**F**	**F**	**F T**	**T**	**F**
F	**F**	**T**	**T**	**F**	**F**	**T**	**T F**	**T**	**T**	**T F**	**F**	**F**
F	**F**	**F**	**F**	**F**	**F**	**T**	**T F**	**F**	**F**	**T F**	**T**	**F**

4.a. Yes. $\mathcal{P}$ and $\mathcal{Q}$ have the same truth-value on every truth-value assignment. On every truth-value assignment on which they are both true, $\sim \mathcal{P}$ and $\sim \mathcal{Q}$ are both false, and on every truth-value assignment on which they are both false, $\sim \mathcal{P}$ and $\sim \mathcal{Q}$ are both true. It follows that $\sim \mathcal{P}$ and $\sim \mathcal{Q}$ are truth-functionally equivalent.

c. If $\mathcal{P}$ and $\mathcal{Q}$ are truth-functionally equivalent then they have the same truth-value on every truth-value assignment. On those assignments on which they are both true, the second disjunct of $\sim \mathcal{P} \vee \mathcal{Q}$ is true and so is the disjunction. On those assignments on which they are both false, the first disjunct of $\sim \mathcal{P} \vee \mathcal{Q}$ is true and so is the disjunction. So $\sim \mathcal{P} \vee \mathcal{Q}$ is true on every truth-value assignment.

Section 3.4E

1.a. Truth-functionally consistent

A	B	C	A	↓ ⊃	B	B	↓ ⊃	C	A	↓ ⊃	C
T	**T**	**T**	**T**	**T**	**T**	**T**	**T**	**T**	**T**	**T**	**T**
T	**T**	**F**	**T**	**T**	**T**	**T**	**F**	**F**	**T**	**F**	**F**
T	**F**	**T**	**T**	**F**	**F**	**F**	**T**	**T**	**T**	**T**	**T**
T	**F**	**F**	**T**	**F**	**F**	**F**	**T**	**F**	**T**	**F**	**F**
F	**T**	**T**	**F**	**T**	**T**	**T**	**T**	**T**	**F**	**T**	**T**
F	**T**	**F**	**F**	**T**	**T**	**T**	**F**	**F**	**F**	**T**	**F**
F	**F**	**T**	**F**	**T**	**F**	**F**	**T**	**T**	**F**	**T**	**T**
F	**F**	**F**	**F**	**T**	**F**	**F**	**T**	**F**	**F**	**T**	**F**

c. Truth-functionally inconsistent

H J L	↓ ~ [J ∨ (H ⊃ L)]	↓ L ≡ (~J ∨ ~H)	↓ H ≡ (J ∨ L)
T T T	**F T T T T T**	**T F F T F F T**	**T T T T T**
T T F	**F T T T F F**	**F T F T F F T**	**T T T T F**
T F T	**F F T T T T**	**T T T F T F T**	**T T F T T**
T F F	**T F F T F F**	**F F T F T F T**	**T F F F F**
F T T	**F T T F T T**	**T T F T T T F**	**F F T T T**
F T F	**F T T F T F**	**F F F T T T F**	**F F T T F**
F F T	**F F T F T T**	**T T T F T T F**	**F F F T T**
F F F	**F F T F T F**	**F F T F T T F**	**F T F F F**

e. Truth-functionally inconsistent

H	J	(J	⊃	J)	↓ ⊃	H	↓ ~J	↓ ~H
T	**T**	**T**	**T**	**T**	**T**	**T**	**F T**	**F T**
T	**F**	**F**	**T**	**F**	**T**	**T**	**T F**	**F T**
F	**T**	**T**	**T**	**T**	**F**	**F**	**F T**	**T F**
F	**F**	**F**	**T**	**F**	**F**	**F**	**T F**	**T F**

g. Truth-functionally consistent

A	B	C	↓ A	↓ B	↓ C
T	**T**	**T**	**T**	**T**	**T**
T	**T**	**F**	**T**	**T**	**F**
T	**F**	**T**	**T**	**F**	**T**
T	**F**	**F**	**T**	**F**	**F**
F	**T**	**T**	**F**	**T**	**T**
F	**T**	**F**	**F**	**T**	**F**
F	**F**	**T**	**F**	**F**	**T**
F	**F**	**F**	**F**	**F**	**F**

i. Truth-functionally consistent

A	B	C	(A	&	B)	↓ ∨	(C	⊃	B)	↓ ~ A	↓ ~ B
T	**T**	**T**	**T**	**T**	**T**	**T**	**T**	**T**	**T**	**FT**	**FT**
T	**T**	**F**	**T**	**T**	**T**	**T**	**F**	**T**	**T**	**FT**	**FT**
T	**F**	**T**	**T**	**F**	**F**	**F**	**T**	**F**	**F**	**FT**	**TF**
T	**F**	**F**	**T**	**F**	**F**	**T**	**F**	**T**	**F**	**FT**	**TF**
F	**T**	**T**	**F**	**F**	**T**	**T**	**T**	**T**	**T**	**TF**	**FT**
F	**T**	**F**	**F**	**F**	**T**	**T**	**F**	**T**	**T**	**TF**	**FT**
F	**F**	**T**	**F**	**F**	**F**	**F**	**T**	**F**	**F**	**TF**	**TF**
F	**F**	**F**	**F**	**F**	**F**	**T**	**F**	**T**	**F**	**TF**	**TF**

2.a. Truth-functionally consistent

B	D	E	B	↓ ⊃	(D	⊃	E)	~ D	↓ &	B
T	**F**	**T**	**T**	**T**	**F**	**T**	**T**	**TF**	**T**	**T**

c. Truth-functionally consistent

F	J	K	F	↓ ⊃	(J	∨	K)	F	↓ ≡	~ J
T	**F**	**T**	**T**	**T**	**F**	**T**	**T**	**T**	**T**	**TF**

e. Truth-functionally consistent

A	B	(A	⊃	B)	↓ ≡	(~ B	∨	B)	↓ A
T	**T**	**T**	**T**	**T**	**T**	**FT**	**T**	**T**	**T**

3.a. Truth-functionally inconsistent

S: Space is infinitely divisible.
Z: Zeno's paradoxes are compelling.
C: Zeno's paradoxes are convincing.

C	S	Z	S	↓ ⊃	Z	↓ ~ (C	∨	Z)	↓ S
T	**T**	**T**	**T**	**T**	**T**	**FT**	**T**	**T**	**T**
T	**T**	**F**	**T**	**F**	**F**	**FT**	**T**	**F**	**T**
T	**F**	**T**	**F**	**T**	**T**	**FT**	**T**	**T**	**F**
T	**F**	**F**	**F**	**T**	**F**	**FT**	**T**	**F**	**F**
F	**T**	**T**	**T**	**T**	**T**	**FF**	**T**	**T**	**T**
F	**T**	**F**	**T**	**F**	**F**	**TF**	**F**	**F**	**T**
F	**F**	**T**	**F**	**T**	**T**	**FF**	**T**	**T**	**F**
F	**F**	**F**	**F**	**T**	**F**	**TF**	**F**	**F**	**F**

c. Truth-functionally consistent

E: Eugene O'Neill was an alcoholic.

P: Eugene O'Neill's plays show that he was an alcoholic.

I: *The Iceman Cometh* must have been written by a teetotaler.

F: Eugene O'Neill was a fake.

				↓	↓	↓		↓	
E	F	I	P	E	P	I	E	∨	F
T	T	T	T	T	T	T	T	T	T
T	T	T	F	T	F	T	T	T	T
T	T	F	T	T	T	F	T	T	T
T	T	F	F	T	F	F	T	T	T
T	F	T	T	T	T	T	T	T	F
T	F	T	F	T	F	T	T	T	F
T	F	F	T	T	T	F	T	T	F
T	F	F	F	T	F	F	T	T	F
F	T	T	T	F	T	T	F	T	T
F	T	T	F	F	F	T	F	T	T
F	T	F	T	F	T	F	F	T	T
F	T	F	F	F	F	F	F	T	T
F	F	T	T	F	T	T	F	F	F
F	F	T	F	F	F	T	F	F	F
F	F	F	T	F	T	F	F	F	F
F	F	F	F	F	F	F	F	F	F

e. Truth-functionally consistent

R: The Red Sox will win next Sunday.

J: Joan bet $5.00.

E: Joan will buy Ed a hamburger.

				↓					↓	
E	J	R	R	⊃	(J	⊃	E)	~R	&	~E
T	T	T	T	T	T	T	T	FT	F	FT
T	T	F	F	T	T	T	T	TF	F	FT
T	F	T	T	T	F	T	T	FT	F	FT
T	F	F	F	T	F	T	T	TF	F	FT
F	T	T	T	F	T	F	F	FT	F	TF
F	T	F	F	T	T	F	F	TF	T	TF
F	F	T	T	T	F	T	F	FT	F	TF
F	F	F	F	T	F	T	F	TF	T	TF

4.a. First assume that {$\mathscr{P}$} is truth-functionally inconsistent. Then, since $\mathscr{P}$ is the only member of {$\mathscr{P}$}, there is no truth-value assignment on which $\mathscr{P}$ is true;

so 𝒫 is false on every truth-value assignment. But then ~ 𝒫 is true on every truth-value assignment, and so ~ 𝒫 is truth-functionally true.

Now assume that ~ 𝒫 is truth-functionally true. Then ~ 𝒫 is true on every truth-value assignment, and so 𝒫 is false on every truth-value assignment. But then there is no truth-value assignment on which 𝒫, the only member of {𝒫}, is true, and so the set is truth-functionally inconsistent.

c. No. For example, 'A' and '~ A' are both truth-functionally indeterminate, but {A, ~ A} is truth-functionally inconsistent.

Section 3.5E

1.a. Truth-functionally valid

				↓					↓		↓		↓	
A	H	J	A	⊃	(H	&	J)	J	≡	H	~	J	~	A
T	**T**	**T**	**T**	**T**	**T**	**T**	**T**	**T**	**T**	**T**	**F**	**T**	**F**	**T**
T	**T**	**F**	**T**	**F**	**T**	**F**	**F**	**F**	**F**	**T**	**T**	**F**	**F**	**T**
T	**F**	**T**	**T**	**F**	**F**	**F**	**T**	**T**	**F**	**F**	**F**	**T**	**F**	**T**
T	**F**	**F**	**T**	**F**	**F**	**F**	**F**	**F**	**T**	**F**	**T**	**F**	**F**	**T**
F	**T**	**T**	**F**	**T**	**T**	**T**	**T**	**T**	**T**	**T**	**F**	**T**	**T**	**F**
F	**T**	**F**	**F**	**T**	**T**	**F**	**F**	**F**	**F**	**T**	**T**	**F**	**T**	**F**
F	**F**	**T**	**F**	**T**	**F**	**F**	**T**	**T**	**F**	**F**	**F**	**T**	**T**	**F**
F	**F**	**F**	**F**	**T**	**F**	**F**	**F**	**F**	**T**	**F**	**T**	**F**	**T**	**F**

c. Truth-functionally valid

							↓									↓				↓		
A	D	G	(D	≡	~	G)	&	G	(G	∨	[(A	⊃	D)	&	A])	⊃	~	D	G	⊃	~	D
T	**T**	**T**	**T**	**F**	**F**	**T**	**F**	**T**	**T**	**T**	**T**	**T**	**T**	**T**	**T**	**F**	**F**	**T**	**T**	**F**	**F**	**T**
T	**T**	**F**	**T**	**T**	**T**	**F**	**F**	**F**	**F**	**T**	**T**	**T**	**T**	**T**	**T**	**F**	**F**	**T**	**F**	**T**	**F**	**T**
T	**F**	**T**	**F**	**T**	**F**	**T**	**T**	**T**	**T**	**T**	**T**	**F**	**F**	**F**	**T**	**T**	**T**	**F**	**T**	**T**	**T**	**F**
T	**F**	**F**	**F**	**F**	**T**	**F**	**F**	**F**	**F**	**F**	**T**	**F**	**F**	**F**	**T**	**T**	**T**	**F**	**F**	**T**	**T**	**F**
F	**T**	**T**	**T**	**F**	**F**	**T**	**F**	**T**	**T**	**T**	**F**	**T**	**T**	**F**	**F**	**F**	**F**	**T**	**T**	**F**	**F**	**T**
F	**T**	**F**	**T**	**T**	**T**	**F**	**F**	**F**	**F**	**F**	**F**	**T**	**T**	**F**	**F**	**T**	**F**	**T**	**F**	**T**	**F**	**T**
F	**F**	**T**	**F**	**T**	**F**	**T**	**T**	**T**	**T**	**T**	**F**	**T**	**F**	**F**	**F**	**T**	**T**	**F**	**T**	**T**	**T**	**F**
F	**F**	**F**	**F**	**F**	**T**	**F**	**F**	**F**	**F**	**F**	**F**	**T**	**F**	**F**	**F**	**T**	**T**	**F**	**F**	**T**	**T**	**F**

e. Truth-functionally valid

						↓				↓		↓	
C	D	E	(C	⊃	D)	⊃	(D	⊃	E)	D	C	⊃	E
T	**T**	**T**	**T**	**T**	**T**	**T**	**T**	**T**	**T**	**T**	**T**	**T**	**T**
T	**T**	**F**	**T**	**T**	**T**	**F**	**T**	**F**	**F**	**T**	**T**	**F**	**F**
T	**F**	**T**	**T**	**F**	**F**	**T**	**F**	**T**	**T**	**F**	**T**	**T**	**T**
T	**F**	**F**	**T**	**F**	**F**	**T**	**F**	**T**	**F**	**F**	**T**	**F**	**F**
F	**T**	**T**	**F**	**T**	**T**	**T**	**T**	**T**	**T**	**T**	**F**	**T**	**T**
F	**T**	**F**	**F**	**T**	**T**	**F**	**T**	**F**	**F**	**T**	**F**	**T**	**F**
F	**F**	**T**	**F**	**T**	**F**	**T**	**F**	**T**	**T**	**F**	**F**	**T**	**T**
F	**F**	**F**	**F**	**T**	**F**	**T**	**F**	**T**	**F**	**F**	**F**	**T**	**F**

g. Truth-functionally valid

G	H	(G	≡	H)	↓ ∨	(~	G	≡	H)	(~	G	≡	~	H)	↓ ∨	~	(G	≡	H)
T	T	T	T	T	T	F	T	F	T	F	T	T	F	T	T	F	T	T	T
T	F	T	F	F	T	F	T	T	F	F	T	F	T	F	T	T	T	F	F
F	T	F	F	T	T	T	F	T	T	T	F	F	F	T	T	T	F	F	T
F	F	F	T	F	T	T	F	F	F	T	F	T	T	F	T	F	F	T	F

i. Truth-functionally invalid

F	G	~	~	F	↓ ⊃	~	~	G	~	G	↓ ⊃	~	F	G	↓ ⊃	F
T	T	T	F	T	T	T	F	T	F	T	T	F	T	T	T	T
T	F	T	F	T	F	F	T	F	T	F	F	F	T	F	T	T
F	T	F	T	F	T	T	F	T	F	T	T	T	F	T	F	F
F	F	F	T	F	T	F	T	F	T	F	T	T	F	F	T	F

2.a. Truth-functionally valid

J	M	(J	∨	M)	↓ ⊃	~	(J	&	M)	M	↓ ≡	(M	⊃	J)	M	↓ ⊃	J
T	T	T	T	T	F	F	T	T	T	T	T	T	T	T	T	T	T
T	F	T	T	F	T	T	T	F	F	F	F	F	T	T	F	T	T
F	T	F	T	T	T	T	F	F	T	T	F	T	F	F	T	F	F
F	F	F	F	F	T	T	F	F	F	F	F	F	T	F	F	T	F

c. Truth-functionally valid

A	B	A	↓ ⊃	~	A	(B	⊃	A)	↓ ⊃	B	A	↓ ≡	~	B
T	T	T	F	F	T	T	T	T	T	T	T	F	F	T
T	F	T	F	F	T	F	T	T	F	F	T	T	T	F
F	T	F	T	T	F	T	F	F	T	T	F	T	F	T
F	F	F	T	T	F	F	T	F	F	F	F	F	T	F

e. Truth-functionally invalid

A	B	C	A	↓ &	~	[(B	&	C)	≡	(C	⊃	A)]	B	↓ ⊃	~	B	~	C	↓ ⊃	C
T	F	F	T	T	T	F	F	F	F	F	T	T	F	T	T	F	T	F	F	F

3.a. Truth-functionally valid

					↓			
B	C	(B	&	C)	⊃	(B	∨	C)
T	**T**	**T**	**T**	**T**	**T**	**T**	**T**	**T**
T	**F**	**T**	**F**	**F**	**T**	**T**	**T**	**F**
F	**T**	**F**	**F**	**T**	**T**	**F**	**T**	**T**
F	**F**	**F**	**F**	**F**	**T**	**F**	**F**	**F**

c. Truth-functionally invalid

													↓					
J	T	([(J	⊃	T)	⊃	J]	&	[(T	⊃	J)	⊃	T])	⊃	(~	J	∨	~	T)
T	**T**	**T**	**T**	**T**	**T**	**T**	**T**	**T**	**T**	**T**	**T**	**T**	**F**	**F**	**T**	**F**	**F**	**T**

e. Truth-functionally invalid

										↓	
B	C	D	[(B	&	C)	&	(B	∨	D)]	⊃	D
T	**T**	**F**	**T**	**T**	**T**	**T**	**T**	**T**	**F**	**F**	**F**

4.a. Truth-functionally invalid

S: 'Stern' means the same as 'star'.
N: 'Nacht' means the same as 'day'.

			↓		↓	↓
N	S	N	⊃	S	~N	~S
T	**T**	**T**	**T**	**T**	**FT**	**FT**
T	**F**	**T**	**F**	**F**	**FT**	**TF**
F	**T**	**F**	**T**	**T**	**TF**	**FT**
F	**F**	**F**	**T**	**F**	**TF**	**TF**

c. Truth-functionally valid

S: September has 30 days.
A: April has 30 days.
N: November has 30 days.
F: February has 40 days.
M: May has 30 days.

A	F	M	N	S	S	↓ &	(A	&	N)	(A	≡	~	M)	↓ &	(N	⊃	M)	↓ F
T	T	T	T	T	T	T	T	T	T	T	F	F	T	F	T	T	T	T
T	T	T	T	F	F	F	T	T	T	T	F	F	T	F	T	T	T	T
T	T	T	F	T	T	F	T	F	F	T	F	F	T	F	F	T	T	T
T	T	T	F	F	F	F	T	F	F	T	F	F	T	F	F	T	T	T
T	T	F	T	T	T	T	T	T	T	T	T	T	F	F	T	F	F	T
T	T	F	T	F	F	F	T	T	T	T	T	T	F	F	T	F	F	T
T	T	F	F	T	T	F	T	F	F	T	T	T	F	T	F	T	F	T
T	T	F	F	F	F	F	T	F	F	T	T	T	F	T	F	T	F	T
T	F	T	T	T	T	T	T	T	T	T	F	F	T	F	T	T	T	F
T	F	T	T	F	F	F	T	T	T	T	F	F	T	F	T	T	T	F
T	F	T	F	T	T	F	T	F	F	T	F	F	T	F	F	T	T	F
T	F	T	F	F	F	F	T	F	F	T	F	F	T	F	F	T	T	F
T	F	F	T	T	T	T	T	T	T	T	T	T	F	F	T	F	F	F
T	F	F	T	F	F	F	T	T	T	T	T	T	F	F	T	F	F	F
T	F	F	F	T	T	F	T	F	F	T	T	T	F	T	F	T	F	F
T	F	F	F	F	F	F	T	F	F	T	T	T	F	T	F	T	F	F
F	T	T	T	T	T	F	F	F	T	F	T	F	T	T	T	T	T	T
F	T	T	T	F	F	F	F	F	T	F	T	F	T	T	T	T	T	T
F	T	T	F	T	T	F	F	F	F	F	T	F	T	T	F	T	T	T
F	T	T	F	F	F	F	F	F	F	F	T	F	T	T	F	T	T	T
F	T	F	T	T	T	F	F	F	T	F	F	T	F	F	T	F	F	T
F	T	F	T	F	F	F	F	F	T	F	F	T	F	F	T	F	F	T
F	T	F	F	T	T	F	F	F	F	F	F	T	F	F	F	T	F	T
F	T	F	F	F	F	F	F	F	F	F	F	T	F	F	F	T	F	T
F	F	T	T	T	T	F	F	F	T	F	T	F	T	T	T	T	T	F
F	F	T	T	F	F	F	F	F	T	F	T	F	T	T	T	T	T	F
F	F	T	F	T	T	F	F	F	F	F	T	F	T	T	F	T	T	F
F	F	T	F	F	F	F	F	F	F	F	T	F	T	T	F	T	T	F
F	F	F	T	T	T	F	F	F	T	F	F	T	F	F	T	F	F	F
F	F	F	T	F	F	F	F	F	T	F	F	T	F	F	T	F	F	F
F	F	F	F	T	T	F	F	F	F	F	F	T	F	F	F	T	F	F
F	F	F	F	F	F	F	F	F	F	F	F	T	F	F	F	T	F	F

e. Truth-functionally valid

D: Computers can have desires.
E: Computers can have emotions.
T: Computers can think.

				↓			↓			↓		↓
D	E	T	T	≡	E	E	⊃	D	D	⊃	~ T	~ T
T	T	T	T	T	T	T	T	T	T	F	F T	F T
T	T	F	F	F	T	T	T	T	T	T	T F	T F
T	F	T	T	F	F	F	T	T	T	F	F T	F T
T	F	F	F	T	F	F	T	T	T	T	T F	T F
F	T	T	T	T	T	T	F	F	F	T	F T	F T
F	T	F	F	F	T	T	F	F	F	T	T F	T F
F	F	T	T	F	F	F	T	F	F	T	F T	F T
F	F	F	F	T	F	F	T	F	F	T	T F	T F

5.a. Suppose that the argument is truth-functionally valid. Then there is no truth-value assignment on which $\mathscr{P}_1, \ldots, \mathscr{P}_n$ are all true and $\mathscr{Q}$ is false. But, by the characteristic truth-table for '&', the iterated conjunction $(\ldots(\mathscr{P}_1 \,\&\, \mathscr{P}_2) \,\&\, \ldots \mathscr{P}_n)$ has the truth-value **T** on a truth-value assignment if and only if all of $\mathscr{P}_1, \ldots, \mathscr{P}_n$ have the truth-value **T** on that assignment. So, on our assumption, there is no truth-value assignment on which the antecedent of $(\ldots(\mathscr{P}_1 \,\&\, \mathscr{P}_2) \,\&\, \ldots \,\&\, \mathscr{P}_n) \supset \mathscr{Q}$ has the truth-value **T** and the consequent has the truth-value **F**. It follows that there is no truth-value assignment on which the corresponding material conditional is false, so it is truth-functionally true.

Assume that $(\ldots(\mathscr{P}_1 \,\&\, \mathscr{P}_2) \,\&\, \ldots \,\&\, \mathscr{P}_n) \supset \mathscr{Q}$ is truth-functionally true. Then there is no truth-value assignment on which the antecedent is true and the consequent false. But the iterated conjunction is true if and only if the sentences $\mathscr{P}_1, \ldots, \mathscr{P}_n$ are all true. So there is no truth-value assignment on which $\mathscr{P}_1, \ldots, \mathscr{P}_n$ are all true and $\mathscr{Q}$ is false; hence the argument is truth-functionally valid.

c. No. For example, {A ⊃ B} ⊨ '~ A ∨ B'. But {A ⊃ B} does not entail '~ A', nor does it entail 'B'.

Section 3.6E

1.a. If $\{\sim \mathscr{P}\}$ is truth-functionally inconsistent, then there is no truth-value assignment on which $\sim \mathscr{P}$ is true (since $\sim \mathscr{P}$ is the only member of its unit set). But then $\sim \mathscr{P}$ is false on every truth-value assignment, so $\mathscr{P}$ is true on every truth-value assignment and is truth-functionally true.

c. If $\Gamma \cup \{\sim \mathscr{P}\}$ is truth-functionally inconsistent, then there is no truth-value assignment on which every member of $\Gamma \cup \{\sim \mathscr{P}\}$ is true. But $\sim \mathscr{P}$ is true on a truth-value assignment if and only if $\mathscr{P}$ is false on that assignment. Hence there is no truth-value assignment on which every member of Γ is true and $\mathcal{P}$ is false. Hence $\Gamma \vDash \mathcal{P}$.

2.a. $\mathcal{P}$ is truth-functionally true if and only if the set $\{\sim \mathcal{P}\}$ is truth-functionally inconsistent. But $\{\sim \mathcal{P}\}$ is the same set as $\varnothing \cup \{\sim \mathcal{P}\}$. So $\mathcal{P}$ is truth-functionally true if and only if $\varnothing \cup \{\sim \mathcal{P}\}$ is truth-functionally inconsistent. But we have already seen, by previous results, that $\varnothing \cup \{\sim \mathcal{P}\}$ is truth-functionally inconsistent if and only if $\varnothing \vDash \mathcal{P}$. Hence $\mathcal{P}$ is truth-functionally true if and only if $\varnothing \vDash \mathcal{P}$.

c. Assume that Γ is truth-functionally inconsistent. Then there is no truth-value assignment on which every member of Γ is true. Let $\mathcal{P}$ be an *arbitrarily* selected sentence of *SL*. Then there is no truth-value assignment on which every member of Γ is true and $\mathcal{P}$ false since there is no truth-value assignment on which every member of Γ is true. Hence $\Gamma \vDash \mathcal{P}$.

3.a. Let Γ be a truth-functionally consistent set. Then there is at least one truth-value assignment on which every member of Γ is true. But $\mathcal{P}$ is also true on such an assignment since a truth-functionally true sentence is true on every truth-value assignment. Hence on at least one truth-value assignment every member of $\Gamma \cup \{\mathcal{P}\}$ is true; so the set is truth-functionally consistent.

4.a. $\mathcal{P}$ is either true or false on each truth-value assignment. On any assignment on which $\mathcal{P}$ is true, $\mathcal{Q}$ is true (because $\{\mathcal{P}\} \vDash \mathcal{Q}$) and so $\mathcal{Q} \vee \mathcal{R}$ is true. On any assignment on which $\mathcal{P}$ is false, $\sim \mathcal{P}$ is true, $\mathcal{R}$ is therefore also true (because $\{\sim \mathcal{P}\} \vDash \mathcal{R}$), and so $\mathcal{Q} \vee \mathcal{R}$ is true as well. Either way, then, $\mathcal{Q} \vee \mathcal{R}$ is true—so the sentence is truth-functionally true.

c. Assume that every member of $\Gamma \cup \Gamma'$ is true on some truth-value assignment. Then every member of Γ is true, and so $\mathcal{P}$ is true (because $\Gamma \vDash \mathcal{P}$). Every member of Γ′ is also true, and so $\mathcal{Q}$ is true (because $\Gamma' \vDash \mathcal{Q}$). Therefore $\mathcal{P}$ & $\mathcal{Q}$ is true. So $\Gamma \cup \Gamma' \vDash \mathcal{P}$ & $\mathcal{Q}$.

CHAPTER FOUR

Section 4.2E

a. 1.	$\sim (H \vee I)$ ✓			SM
2.	$H \vee I$ ✓			SM
3.	$\sim H$			$1 \sim\vee D$
4.	$\sim I$			$1 \sim\vee D$
5.		H	I	$2 \vee D$
		×	×	

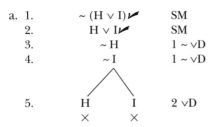

Since the truth-tree is closed, the set is truth-functionally inconsistent.

c.	1.	~ (H ∨ I) ✓		SM
	2.	H ∨ ~ I ✓		SM
	3.	~ H		1 ~ ∨D
	4.	~ I		1 ~ ∨D
	5.	H	~ I	2 ∨D
		×		

Since the truth-tree has at least one completed open branch, the set is truth-functionally consistent. The recoverable fragment is

H	I
F	**F**

e.	1.	A & (B & C) ✓			SM
	2.	~ (A & (B & C)) ✓			SM
	3.	A			1 &D
	4.	B & C ✓			1 &D
	5.	B			4 &D
	6.	C			4 &D
	7.	~ A	~ (B & C) ✓		2 ~ &D
		×			
	8.		~ B	~ C	7 ~ &D
			×	×	

Since the truth-tree is closed, the set is truth-functionally inconsistent.

g.	1.	~ C ∨ (A & B) ✓			SM
	2.	C			SM
	3.	~ (A & B) ✓			SM
	4.	~ C	A & B ✓		1 ∨D
	5.	×	A		4 &D
	6.		B		4 &D
	7.		~ A	~ B	3 ~ &D
			×	×	

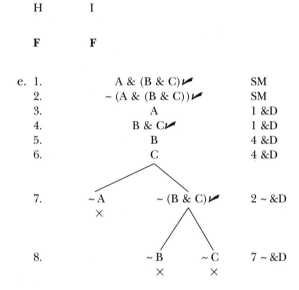

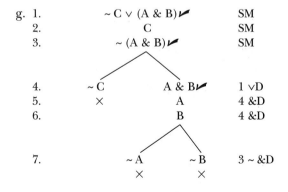

Since the truth-tree is closed, the set is truth-functionally inconsistent.

i. 1.	(~ F & ~ G) & ((G ∨ ~ I) & (I ∨ ~ H))✔	SM
2.	~ F & ~ G✔	1 &D
3.	(G ∨ ~ I) & (I ∨ ~ H)✔	1 &D
4.	~ F	2 &D
5.	~ G	2 &D
6.	G ∨ ~ I✔	3 &D
7.	I ∨ ~ H✔	3 &D
8.	G × ~ I	6 ∨D
9.	I × ~ H	7 ∨D

Since the truth-tree has at least one completed open branch, the set is truth-functionally consistent. The recoverable fragment is

F	G	H	I
F	**F**	**F**	**F**

k. 1.	(F ∨ ~ G) & ((G ∨ ~ I) & (I ∨ ~ H))✔	SM
2.	F ∨ ~ G✔	1 &D
3.	(G ∨ ~ I) & (I ∨ ~ H)✔	1 &D
4.	G ∨ ~ I✔	3 &D
5.	I ∨ ~ H✔	3 &D
6.	F ~ G	2 ∨D
7.	G ~I G × ~ I	4 ∨D
8.	I ~ H I × ~ H I × ~ H	5 ∨D

Since the truth-tree has at least one completed open branch, the set is truth-functionally consistent. The recoverable fragments are

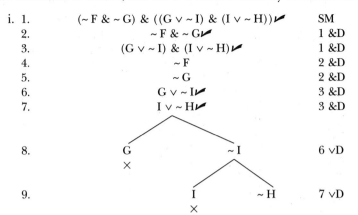

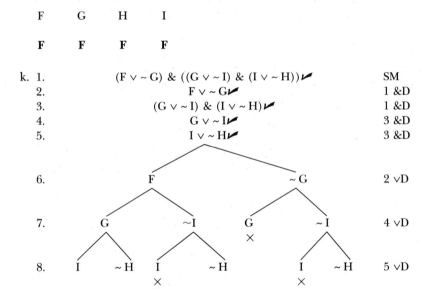

F	G	H	I
T	**T**	**T**	**T**
T	**T**	**F**	**T**
T	**T**	**F**	**F**
T	**F**	**F**	**F**
F	**F**	**F**	**F**

m.

1.	A ∨ (B ∨ C) ✓	SM
2.	~ (A ∨ B) ✓	SM
3.	~ (B & C) ✓	SM
4.	~ (A & C) ✓	SM
5.	~ A	2 ~ ∨D
6.	~ B	2 ~ ∨D
7.	A × B ∨ C ✓	1 ∨D
8.	~ B ~ C	3 ~ &D
9.	~ A ~ C ~ A ~ C	4 ~ &D
10.	B × C B × C × B × C × B × C ×	7 ∨D

Since the truth-tree has at least one completed open branch, the set is truth-functionally consistent. The recoverable fragment is

A	B	C
F	**F**	**T**.

Section 4.3E

a.

1.	~ (A ⊃ B) ✓	SM
2.	~ (B ⊃ A) ✓	SM
3.	A	1 ~ ⊃D
4.	~ B	1 ~ ⊃D
5.	B	2 ~ ⊃D
6.	~ A ×	2 ~ ⊃D

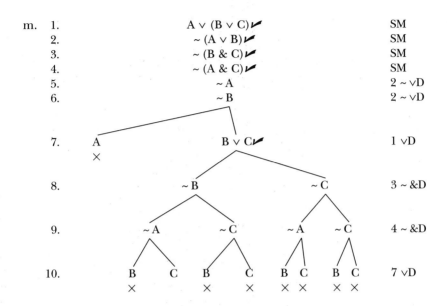

Since the truth-tree is closed, the set is truth-functionally inconsistent.

c.

1.	$\sim((A \supset \sim B) \supset (B \supset A))$ ✓		SM
2.	$\sim(\sim A \supset \sim B)$ ✓		SM
3.	$A \supset \sim B$ ✓		$1 \sim\supset D$
4.	$\sim(B \supset A)$ ✓		$1 \sim\supset D$
5.	$\sim A$		$2 \sim\supset D$
6.	$\sim\sim B$ ✓		$2 \sim\supset D$
7.	B		$4 \sim\supset D$
8.	$\sim A$		$4 \sim\supset D$
9.	B		$6 \sim\sim D$
10.	$\sim A$	$\sim B$	$3 \supset D$
		×	

Since the truth-tree has at least one completed open branch, the set is truth-functionally consistent. The recoverable fragment is

A	B
F	**T**

e.

1.	$H \equiv G$ ✓		SM
2.	$\sim G$		SM
3.	H	$\sim H$	$1 \equiv D$
4.	G	$\sim G$	$1 \equiv D$
	×		

Since the truth-tree has at least one completed open branch, the set is truth-functionally consistent. The recoverable fragment is

H	G
F	**F**

g.

1.	$H \equiv G$ ✓		SM
2.	$\sim(H \supset G)$ ✓		SM
3.	H		$2 \sim\supset D$
4.	$\sim G$		$2 \sim\supset D$
5.	H	$\sim H$	$1 \equiv D$
6.	G	$\sim G$	$1 \equiv D$
	×	×	

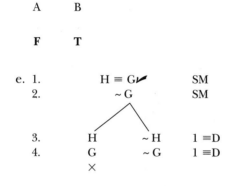

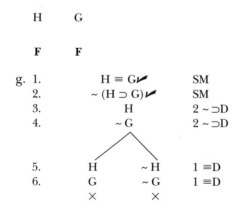

Since the truth-tree is closed, the set is truth-functionally inconsistent.

```
i.  1.            H ≡ G✓                    SM
    2.            G ≡ I✓                    SM
    3.          ~ (H ⊃ I)✓                  SM
    4.              H                       3 ~⊃D
    5.             ~ I                      3 ~⊃D
                  /    \
    6.          H        ~ H                1 ≡D
    7.          G        ~ G                1 ≡D
               / \        ×
    8.       G    ~ G                       2 ≡D
    9.       I    ~ I                       2 ≡D
             ×     ×
```

Since the truth-tree is closed, the set is truth-functionally inconsistent.

```
k.  1.                    A ≡ (~ B ≡ C)✓                         SM
    2.                  ~ A ⊃ (B ⊃ ~ C)✓                         SM
    3.                    ~ (A ⊃ ~ C)✓                           SM
    4.                          A                                3 ~⊃D
    5.                        ~ ~ C✓                             3 ~⊃D
    6.                          C                                5 ~ ~D
                      /                 \
    7.              A                        ~ A                 1 ≡D
    8.          ~ B ≡ C✓                 ~ (~ B ≡ C)             1 ≡D
            /              \                  ×
    9.   ~ ~ A✓               B ⊃ ~ C✓                           2 ⊃D
   10.     A                                                     9 ~ ~D
          / \                 /        \
   11.  ~ B  ~ ~ B         ~ B          ~ ~ B                    8 ≡D
   12.   C    ~ C           C            ~ C                     8 ≡D
               ×           / \             ×
   13.                   ~ B   ~ C                               9 ⊃D
                                ×
```

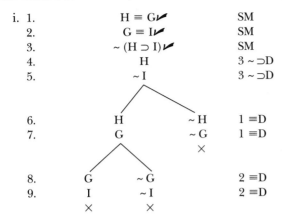

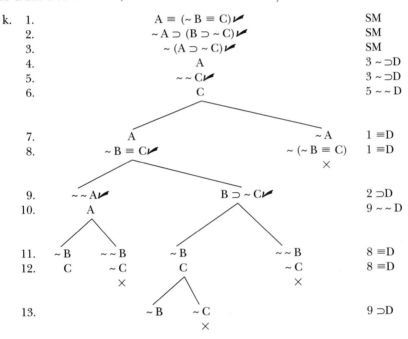

Since the truth-tree has at least one completed open branch, the set is truth-functionally consistent. The recoverable fragment is

A	B	C
T	**F**	**T**

m.

1.	$J \supset (H \equiv \sim I)$ ✓					SM
2.	$\sim (J \equiv H)$ ✓					SM
3.	$\sim J$		$H \equiv \sim I$ ✓			1 ⊃D
4.	J	$\sim J$	J		$\sim J$	2 ~ ≡D
5.	$\sim H$	H	$\sim H$		H	2 ~ ≡D
	×					
6.			H	$\sim H$	H	$\sim H$	3 ≡D
7.			$\sim I$	$\sim \sim I$ ✓	$\sim I$	$\sim \sim I$	3 ≡D
8.			×	I		×	7 ~ ~D

Since the truth-tree has at least one completed open branch, the set is truth-functionally consistent. The recoverable fragments are

H	I	J
T	**T**	**F**
T	**F**	**F**
F	**T**	**T**

Section 4.4E

1.a.

1.	$H \vee G$ ✓		SM
2.	$\sim G \& \sim H$ ✓		SM
3.	$\sim G$		2 &D
4.	$\sim H$		2 &D
5.	H	G	1 ∨D
	×	×	

Since the truth-tree is closed, the set is truth-functionally inconsistent.

c.

1.	~ ~ C✓		SM
2.	C & [U ∨ (~ C & B)]✓		SM
3.	C		1 ~ ~ D
4.	C		2 &D
5.	U ∨ (~ C & B)✓		2 &D
6.	U	~ C & B✓	5 ∨D
7.		~ C	6 &D
8.		B	6 &D
		×	

Since the truth-tree has at least one completed open branch, the set is truth-functionally consistent. The recoverable fragments are

B	C	U
F	**T**	**T**
T	**T**	**T**

e.

1.	~ [~ (E ∨ ~ C) & A]✓			SM
2.	~ (E ∨ ~ C) & A✓			SM
3.	~ (E ∨ ~ C)✓			2 &D
4.	A			2 &D
5.	~ E			3 ~ ∨D
6.	~ ~ C✓			3 ~ ∨D
7.	~ ~ (E ∨ ~ C)✓		~ A	1 ~ &D
			×	
8.	E ∨ ~ C✓			7 ~ ~ D
9.	E	~ C		8 ∨D
	×			
10.		C		6 ~ ~ D
		×		

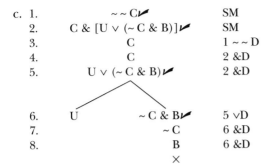

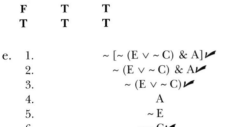

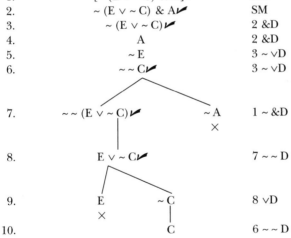

Since the truth-tree is closed, the set is truth-functionally inconsistent.

g.	1.	~ A ∨ ~ ~ [~ (K & ~ A) ∨ R] ✓	SM
	2.	~ [D ∨ (A & ~ K)] ✓	SM
	3.	A & (R ∨ K) ✓	SM
	4.	A	3 &D
	5.	R ∨ K ✓	3 &D
	6.	~ D	2 ~ ∨D
	7.	~ (A & ~ K) ✓	2 ~ ∨D
	8.	~ A × | ~ ~ K ✓	7 ~ &D
	9.	K	8 ~ ~ D
	10.	~ A × | ~ ~ [~ (K & ~ A) ∨ R] ✓	1 ∨D
	11.	~ (K & ~ A) ∨ R ✓	10 ~ ~ D
	12.	~ (K & ~ A) ✓ | R	11 ∨D
	13.	~ K × | ~ ~ A ✓	12 ~ &D
	14.	A	13 ~ ~ D
	15.	R | K | R | K	5 ∨D

Since the truth-tree has at least one completed open branch, the set is truth-functionally consistent. The recoverable fragments are

A	D	K	R
T	**F**	**T**	**T**
T	**F**	**T**	**F**

i.

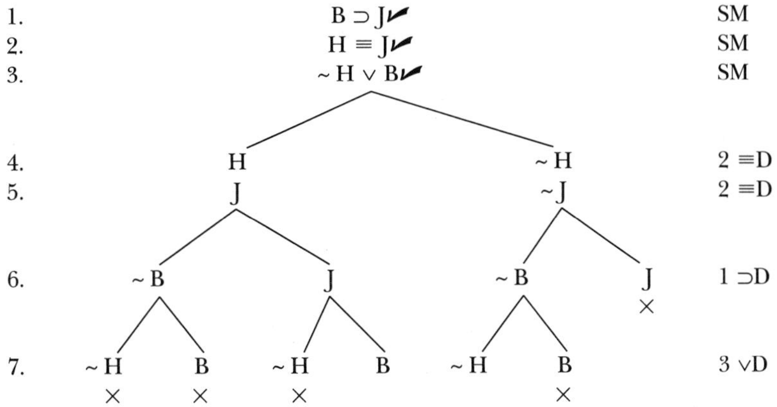

Since the truth-tree has at least one completed open branch, the set is truth-functionally consistent. The recoverable fragments are

B	H	J
T	**T**	**T**
F	**F**	**F**

k.

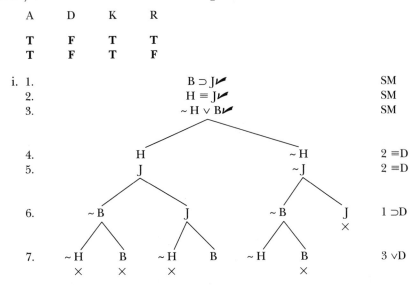

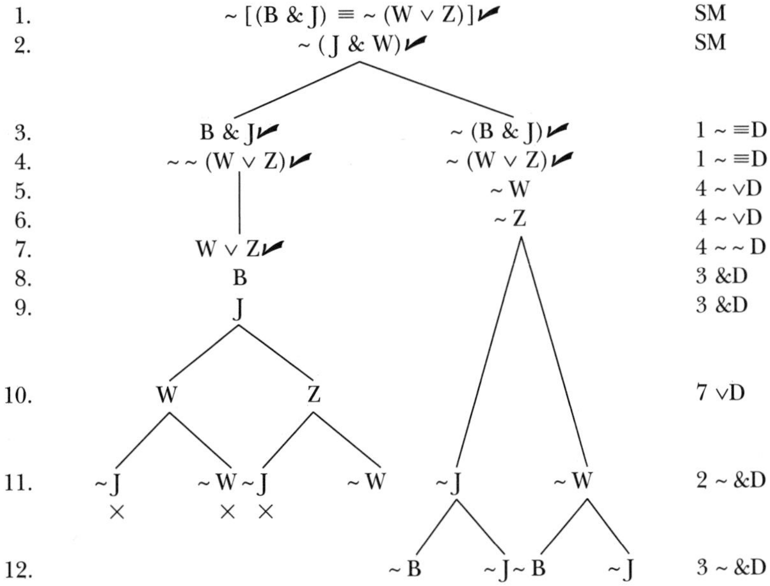

Since the truth-tree has at least one completed open branch, the set is truth-functionally consistent. The recoverable fragments are

B	J	W	Z
T	T	F	T
T	F	F	F
F	T	F	F
F	F	F	F

2.a. True. Truth-trees test for consistency. An open branch shows that the set is consistent because it yields at least one truth-value assignment on which all the members of the set being tested are true.

c. True. If a set has an open truth-tree, then we can recover from that tree a truth-value assignment on which every member of the set is true. And a set is, by definition, consistent if and only if there is at least one truth-value assignment on which all its members are true.

e. True. If all the branches are closed, there is no truth-value assignment on which all the members of the set being tested are true, and if there is no such assignment, that set is truth-functionally inconsistent.

g. False. The number of branches on a completed tree and the number of distinct atomic components of the members of the set being tested are not related.

i. False. Closed branches represent unsuccessful attempts to find truth-value assignments on which all the members of the set being tested are true. No fragments of truth-value assignments are recoverable from them; hence they do not yield assignments on which all the members of the set being tested are false.

k. False. The truth-tree for {A ⊃ B, A} has a closed branch.

1.	A ⊃ B✓		SM
2.	A		SM
3.	~ A	B	1 ⊃D
	×		

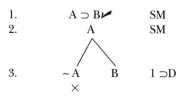

3.a.

1.	D ≡ (B ∨ S) ✓			SM
2.	~ (B ∨ S) & M ✓			SM
3.	N ⊃ M			SM
4.	D ∨ ~ M ✓			SM
5.	~ (B ∨ S) ✓			2 &D
6.	M			2 &D
7.	~ B			5 ~ ∨D
8.	~ S			5 ~ ∨D
9.	D		~ M ×	4 ∨D
10.	D	~ D		1 ≡D
11.	B ∨ S ✓	~ (B ∨ S) ×		1 ≡D
12.	B × S ×			11 ∨D

The truth-tree closes so the set is truth-functionally inconsistent.

c.

1.	[(B ∨ M) ∨ G] & ~ [(B & M) & G] ✓			SM
2.	(B ⊃ I) & (~ I ⊃ ~ G) ✓			SM
3.	[U ⊃ (B ∨ M)] & ~ M ✓			SM
4.	U & ~ I ✓			SM
5.	U			4 &D
6.	~ I			4 &D
7.	U ⊃ (B ∨ M)			3 &D
8.	~ M			3 &D
9.	B ⊃ I ✓			2 &D
10.	~ I ⊃ ~ G ✓			2 &D
11.	(B ∨ M) ∨ G ✓			1 &D
12.	~ [(B & M) & G]			1 &D
13.	~ B		I ×	9 ⊃D
14.	~ ~ I ✓	~ G		10 ⊃D
15.	I ×			14 ~ ~ D
16.		B ∨ M ✓ G ×		11 ∨D
17.		B × M ×		16 ∨D

Since the truth-tree is closed, the set is truth-functionally inconsistent.

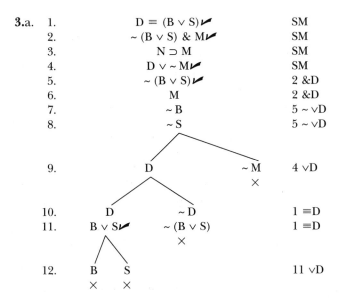

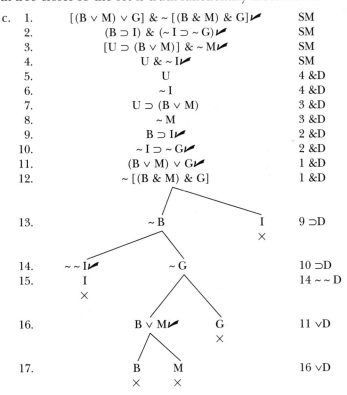

Section 4.5E

1.a.

1.	M & ~ M ✓	SM
2.	M	1 &D
3.	~ M	1 &D
	×	

Since the truth-tree is closed, the sentence we are testing is truth-functionally false.

c.

1.	~ M ∨ ~ M ✓		SM
2.	~ M	~ M	1 ∨D

1.	~ (~ M ∨ ~ M) ✓	SM
2.	~ ~ M ✓	1 ~ ∨D
3.	~ ~ M ✓	1 ~ ∨D
4.	M	2 ~ ~ D
5.	M	3 ~ ~ D

Since neither the tree for '~ M ∨ ~ M' nor the tree for '~ (~ M ∨ ~ M)' is closed, '~ M ∨ ~ M' is truth-functionally indeterminate.

e.

1.	(C ⊃ R) & [(C ⊃ ~ R) & ~ (~ C ∨ R)] ✓		SM
2.	C ⊃ R ✓		1 &D
3.	(C ⊃ ~ R) & ~ (~ C ∨ R) ✓		1 &D
4.	C ⊃ ~ R		3 &D
5.	~ (~ C ∨ R) ✓		3 &D
6.	~ ~ C ✓		5 ~ ∨D
7.	~ R		5 ~ ∨D
8.	C		6 ~ ~ D
9.	~ C	R	2 ⊃D
	×	×	

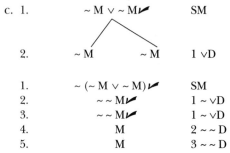

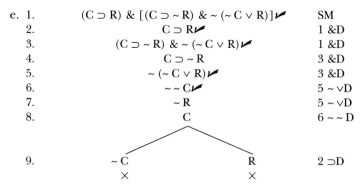

Since the truth-tree is closed, the sentence we are testing is truth-functionally false.

g. 1.   (~ A ≡ ~ Z) & (A & ~ Z)✔   SM
2.   ~ A ≡ ~ Z✔   1 &D
3.   A & ~ Z✔   1 &D
4.   A   3 &D
5.   ~ Z   3 &D

6.   ~ A   ~ ~ A   2 ≡D
7.   ~ Z   ~ ~ Z✔   2 ≡D
    ×
8.   Z   7 ~ ~ D
    ×

Since the truth-tree is closed, the sentence we are testing is truth-functionally false.

i. 1.   (A ∨ B) & ~ (A ∨ B)✔   SM
2.   A ∨ B✔   1 &D
3.   ~ (A ∨ B)✔   1 &D
4.   ~ A   3 ~ ∨D
5.   ~ B   3 ~ ∨D

6.   A   B   2 ∨D
    ×   ×

The tree is closed, so the sentence is truth-functionally false.

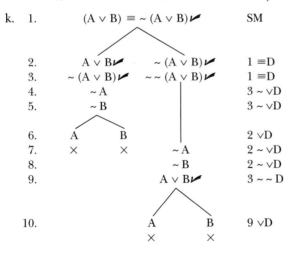

k. 1.   (A ∨ B) ≡ ~ (A ∨ B)✔   SM

2.   A ∨ B✔   ~ (A ∨ B)✔   1 ≡D
3.   ~ (A ∨ B)✔   ~ ~ (A ∨ B)✔   1 ≡D
4.   ~ A   3 ~ ∨D
5.   ~ B   3 ~ ∨D

6.   A   B   2 ∨D
7.   ×   ×   ~ A   2 ~ ∨D
8.   ~ B   2 ~ ∨D
9.   A ∨ B✔   3 ~ ~ D

10.   A   B   9 ∨D
    ×   ×

The tree is closed, so the sentence is truth-functionally false.

m. 1. ~ (D ∨ F) ≡ (~ D ∨ ~ F) SM

	Left branch	Right branch	
2.	~ (D ∨ F) ✓	~ ~ (D ∨ F) ✓	1 ≡D
3.	~ D ∨ ~ F ✓	~ (~ D ∨ ~ F) ✓	1 ≡D
4.		D ∨ F ✓	2 ~ ~ D
5.		~ ~ D ✓	3 ~ ∨D
6.		~ ~ F ✓	3 ~ ∨D
7.		D	5 ~ ~ D
8.		F	6 ~ ~ D
9.		D F	4 ∨D
10.	~ D		2 ~ ∨D
11.	~ F		2 ~ ∨D
12.	~ D ~ F		3 ∨ D

1. ~ (~ (D ∨ F) ≡ (~ D ∨ ~ F)) ✓ SM

	Left branch	Right branch	
2.	~ (D ∨ F) ✓	~ ~ (D ∨ F) ✓	1 ~ ≡D
3.	~ (~ D ∨ ~ F) ✓	~ D ∨ ~ F ✓	1 ~ ≡D
4.		D ∨ F ✓	2 ~ ~ D
5.		~ D ~ F	3 ∨D
6.		D F D F	4 ∨D
7.	~ D	× ×	2 ~ ∨D
8.	~ F		2 ~ ∨D
9.	~ ~ D ✓		3 ~ ∨D
10.	~ ~ F		3 ~ ∨D
11.	D		9 ~ ~ D
	×		

Neither the tree for the sentence nor the tree for its negation is closed. Therefore the sentence is truth-functionally indeterminate.

2.a. 1.	~ [(B ⊃ L) ∨ (L ⊃ B)] ✓	SM
2.	~ (B ⊃ L) ✓	1 ~ ∨D
3.	~ (L ⊃ B) ✓	1 ~ ∨D
4.	B	2 ~ ⊃D
5.	~ L	2 ~ ⊃D
6.	L	3 ~ ⊃D
7.	~ B	3 ~ ⊃D
	×	

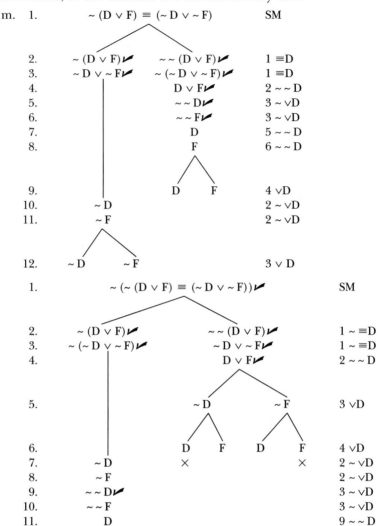

Since the truth-tree for the negation of the given sentence is closed, the given sentence is truth-functionally true.

c.

1.	$\sim [(A \equiv K) \supset (A \vee K)]$ ✓		SM
2.	$A \equiv K$ ✓		1 $\sim\vee$D
3.	$\sim (A \vee K)$ ✓		1 $\sim\vee$D
4.	$\sim A$		3 $\sim\vee$D
5.	$\sim K$		3 $\sim\vee$D
6.	A	$\sim A$	2 $\equiv$D
7.	K	$\sim K$	2 $\equiv$D
	×		

Since the truth-tree for the negation of the given sentence is not closed, the given sentence is not truth-functionally true. The recoverable fragment is

A	K
F	**F**

e.

1.	$\sim [[(J \supset Z) \ \& \sim Z] \supset \sim J]$ ✓		SM
2.	$(J \supset Z) \ \& \sim Z$ ✓		1 $\sim\vee$D
3.	$\sim\sim J$ ✓		1 $\sim\vee$D
4.	J		3 $\sim\sim$D
5.	$J \supset Z$ ✓		2 &D
6.	$\sim Z$		2 &D
7.	$\sim J$	Z	5 $\supset$D
	×	×	

Since the truth-tree for the negation of the given sentence is closed, the given sentence is truth-functionally true.

g. 1.	~ [(B ⊃ (M ⊃ H)) ≡ [(B ⊃ M) ⊃ (B ⊃ H)]] ✓					SM
2.	B ⊃ (M ⊃ H) ✓			~ (B ⊃ (M ⊃ H)) ✓		1 ~ ≡D
3.	~ [(B ⊃ M) ⊃ (B ⊃ H)] ✓			(B ⊃ M) ⊃ (B ⊃ H) ✓		1 ~ ≡D
4.	B ⊃ M ✓					3 ~ ⊃D
5.	~ (B ⊃ H) ✓					3 ~ ⊃D
6.	B					5 ~ ⊃D
7.	~ H					5 ~ ⊃D
8.	~ B ×	M				4 ⊃D
9.		~ B ×	M ⊃ H ✓			2 ⊃D
10.			~ M × H ×			9 ⊃D
11.				B		2 ~ ⊃D
12.				~ (M ⊃ H) ✓		2 ~ ⊃D
13.				M		12 ~ ⊃D
14.				~ H		12 ~ ⊃D
15.				~ (B ⊃ M) ✓	B ⊃ H ✓	3 ⊃D
16.				B		15 ~ ⊃D
17.				~ M ×		15 ~ ⊃D
18.					~ B × H ×	15 ⊃D

Since the truth-tree for the negation of the given sentence is closed, the given sentence is truth-functionally true.

i. 1.	~ ((A & ~ B) ⊃ ~ (A ∨ B)) ✓		SM
2.	A & ~ B ✓		1 ~ ⊃D
3.	~ ~ (A ∨ B) ✓		1 ~ ⊃D
4.	A		2 &D
5.	~ B		2 &D
6.	A ∨ B ✓		3 ~ ~ D
7.	A	B ×	6 ∨D

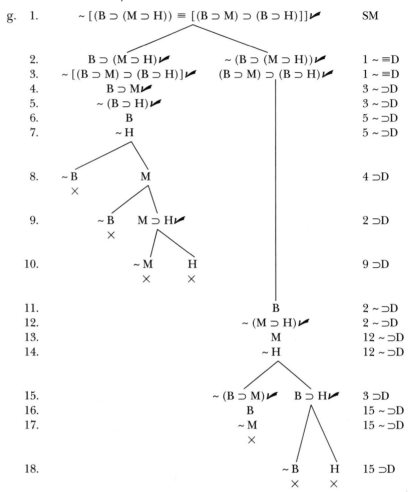

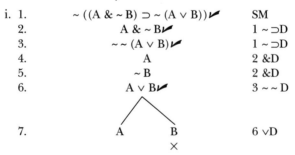

The tree for the negation of the sentence is not closed. Therefore the sentence is not truth-functionally true. The recoverable fragment is

A	B
T	**F**

k.

Line	Left branch		Right branch		Rule
1.	~(((A & B) ⊃ C) ≡ ((A ⊃ ~B) ∨ C))✓				SM
2.	(A & B) ⊃ C✓		~((A & B) ⊃ C)✓		1 ~≡D
3.	~((A ⊃ ~B) ∨ C)✓		(A ⊃ ~B) ∨ C✓		1 ~≡D
4.	~(A ⊃ ~B)✓				3 ~∨D
5.	~C				3 ~∨D
6.	A				4 ~⊃D
7.	~~B✓				4 ~⊃D
8.	B				7 ~~D
9.	~(A & B)✓	C ×			2 ⊃D
10.	~A × / ~B ×				9 ~&D
11.			A & B✓		2 ~⊃D
12.			~C		2 ~⊃D
13.			A		11 &D
14.			B		11 &D
15.			A ⊃ ~B✓	C ×	3 ∨D
16.			~A × / ~B ×		15 ⊃D

The tree for the negation of the sentence is closed. Therefore the sentence is truth-functionally true.

m.

Line	Left branch	Right branch	Rule
1.	~((A ⊃ (B & C)) ⊃ (A ⊃ (B ⊃ C)))✓		SM
2.	A ⊃ (B & C)✓		1 ~⊃D
3.	~(A ⊃ (B ⊃ C))✓		1 ~⊃D
4.	A		3 ~⊃D
5.	~(B ⊃ C)✓		3 ~⊃D
6.	B		5 ~⊃D
7.	~C		5 ~⊃D
8.	~A	B & C✓	2 ⊃D
9.	×	B	8 &D
10.		C	8 &D
		×	

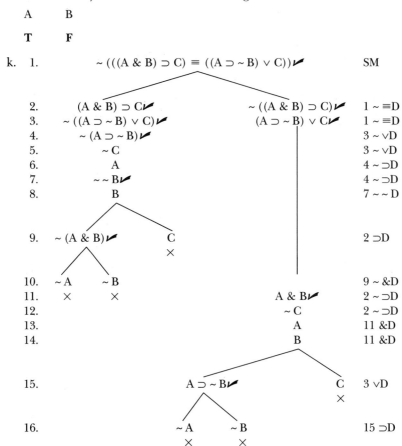

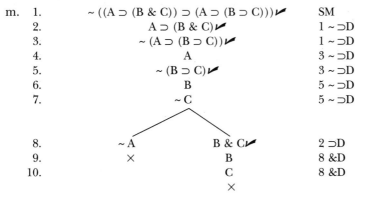

The tree for the negation of the sentence is closed. Therefore the sentence is truth-functionally true.

o.

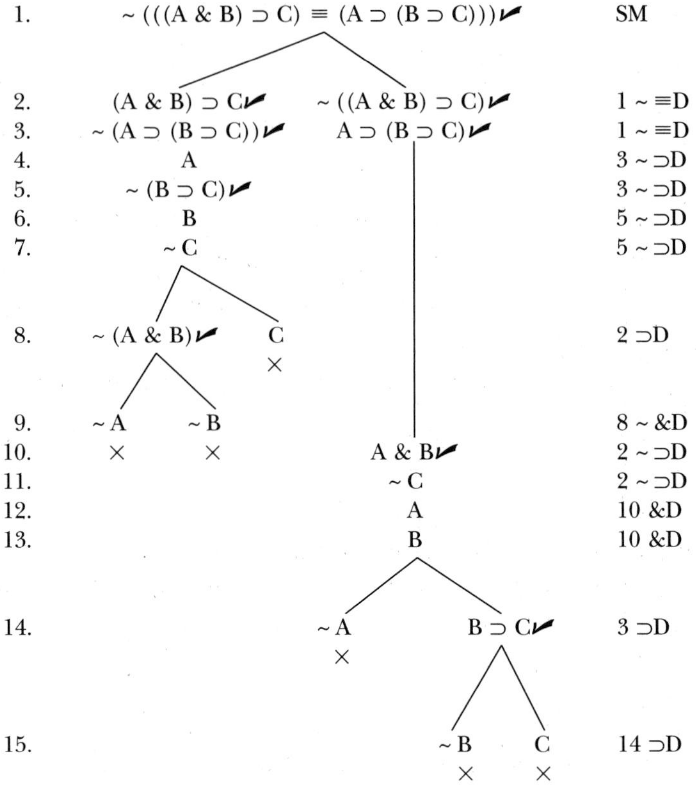

The tree for the negation of the sentence is closed. Therefore the sentence is truth-functionally true.

3.a.	1.	~ (~ A ⊃ A) ✓	SM
	2.	~ A	1 ~ ⊃D
	3.	~ A	1 ~ ⊃D

The tree for the sentence does not close. Therefore the sentence is not truth-functionally false. The recoverable fragment is

A
F

Since only one of the two relevant fragments is recoverable, the sentence is not truth-functionally true. Therefore it is truth-functionally indeterminate.

c.

1.	(A ≡ ~ A) ⊃ ~ (A ≡ ~ A)✓				SM
2.	~ (A ≡ ~ A)✓		~ (A ≡ ~ A)✓		1 ⊃D
3.	A	~ A	A	~ A	2 ~ ≡D
4.	~ ~ A✓	~ A	~ ~ A✓	~ A	2 ~ ≡D
5.	A		A		4 ~ ~ D

The tree for the sentence does not close. Therefore the sentence is not truth-functionally false. The recoverable fragments are

A
T
F

Since both the two relevant fragments are recoverable, the sentence is truth-functionally true.

e.

1.	(~ B & ~ D) ∨ ~ (B ∨ D)✓		SM
2.	~ B & ~ D✓	~ (B ∨ D)✓	1 ∨D
3.	~ B		2 &D
4.	~ D		2 &D
5.		~ B	2 ~ ∨D
6.		~ D	2 ~ ∨D

The tree for the sentence does not close. Therefore the sentence is not truth-functionally false. The recoverable fragment is

B	D
F	**F**

Since only one of the four relevant fragments is recoverable, the sentence is not truth-functionally true. Therefore it is truth-functionally indeterminate.

g.

1.	[(A ∨ B) & (A ∨ C)] ⊃ ~ (B & C)✓				SM
2.	~ ((A ∨ B) & (A ∨ C))✓		~ (B & C)✓		1 ⊃D
3.	~ (A ∨ B)✓	~ (A ∨ C)✓	~ B	~ C	2 ~ &D
4.	~ A	~ A			3 ~ ∨D
5.	~ B	~ C			3 ~ ∨D

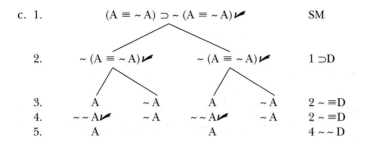

The tree for the sentence does not close. Therefore the sentence is not truth-functionally false. The recoverable fragments are

A	B	C
F	**F**	**T**
F	**F**	**F**
F	**T**	**F**
T	**F**	**T**
T	**F**	**F**
T	**T**	**F**

Since only six of the eight relevant fragments are recoverable, the sentence is not truth-functionally true. Therefore it is truth-functionally indeterminate.

i.

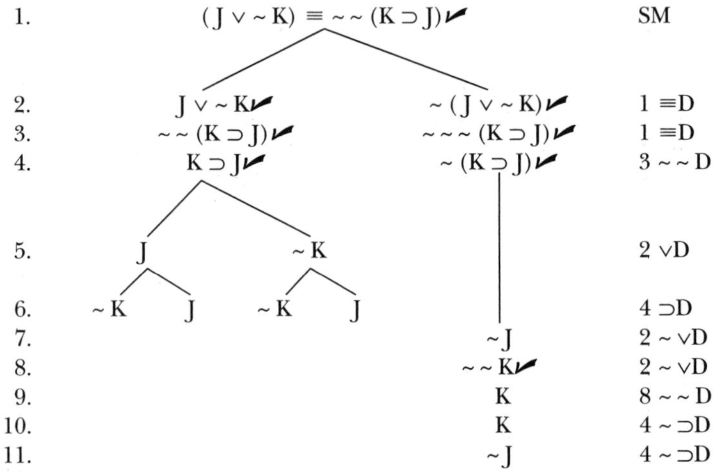

The tree for the sentence does not close. Therefore the sentence is not truth-functionally false. The recoverable fragments are

J	K
T	**F**
T	**T**
F	**T**
F	**F**

Since all four of the four relevant fragments are recoverable, the sentence is truth-functionally true.

4.a. False. A tree for a truth-functionally true sentence can have some open and some closed branches. '(H ∨ ~ H) ∨ (~ H & H)' is clearly truth-functionally true, inasmuch as its left disjunct is truth-functionally true. Yet the tree for this sentence has two open branches and one closed branch.

1.	(H ∨ ~ H) ∨ (~ H & H) ✓		SM
2.	H ∨ ~ H ✓	~ H & H ✓	1 ∨D
3.		~ H	2 &D
4.		H	2 &D
		×	
5.	H ~ H		2 ∨D

c. False. Many truth-functionally indeterminate sentences have completed trees all of whose branches are open. A simple example is

1.	H ∨ G ✓	SM
2.	H G	1 ∨D

e. False. Some such unit sets have open trees; for example, {𝒫 ∨ 𝒬} does, but not all such unit sets have open trees. For example, {𝒫 & 𝒬} has a closed tree if 𝒫 is 'H & G' and 𝒬 is '~ H & K'.

1.	(H & G) & (~ H & K) ✓	SM
2.	H & G ✓	1 &D
3.	~ H & K ✓	1 &D
4.	H	2 &D
5.	G	2 &D
6.	~ H	3 &D
7.	K	3 &D
	×	

Section 4.6E

1.a.

1.	~ [~ (Z ∨ K) ≡ (~ Z & ~ K)] ✓				SM
2.	~ (Z ∨ K) ✓		~ ~ (Z ∨ K) ✓		1 ~ ≡D
3.	~ (~ Z & ~ K) ✓		~ Z & ~ K ✓		1 ~ ≡D
4.	~ Z				2 ~ ∨D
5.	~ K				2 ~ ∨D
6.	~ ~ Z ✓	~ ~ K ✓			3 ~ &D
7.	Z	K			6 ~ ~ D
	×	×			
8.			Z ∨ K ✓		2 ~ ~ D
9.			~ Z		3 &D
10.			~ K		3 &D
11.			Z	K	8 ∨D
			×	×	

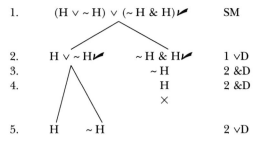

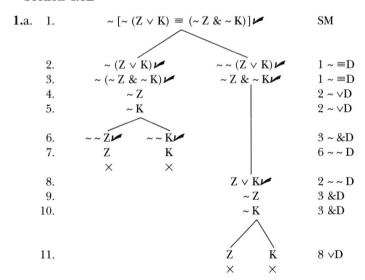

Our truth-tree for the negation of the biconditional of the sentences we are testing, '~ (Z ∨ K)' and '~ Z & ~ K', is closed. Therefore that negation is truth-functionally false, the biconditional it is a negation of is truth-functional true, and the sentences we are testing are truth-functionally equivalent.

c.

1.	~ [[(B & C) ⊃ R] ≡ [(B ⊃ R) & (C ⊃ R)]]✓					SM
2.	(B & C) ⊃ R✓				~ [(B & C) ⊃ R]✓	1 ~ ≡D
3.	~ [(B ⊃ R) & (C ⊃ R)]				(B ⊃ R) & (C ⊃ R)✓	1 ~ ≡D
4.	~ (B ⊃ R)✓		~ (C ⊃ R)✓			3 ~ &D
5.	B		C			4 ~ ⊃D
6.	~ R		~ R			4 ~ ⊃D
7.	~ (B & C)✓	R ✕	~ (B & C)✓	R ✕		2 ⊃D
8.	~ B ✕ ~ C		~ B ~ C ✕			7 ~ &D
9.					B & C✓	2 ~ ⊃D
10.					~ R	2 ~ ⊃D
11.					B	9 &D
12.					C	9 &D
13.					B ⊃ R✓	3 &D
14.					C ⊃ R	3 &D
15.					~ B ✕ R ✕	13 ⊃D

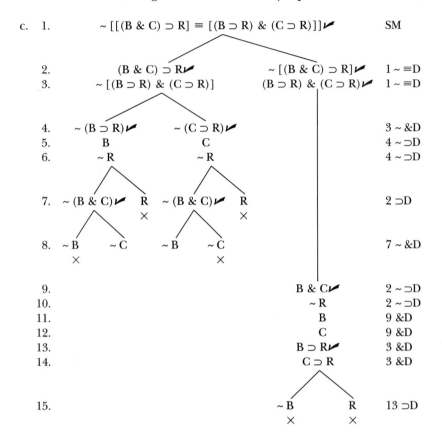

Since our truth-tree for the negation of the biconditional of the sentences we are testing is open, those sentences are not truth-functionally equivalent. The recoverable fragments are

B	C	R
T	**F**	**F**
F	**T**	**F**

e.

Line	Left branch	Right branch	Justification
1.	~ ([A & (B ∨ C)] ≡ [(A & B) ∨ (A & C)]✓		SM
2.	A & (B ∨ C)✓	~ [A & (B ∨ C)]✓	1 ~ ≡D
3.	~ [(A & B) ∨ (A & C)]✓	(A & B) ∨ (A & C)✓	1 ~ ≡D
4.	A		2 &D
5.	B ∨ C✓		2 &D
6.	~ (A & B)✓		3 ~ ∨D
7.	~ (A & C)✓		3 ~ ∨D
8.	~ A × ~ C		7 ~ &D
9.	~ A × ~ B		6 ~ &D
10.	B × C ×		5 ∨D
11.		A & B✓ A & C	3 ∨D
12.		A A	11 &D
13.		B C	11 &D
14.		~ A × ~ (B ∨ C)✓ ~ A × ~ (B ∨ C)✓	2 ~ &D
15.		~ B ~ B	14 ~ ∨D
16.		~ C × ~ C ×	14 ~ ∨D

Since our truth-tree for the negation of the biconditional of the sentences we are testing is closed, those sentences are truth-functionally equivalent.

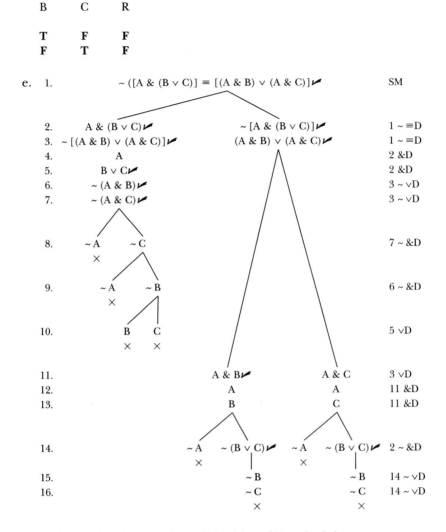

g. 1.	$\sim [(D \supset (L \supset M)) \equiv ((D \supset L) \supset M)]$✓		SM
2.	$D \supset (L \supset M)$✓	$\sim [D \supset (L \supset M)]$✓	$1 \sim \equiv D$
3.	$\sim [(D \supset L) \supset M]$✓	$(D \supset L) \supset M$✓	$1 \sim \equiv D$
4.	$D \supset L$✓		$3 \sim \supset D$
5.	$\sim M$		$3 \sim \supset D$
6.	$\sim D$ $L \supset M$✓		$2 \supset D$
7.	$\sim L$ M ×		$6 \supset D$
8.	$\sim D$ L $\sim D$ L ×		$4 \supset D$
9.		D	$2 \sim \supset D$
10.		$\sim (L \supset M)$✓	$2 \sim \supset D$
11.		L	$10 \sim \supset D$
12.		$\sim M$	$10 \sim \supset D$
13.		$\sim (D \supset L)$✓ M ×	$3 \supset D$
14.		D	$13 \sim \supset D$
15.		$\sim L$ ×	$13 \sim \supset D$

Since our truth-tree for the negation of the biconditional of the sentences we are testing is open, those sentences are not truth-functionally equivalent. The recoverable fragments are

D	L	M
F	**T**	**F**
F	**F**	**F**

2.a. True. If $\mathscr{P}$ and $\mathscr{Q}$ are truth-functionally equivalent, their biconditional is truth-functionally true. And all truth-functionally true sentences have open trees.

c. False. The tree for the set $\{\mathscr{P}, \mathscr{Q}\}$ may close, for $\mathscr{P}$ and $\mathscr{Q}$ may both be truth-functionally false. Remember that all truth-functionally false sentences are truth-functionally equivalent and a set composed of one or more truth-functionally false sentences has a closed tree.

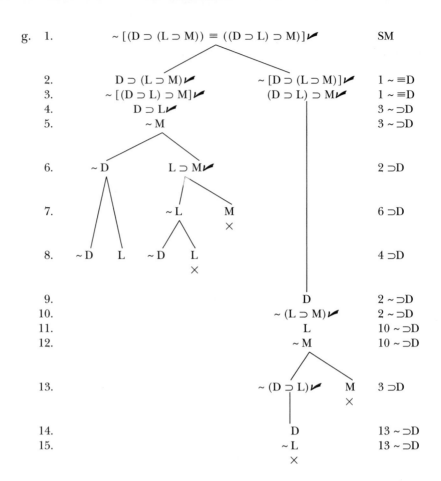

Section 4.7E

1.a.

1.	$A \supset (B \& C)$ ✓		SM
2.	$C \equiv B$		SM
3.	$\sim C$		SM
4.	$\sim \sim A$ ✓		SM
5.	A		$4 \sim \sim D$
6.	$\sim A$	$B \& C$ ✓	$1 \supset D$
7.	×	B	6 &D
8.		C	6 &D
		×	

Our tree is closed, so the set $\{A \supset (B \& C), C \equiv B, \sim C\}$ does truth-functionally entail '$\sim A$'.

c.

1.	$\sim (A \equiv B)$ ✓		SM
2.	$\sim A$		SM
3.	$\sim B$		SM
4.	$\sim (C \& \sim C)$		SM
5.	A	$\sim A$	$1 \sim \equiv D$
6.	$\sim B$	B	$1 \sim \equiv D$
	×	×	

Our tree is closed, so the set $\{\sim (A \equiv B), \sim A, \sim B\}$ does truth-functionally entail '$C \& \sim C$'.

e.

1.	$\sim \sim F \supset \sim \sim G$ ✓				SM
2.	$\sim G \supset \sim F$ ✓				SM
3.	$\sim (G \supset F)$ ✓				SM
4.	G				$3 \sim \supset D$
5.	$\sim F$				$3 \sim \supset D$
6.	$\sim \sim \sim F$ ✓		$\sim \sim G$ ✓		$1 \supset D$
7.	$\sim F$		G		$6 \sim \sim D$
8.	$\sim \sim G$ ✓	$\sim F$	$\sim \sim G$ ✓	$\sim F$	$2 \supset D$
9.	G		G		$8 \sim \sim D$

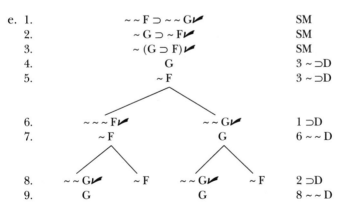

Our truth-tree is open, so the set {~ ~ F ⊃ ~ ~ G, ~ G ⊃ ~ F} does not truth-functionally entail ‘G ⊃ F’. The relevant fragment of the recoverable truth-value assignments is

F	G
F	**T**

g.

1.	[(C ∨ D) & H] ⊃ A✓		SM
2.	D		SM
3.	~ (H ⊃ A)✓		SM
4.	H		3 ~ ⊃D
5.	~ A		3 ~ ⊃D
6.	~ [(C ∨ D) & H]✓	A ✕	1 ⊃D
7.	~ (C ∨ D)✓ ~ H ✕		6 ~ &D
8.	~ C		7 ~ ∨D
9.	~ D ✕		7 ~ ∨D

Our truth-tree is closed, so the given set does truth-functionally entail ‘H ⊃ A’.

i.

1.	(J ∨ M) ⊃ ~ (J & M)✓		SM
2.	M ≡ (M ⊃ J)✓		SM
3.	~ (M ⊃ J)✓		SM
4.	M		3 ~ ⊃D
5.	~ J		3 ~ ⊃D
6.	~ (J ∨ M)✓	~ (J & M)✓	1 ⊃D
7.	~ J		6 ~ ∨D
8.	~ M ✕		6 ~ ∨D
9.		M ~ M	2 ≡D
10.		M ⊃ J✓ ~ (M ⊃ J) ✕	2 ≡D
11.		~ J ~ M ✕	6 ~ &D
12.		~ M ✕ J ✕	10 ⊃D

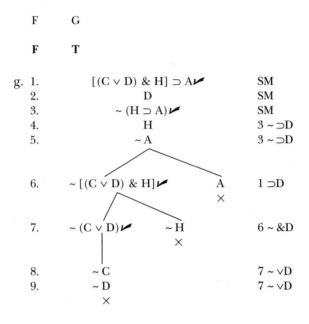

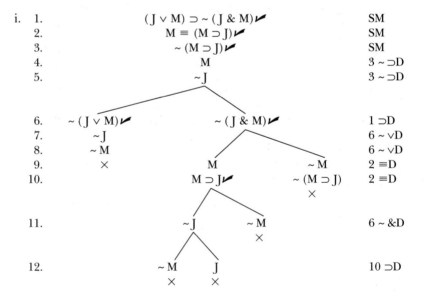

The tree is closed, so the set {(J ∨ M) ⊃ ~ (J & M), M ≡ (M ⊃ J)} does truth-functionally entail 'M ⊃ J'.

k.

1.		~ (~ (A ≡ B) ⊃ (~ A ≡ ~ B)) ✓			SM
2.		~ (A ≡ B) ✓			1 ~ ⊃D
3.		~ (~ A ≡ ~ B) ✓			1 ~ ⊃D
4.	A		~ A		2 ~ ≡D
5.	~ B		B		2 ~ ≡D
6.	~ A	~ ~ A ✓	~ A	~ ~ A ✓	3 ~ ≡D
7.	~ ~ B	~ B	~ ~ B ✓	~ B	3 ~ ≡D
8.	×	A	|	A	6 ~ ~ D
9.			B	×	7 ~ ~ D

Our truth-tree is open, so the empty set does not truth-functionally entail '~ (A ≡ B) ⊃ (~ A ≡ ~ B)'. The relevant fragments of the recoverable truth-value assignments are

A	B
T	**F**
F	**T**

m.

1.	~ (((A ⊃ B) ⊃ (C ⊃ D)) ⊃ (C ⊃ (B ⊃ D))) ✓			SM
2.	(A ⊃ B) ⊃ (C ⊃ D) ✓			1 ~ ⊃D
3.	~ (C ⊃ (B ⊃ D)) ✓			1 ~ ⊃D
4.	C			3 ~ ⊃D
5.	~ (B ⊃ D) ✓			3 ~ ⊃D
6.	B			5 ~ ⊃D
7.	~ D			5 ~ ⊃D
8.	~ (A ⊃ B) ✓	C ⊃ D ✓		2 ⊃D
9.	A			8 ~ ⊃D
10.	~ B			8 ~ ⊃D
11.	×	~ C	D	8 ⊃D
		×	×	

The tree is closed, so the empty set does truth-functionally entail '[(A ⊃ B) ⊃ (C ⊃ D)] ⊃ [C ⊃ (B ⊃ D)]'.

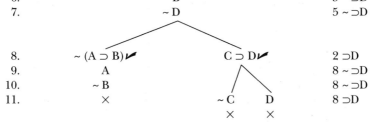

2.a.

1.	$M \supset (K \supset B)$ ✓			SM
2.	$\sim K \supset \sim M$ ✓			SM
3.	$L \& M$ ✓			SM
4.	$\sim B$			SM
5.	L			3 &D
6.	M			3 &D
7.	$\sim M$ ×	$K \supset B$ ✓		1 ⊃D
8.		$\sim K$	B ×	7 ⊃D
9.		$\sim \sim K$ ✓	$\sim M$ ×	2 ⊃D
10.		K ×		9 ~ ~ D

Our truth-tree for the premises and the negation of the conclusion of the argument we are testing is closed. Therefore there is no truth-value assignment on which the premises and the negation of the conclusion are all true, hence no assignment on which the premises are true and the conclusion false. So the argument is truth-functionally valid.

c.

1.	$A \& (B \vee C)$ ✓				SM
2.	$(\sim C \vee H) \& (H \supset \sim H)$ ✓				SM
3.	$\sim (A \& B)$ ✓				SM
4.	A				1 &D
5.	$B \vee C$ ✓				1 &D
6.	$\sim C \vee H$ ✓				2 &D
7.	$H \supset \sim H$ ✓				2 &D
8.	$\sim A$ ×	$\sim B$			3 ~ &D
9.		B ×	C		5 ∨D
10.			$\sim C$ ×	H	6 ∨D
11.			$\sim H$ ×	$\sim H$ ×	7 ⊃D

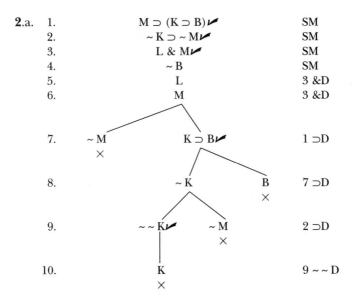

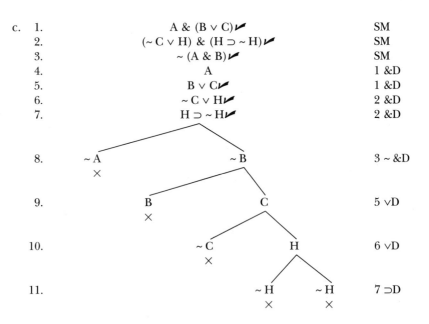

Our truth-tree for the premises and the negation of the conclusion of the argument we are testing is closed. Therefore the argument is truth-functionally valid.

e.

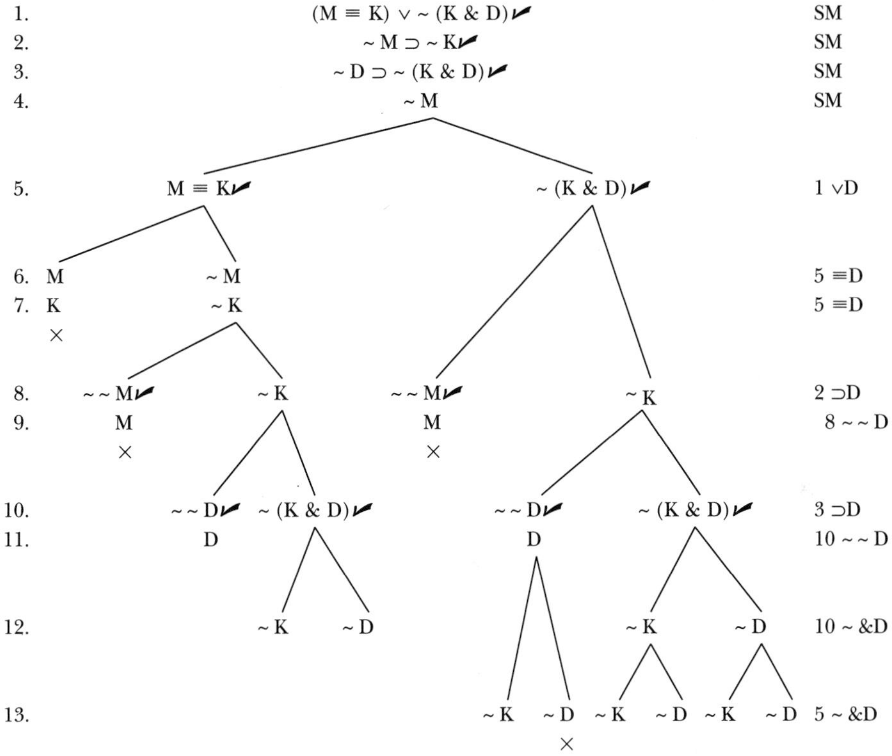

Our truth-tree for the premises and the negation of the conclusion of the argument we are testing is open. Therefore that argument is truth-functionally invalid. The recoverable fragments are

D	K	M
T	**F**	**F**
F	**F**	**F**

g.

1.			B & (H ∨ Z) ✓			SM
2.			~ Z ⊃ K ✓			SM
3.			(B ≡ Z) ⊃ ~ Z ✓			SM
4.			~ K			SM
5.			~ (M & N)			SM
6.			B			1 &D
7.			H ∨ Z			1 &D
8.			~ ~ Z ✓		K ×	2 ⊃D
9.			Z			8 ~ ~ D
10.	~ (B ≡ Z) ✓			~ Z ×		3 ⊃D
11.	B	~ B				10 ~ ≡D
12.	~ Z ×	Z ×				10 ~ ≡D

Our truth-tree for the premises and the negation of the conclusion of the argument we are testing is closed. Therefore that argument is truth-functionally valid. Notice that our tree closed before we decomposed the negation of the conclusion. Thus the premises of the argument form a truth-functionally inconsistent set, and therefore those premises and any conclusion constitute a truth-functionally valid argument, even where the conclusion has no atomic components in common with the premises.

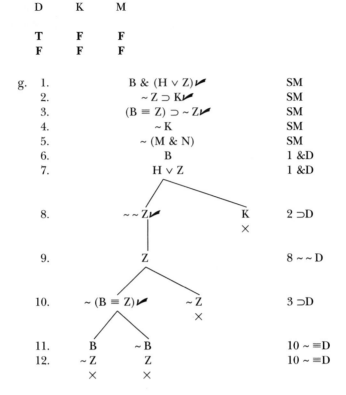

i.

Line						
1.	A & (B ⊃ C) ✓					SM
2.	~ ((A & C) ∨ (A & ~ B)) ✓					SM
3.	A					1 &D
4.	B ⊃ C ✓					1 &D
5.	~ (A & C) ✓					2 ~ ∨D
6.	~ (A & ~ B) ✓					2 ~ ∨D
7.	~ B			C		4 ⊃D
8.	~ A	~ C		~ A	~ C	5 ~ &D
	×			×	×	
9.		~ A	~ ~ B ✓			6 ~ &D
10.		×	B			9 ~ ~ D
			×			

Our truth-tree for the premise and the negation of the conclusion is closed. Therefore the argument is truth-functionally valid.

k.

Line						
1.	A ⊃ ~ A ✓					SM
2.	(B ⊃ A) ⊃ B ✓					SM
3.	~ (A ≡ ~ B) ✓					SM
4.	A			~ A		3 ~ ≡D
5.	~ ~ B ✓			~ B		3 ~ ≡D
6.	B					5 ~ ~ D
7.	~ (B ⊃ A) ✓	B		~ (B ⊃ A) ✓	B	2 ⊃D
8.	B			B	×	7 ~ ⊃D
9.	~ A			~ A		7 ~ ⊃D
10.	×	~ A	~ A	×		1 ⊃D
		×	×			

Our truth-tree for the premise and the negation of the conclusion is closed. Therefore the argument is truth-functionally valid.

3.a. In symbolizing the argument we use the following abbreviations:

C: Members of Congress claim to be sympathetic to senior citizens.
M: More money will be collected through social security taxes.
S: The social security system will succeed.
T: Many senior citizens will be in trouble.

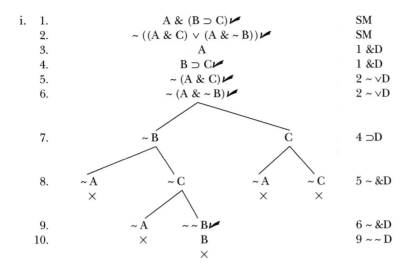

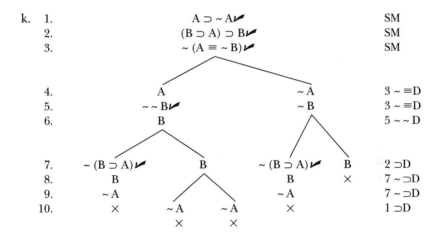

Here is our tree for the premises and the negation of the conclusion:

1.	S ≡ M ✓		SM
2.	S ∨ T		SM
3.	C & ~ M ✓		SM
4.	~ ~ S ✓		SM
5.	S		4 ~ ~ D
6.	C		3 &D
7.	~ M		3 &D
8.	S	~ S	1 ≡D
9.	M	~ M	1 ≡D
	×	×	

Since our truth-tree is closed, the argument is truth-functionally valid.

c. In symbolizing the argument we use the following abbreviations:

A: The President acts quickly.
C: The President is pressured by senior citizens.
D: Senior citizens will be delighted.
H: The President is pressured by members of the House.
M: The President is pressured by members of the Senate.
S: The social security system will be saved.

Here is our tree for the premises and the negation of the conclusion.

1.	(A ⊃ S) & (S ⊃ D) ✓				SM
2.	[(M ∨ H) ∨ C] ⊃ A ✓				SM
3.	~ (M ∨ H) & C ✓				SM
4.	~ D				SM
5.	~ (M ∨ H) ✓				3 &D
6.	C				3 &D
7.	~ M				5 ~ ∨D
8.	~ H				5 ~ ∨D
9.	A ⊃ S ✓				1 &D
10.	S ⊃ D ✓				1 &D
11.	~ [(M ∨ H) ∨ C] ✓	A			2 ⊃D
12.	~ (M ∨ H)				11 ~ ∨D
13.	~ C				11 ~ ∨D
	×				
14.		~ S		D	10 ⊃D
				×	
15.		~ A	S		9 ⊃D
		×	×		

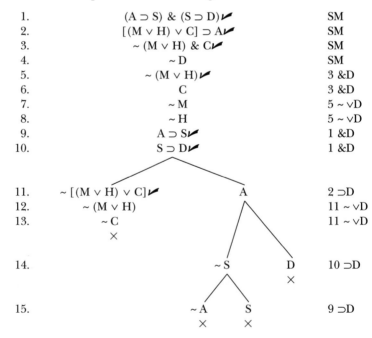

Since our tree is closed, the argument is truth-functionally valid.

e. In symbolizing the argument we use the following abbreviations:

H: The House of Representatives will pass the bill.
S: The Senate will pass the bill.
T: The President will be pleased.
V: The voters will be pleased.
W: All the members of the White House will be happy.

Here is our tree for the premises and the negation of the conclusion.

1.	~ (S & H)✔	SM
2.	[(H ∨ S) ⊃ V] & [(S & H) ⊃ ~ T]✔	SM
3.	~ T ⊃ ~ W✔	SM
4.	~ ~ W✔	SM
5.	W	4 ~ ~ D
6.	(H ∨ S) ⊃ V✔	2 &D
7.	(S & H) ⊃ ~ T✔	2 &D
8.	~ ~ T✔ ~ W	3 ⊃D
9.	T	8 ~ ~ D
10.	~ (S & H)✔ ~ T	7 ⊃D
11.	~ (H ∨ S)✔ V	6 ⊃D
12.	~ H	11 ~ ∨D
13.	~ S	11 ~ ∨D
14.	~ S ~ H ~ S ~ H	10 ~ &D
15.	~ S ~ H ~ S ~ H ~ S ~ H ~ S ~ H	1 ~ &D

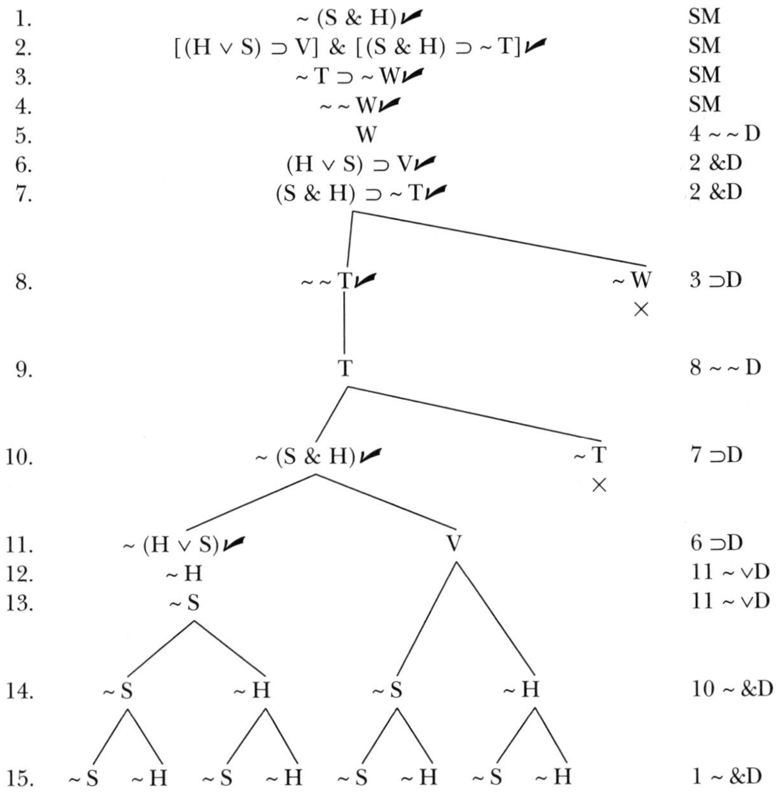

Since our truth-tree is open, the argument is truth-functionally invalid. The recoverable fragments are

H	S	T	W	V
T	**F**	**T**	**T**	**T**
F	**T**	**T**	**T**	**T**
F	**F**	**T**	**T**	**T**
F	**F**	**T**	**T**	**F**

5. The needed rules are

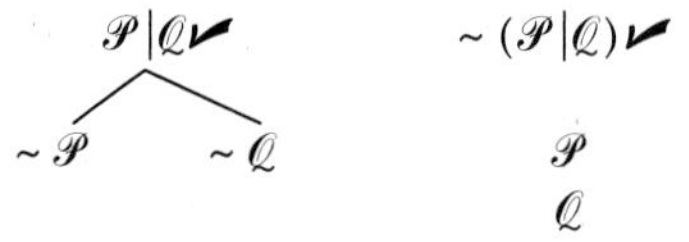

The tree for the negation of the biconditional of the given sentences is

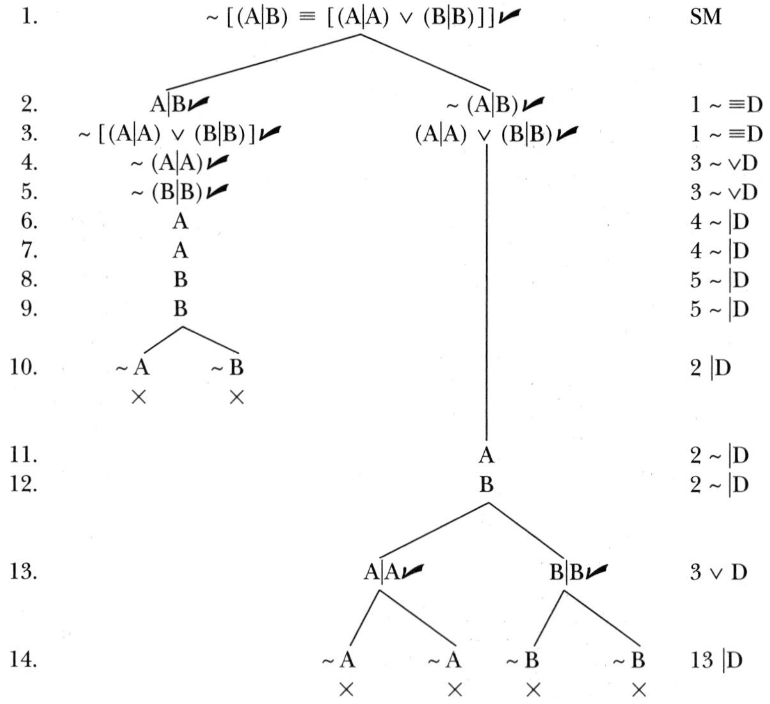

Since our tree closes, the sentences we are testing are truth-functionally equivalent.

CHAPTER FIVE

Section 5.1.1E

a. Derive: Q & R

1	R & Q	Assumption
2	Q	1 &E
3	R	1 &E
4	Q & R	2, 3 &I

c. Derive: K

1	S & [~ T & (K & ~ F)]	Assumption
2	~ T & (K & ~ F)	1 &E
3	K & ~ F	2 &E
4	K	3 &E

e. Derive: [(J ⊃ T) & ~ R] & (~ U ∨ G)

1	N & ~ R	Assumption
2	K & (J ⊃ T)	Assumption
3	(~ U ∨ G) & ~ J	Assumption
4	J ⊃ T	2 &E
5	~ R	1 &E
6	~ U ∨ G	3 &E
7	(J ⊃ T) & ~ R	4, 5 &I
8	[(J ⊃ T) & ~ R] & (~ U ∨ G)	6, 7 &I

Section 5.1.2E

a. Derive: U

1	H ⊃ U	Assumption
2	S & H	Assumption
3	H	2 &E
4	U	1, 3 ⊃E

c. Derive: J ⊃ T

1	J ⊃ (S & T)	Assumption
2	| J	Assumption
3	| S & T	1, 2 ⊃E
4	| T	3 &E
5	J ⊃ T	2–4 ⊃I

e. Derive: (S & B) ⊃ ~ N

1	S ⊃ (L & ~ N)	Assumption
2	S & B	Assumption
3	S	2 &E
4	L & ~ N	1, 3 ⊃E
5	~ N	4 &E
6	(S & B) ⊃ ~ N	2–5 ⊃I

Section 5.1.3E

a. Derive: ~ G

1	(G ⊃ I) & ~ I	Assumption
2	G	Assumption
3	G ⊃ I	1 &E
4	I	2, 3 ⊃E
5	~ I	1 &E
6	~ G	2–5 ~ I

c. Derive: ~ ~ R

1	~ R ⊃ A	Assumption
2	~ R ⊃ ~ A	Assumption
3	~ R	Assumption
4	A	1, 3 ⊃E
5	~ A	2, 3 ⊃E
6	~ ~ R	3–5 ~ I

e. Derive: P

1	(~ P ⊃ ~ L) & (~ L ⊃ L)	Assumption
2	~ P	Assumption
3	~ P ⊃ ~ L	1 &E
4	~ L	2, 3 ⊃E
5	~ L ⊃ L	1 &E
6	L	4, 5 ⊃E
7	P	2–6 ~ E

Section 5.1.4E

a. Derive: B ∨ (K ∨ G)

1	K	Assumption
2	K ∨ G	1 ∨I
3	B ∨ (K ∨ G)	2 ∨I

c. Derive: D

1	D ∨ D	Assumption
2	| D	Assumption
3	| D	2 R
4	D	1, 2–3, 2–3 ∨E

e. Derive: X

1	~ E ∨ X	Assumption
2	~ E ⊃ X	Assumption
3	| ~ E	Assumption
4	| X	2, 3 ⊃E
5	| X	Assumption
6	| X	5 R
7	X	1, 3–4, 5–6 ∨E

Section 5.1.5E

a. Derive: Q

1	K ≡ (~ E & Q)	Assumption
2	K	Assumption
3	~ E & Q	1, 2 ≡E
4	Q	3 &E

c. Derive: S & ~ A

1	(S ≡ ~ I) & N	Assumption
2	(N ≡ ~ I) & ~ A	Assumption
3	~ A	2 &E
4	N ≡ ~ I	2 &E
5	N	1 &E
6	~ I	4, 5 ≡E
7	S ≡ ~ I	1 &E
8	S	6, 7 ≡E
9	S & ~ A	3, 8 &I

e. Derive: (E ≡ O) & (O ≡ E)

1	(E ⊃ T) & (T ⊃ O)	Assumption
2	O ⊃ E	Assumption
3	E	Assumption
4	E ⊃ T	1 &E
5	T	3, 4 ⊃E
6	T ⊃ O	1 &E
7	O	5, 6 ⊃E
8	O	Assumption
9	E	2, 8 ⊃E
10	E ≡ O	3–7, 8–9 ≡I
11	O ≡ E	3–7, 8–9 ≡I
12	(E ≡ O) & (O ≡ E)	10, 11 &I

Section 5.2E

1.a. Derive: (A & C) ∨ (B & C)

1	(A ∨ B) & C	Assumption
2	A ∨ B	1 &E
3	C	1 &E
4	A	Assumption
5	A & C	3, 4 &I
6	(A & C) ∨ (B & C)	5 ∨I
7	B	Assumption
8	B & C	3, 7 &I
9	(A & C) ∨ (B & C)	8 ∨I
10	(A & C) ∨ (B & C)	2, 4–6, 7–9 ∨E

c. Derive: ~ B

1	B ⊃ (A & ~ B)	Assumption
2	B	Assumption
3	A & ~ B	1, 2 ⊃E
4	~ B	3 &E
5	B	2 R
6	~ B	2–5 ~ I

e. Derive: $C \supset (\sim A \,\&\, B)$

1	$\sim D$	Assumption
2	$C \supset (A \equiv B)$	Assumption
3	$(D \vee B) \supset \sim A$	Assumption
4	$(A \equiv B) \supset (D \,\&\, E)$	Assumption
5	$\sim B \supset D$	Assumption
6	│ C	Assumption
7	│ $A \equiv B$	2, 6 $\supset$E
8	│ $D \,\&\, E$	7, 4 $\supset$E
9	│ D	8 &E
10	│ $D \vee B$	9 $\vee$I
11	│ $\sim A$	3, 10 $\supset$E
12	│ │ $\sim B$	Assumption
13	│ │ D	5, 12 $\supset$E
14	│ │ $\sim D$	1 R
15	│ B	12–14 $\sim$E
16	│ $\sim A \,\&\, B$	11, 15 &I
17	$C \supset (\sim A \,\&\, B)$	6–16 $\supset$I

g. Derive: $A \equiv B$

1	$\sim A \,\&\, \sim B$	Assumption
2	│ A	Assumption
3	│ │ $\sim B$	Assumption
4	│ │ $\sim A$	1 &E
5	│ │ A	2 R
6	│ B	3–5 $\sim$E
7	│ B	Assumption
8	│ │ $\sim A$	Assumption
9	│ │ B	7 R
10	│ │ $\sim B$	1 &E
11	│ A	8–10 $\sim$E
12	$A \equiv B$	2–6, 7–11 $\equiv$I

2.a. Derive: $\sim D$

1	$\sim \sim P \supset (W \,\&\, \sim D)$	Assumption
2	$\sim P$	Assumption
3	$W \,\&\, \sim D$	1,2 $\supset$E ⟵ ERROR!
4	$\sim D$	3 &E

This is not an application of the rule Conditional Elimination because the antecedent of the conditional is '~ ~ P' and the sentence on line 2 is '~ P'. They are not the same sentence.

c. Derive: H & A

1	B ⊃ A	Assumption
2	H	Assumption
3	B	Assumption
4	A	1, 3 ⊃E
5	A & A	4, 4 &I
6	B ⊃ (A & A)	3–5 ⊃I
7	H & A	2, 4 &I ⟵ ERROR!

Line 4 is not accessible at line 7. The subderivation ends at line 5. Note that line 5, which cites line 4 twice, is acceptable.

e. Derive: X

1	(K & H) ⊃ L	Assumption
2	X ≡ L	Assumption
3	K & H	Assumption
4	L	1, 3 ⊃E
5	L	4 R ⟵ ERROR!
6	X	2, 5 ≡E

'L' on line 4 is not accessible at line 5. '(K & H) ⊃ L' is derivable on line 5 by Conditional Introduction, but that would not help complete the derivation. In fact, 'X' is not derivable from the set of primary assumptions.

Section 5.4E

1. Goal analysis

Part (i)

a. Derive: L & ~ G

	1	(L & T) & (~ G & S)	Assumption
Subgoal ⟶		L	
Subgoal ⟶		~ G	
Goal ⟶		L & ~ G	_, _ &I

c. Derive: S ⊃ ~ B

	1	~ B ≡ S	Assumption
		S	Assumption
Subgoal ⟶		~ B	
Goal ⟶		S ⊃ ~ B	_–_ ⊃I

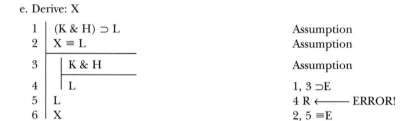

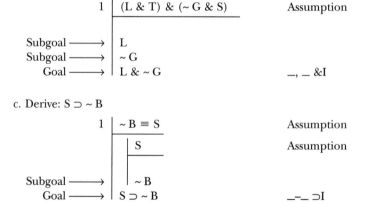

e. Derive: ~ M

	1	M ≡ P	Assumption
	2	~ P	Assumption
		| M	Assumption
Subgoal ⟶		| P	
Subgoal ⟶		| ~ P	
Goal ⟶		~ M	_–_ ~ I

g. Derive S & I

	1	~ G & ~ H	Assumption
	2	G	Assumption
		| ~ (S & I)	Assumption
Subgoal ⟶		| G	
Subgoal ⟶		| ~ G	
Goal ⟶		S & I	_, _ ~ E

i. Derive B

	1	~ Q ⊃ (K ≡ (J & B))	Assumption
	2	~ Q & K	Assumption
Subgoal ⟶		K ≡ (J & B)	
Goal ⟶		J & B	_, _ ≡E
		B	_ &E

k. Derive: N ⊃ (C ⊃ ~ D)

	1	~ D & (N ∨ H)	Assumption
	2	| N	Assumption
	3	| | C	Assumption
Subgoal ⟶		| | ~ D	
Goal ⟶		| C ⊃ ~ D	3–_ ⊃I
		N ⊃ (C ⊃ ~ D)	2–_ ⊃I

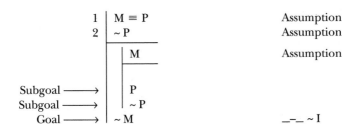

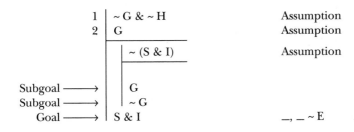

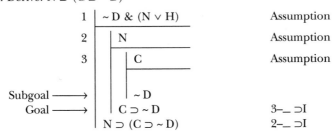

Part (ii)

a. Derive: L & ~ G

1	(L & T) & (~ G & S)	Assumption
2	L & T	1 &E
3	~ G & S	1 &E
4	L	2 &E
5	~ G	3 &E
6	L & ~ G	4, 5 &I

c. Derive: S ⊃ ~ B

1	~ B ≡ S	Assumption
2	│ S	Assumption
3	│ ~ B	1, 2 ≡E
4	S ⊃ ~ B	2–3 ⊃I

e. Derive: ~ M

1	M ≡ P	Assumption
2	~ P	Assumption
3	│ M	Assumption
4	│ P	1, 3 ≡E
5	│ ~ P	2 R
6	~ M	3–5 ~ I

g. Derive S & I

1	~ G & ~ H	Assumption
2	G	Assumption
3	│ ~ (S & I)	Assumption
4	│ G	2 R
5	│ ~ G	1 &E
6	S & I	3–5 ~ E

i. Derive B

1	~ Q ⊃ (K ≡ (J & B))	Assumption
2	~ Q & K	Assumption
3	~ Q	2 &E
4	K	2 &E
5	K ≡ (J & B)	1, 3 ⊃E
6	J & B	4, 5 ≡E
7	B	6 &E

k. Derive: N ⊃ (C ⊃ ~ D)

```
1 | ~ D & (N ∨ H)              Assumption
  |---
2 | | N                        Assumption
  | |---
3 | | | C                      Assumption
  | | |---
4 | | | ~ D                    1 &E
5 | | C ⊃ ~ D                  3–4 ⊃I
6 | N ⊃ (C ⊃ ~ D)              2–5 ⊃I
```

2. Derivability

a. Derive: H & (K ⊃ J)

```
1 | (Z ≡ R) & H                Assumption
2 | (K ⊃ J) & ~ ~ Y            Assumption
3 | D ∨ B                      Assumption
  |---
4 | H                          1 &E
5 | K ⊃ J                      2 &E
6 | H & (K ⊃ J)                4, 5 &I
```

c. Derive: A ⊃ B

```
1 | A ≡ (A ⊃ B)                Assumption
  |---
2 | | A                        Assumption
  | |---
3 | | A ⊃ B                    1, 2 ≡E
4 | | B                        2, 3 ⊃E
5 | A ⊃ B                      2–4 ⊃I
```

e. Derive: ~ G

```
1 | B & F                      Assumption
2 | ~ (B & G)                  Assumption
  |---
3 | | G                        Assumption
  | |---
4 | | B                        1 &E
5 | | B & G                    4, 3 &I
6 | | ~ (B & G)                2 R
7 | ~ G                        3–6 ~ I
```

3. Validity

a. Derive: L ∨ P

```
1 | ~ (L & E)                  Assumption
2 | ~ (L & E) ≡ P              Assumption
  |---
3 | P                          1, 2 ≡E
4 | L ∨ P                      3 ∨I
```

c. Derive: R ⊃ T

1	R ⊃ S		Assumption
2	S ⊃ T		Assumption
3		R	Assumption
4		S	1, 3 ⊃E
5		T	2, 4 ⊃E
6	R ⊃ T		3–5 ⊃I

e. Derive: ~ (A & D)

1	A ⊃ (B & C)		Assumption
2	~ C		Assumption
3		A & D	Assumption
4		A	3 &E
5		B & C	1, 4 ⊃E
6		C	5 &E
7		~ C	2 R
8	~ (A & D)		3–7 ~ I

g. Derive: A ≡ C

1	A ≡ B		Assumption
2	B ≡ C		Assumption
3		A	Assumption
4		B	1, 3 ≡E
5		C	4, 2 ≡E
6		C	Assumption
7		B	6, 2 ≡E
8		A	7, 1 ≡E
9	A ≡ C		3–5, 6–8 ≡I

i. Derive: F & G

1	F ≡ G		Assumption
2	F ∨ G		Assumption
3		F	Assumption
4		F	3 R
5		G	Assumption
6		F	5, 1 ≡E
7	F		2, 3–4, 5–6 ∨E
8	G		1, 7 ≡E
9	F & G		7, 8 &I

4. Theorems

a. Derive: $A \supset (A \vee B)$

Line	Formula	Justification
1	│ │ A	Assumption
2	│ │ $A \vee B$	1 $\vee$I
3	│ $A \supset (A \vee B)$	1–2 $\supset$I

c. Derive: $(A \equiv B) \supset (A \supset B)$

Line	Formula	Justification
1	│ │ $A \equiv B$	Assumption
2	│ │ │ A	Assumption
3	│ │ │ B	1, 2 $\equiv$E
4	│ │ $A \supset B$	2–3 $\supset$I
5	│ $(A \equiv B) \supset (A \supset B)$	1–4 $\supset$I

e. Derive: $(A \supset B) \supset [(C \supset A) \supset (C \supset B)]$

Line	Formula	Justification
1	│ │ $A \supset B$	Assumption
2	│ │ │ $C \supset A$	Assumption
3	│ │ │ │ C	Assumption
4	│ │ │ │ A	2, 3 $\supset$E
5	│ │ │ │ B	1, 4 $\supset$E
6	│ │ │ $C \supset B$	3–5 $\supset$I
7	│ │ $(C \supset A) \supset (C \supset B)$	2–6 $\supset$I
8	│ $(A \supset B) \supset [(C \supset A) \supset (C \supset B)]$	1–7 $\supset$I

g. Derive: $[(A \supset B) \,\&\, {\sim} B] \supset {\sim} A$

Line	Formula	Justification
1	│ │ $(A \supset B) \,\&\, {\sim} B$	Assumption
2	│ │ $A \supset B$	1 &E
3	│ │ │ A	Assumption
4	│ │ │ B	2, 3 $\supset$E
5	│ │ │ ${\sim} B$	1 &E
6	│ │ ${\sim} A$	3–5 ${\sim}$I
7	│ $[(A \supset B) \,\&\, {\sim} B] \supset {\sim} A$	1–6 $\supset$I

i. Derive: $A \supset [B \supset (A \supset B)]$

Line	Formula	Justification
1	│ │ A	Assumption
2	│ │ │ B	Assumption
3	│ │ │ │ A	Assumption
4	│ │ │ │ B	2 R
5	│ │ │ $A \supset B$	3–4 $\supset$I
6	│ │ $B \supset (A \supset B)$	2–5 $\supset$I
7	│ $A \supset [B \supset (A \supset B)]$	1–6 $\supset$I

k. Derive: $(A \supset B) \supset [\sim B \supset \sim (A \,\&\, D)]$

1	$\vert\ \vert\ A \supset B$	Assumption
2	$\vert\ \vert\ \vert\ \sim B$	Assumption
3	$\vert\ \vert\ \vert\ \vert\ A \,\&\, D$	Assumption
4	$\vert\ \vert\ \vert\ \vert\ A$	3 &E
5	$\vert\ \vert\ \vert\ \vert\ B$	1, 4 ⊃E
6	$\vert\ \vert\ \vert\ \vert\ \sim B$	2 R
7	$\vert\ \vert\ \vert\ \sim (A \,\&\, D)$	3–6 ~ I
8	$\vert\ \vert\ \sim B \supset \sim (A \,\&\, D)$	2–7 ⊃I
9	$\vert\ (A \supset B) \supset [\sim B \supset \sim (A \,\&\, D)]$	1–8 ⊃I

5. Equivalence

a. Derive: $(A \vee \sim\sim B) \,\&\, C$

1	$\vert\ (A \vee \sim\sim B) \,\&\, C$	Assumption
2	$\vert\ (A \vee \sim\sim B) \,\&\, C$	1 R

Derive: $(A \vee \sim\sim B) \,\&\, C$

1	$\vert\ (A \vee \sim\sim B) \,\&\, C$	Assumption
2	$\vert\ (A \vee \sim\sim B) \,\&\, C$	1 R

c. Derive: $\sim\sim A$

1	$\vert\ A$	Assumption
2	$\vert\ \vert\ \sim A$	Assumption
3	$\vert\ \vert\ A$	1 R
4	$\vert\ \vert\ \sim A$	2 R
5	$\vert\ \sim\sim A$	2–4 ~ I

Derive: A

1	$\vert\ \sim\sim A$	Assumption
2	$\vert\ \vert\ \sim A$	Assumption
3	$\vert\ \vert\ \sim\sim A$	1 R
4	$\vert\ \vert\ \sim A$	2 R
5	$\vert\ A$	2–4 ~ E

e. Derive: ~ B ⊃ ~ A

1	A ⊃ B	Assumption
2	~ B	Assumption
3	A	Assumption
4	B	1, 3 ⊃E
5	~ B	2 R
6	~ A	3–5 ~ I
7	~ B ⊃ ~ A	2–6 ⊃I

Derive: A ⊃ B

1	~ B ⊃ ~ A	Assumption
2	A	Assumption
3	~ B	Assumption
4	~ A	1, 3 ⊃E
5	A	2 R
6	B	3–5 ~ E
7	A ⊃ B	2–6 ⊃I

6. Inconsistency

a.	1	A ≡ ~ (A ≡ A)	Assumption
	2	A	Assumption
	3	~ (A ≡ A)	1, 2 ≡E
	4	A	Assumption
	5	A	4 R
	6	A ≡ A	4–5, 4–5 ≡I

c.	1	M ⊃ (K ⊃ B)	Assumption
	2	~ K ⊃ ~ M	Assumption
	3	(L & M) & ~ B	Assumption
	4	L & M	3 &E
	5	M	4 &E
	6	K ⊃ B	5, 1 ⊃E
	7	~ K	Assumption
	8	~ M	7, 2 ⊃E
	9	M	4 &E
	10	K	7–9 ~ E
	11	B	6, 10 ⊃E
	12	~ B	3 &E

e.	1	$\sim (Y \equiv A)$	Assumption
	2	$\sim Y$	Assumption
	3	$\sim A$	Assumption
	4	│ $\sim Y$	Assumption
	5	│ │ $\sim A$	Assumption
	6	│ │ $\sim Y$	2 R
	7	│ │ Y	4 R
	8	│ A	5–7 $\sim$ E
	9	│ A	Assumption
	10	│ │ $\sim Y$	Assumption
	11	│ │ A	9 R
	12	│ │ $\sim A$	3 R
	13	│ Y	10–12 $\sim$ E
	14	$Y \equiv A$	4–8, 9–13 $\equiv$I
	15	$\sim (Y \equiv A)$	1 R

g.	1	$(\sim C \supset \sim D)\ \&\ (C \supset D)$	Assumption
	2	$D \supset \sim C$	Assumption
	3	$\sim (B\ \&\ \sim D)$	Assumption
	4	$B \equiv (\sim C \vee D)$	Assumption
	5	│ D	Assumption
	6	│ $\sim C$	2, 5 $\supset$E
	7	│ $\sim C \supset \sim D$	1 &E
	8	│ $\sim D$	6, 7 $\supset$E
	9	│ D	5 R
	10	$\sim D$	5–9 $\sim$ I
	11	│ $\sim D$	Assumption
	12	│ $C \supset D$	1 &E
	13	│ │ C	Assumption
	14	│ │ D	12, 13 $\supset$E
	15	│ │ $\sim D$	11 R
	16	│ $\sim C$	13–15 $\sim$ I
	17	│ $\sim C \vee D$	16 $\vee$I
	18	│ B	4, 17 $\equiv$E
	19	│ $B\ \&\ \sim D$	18, 11 &I
	20	│ $\sim (B\ \&\ \sim D)$	3 R
	21	D	11–20 $\sim$ E

7. Derivability

a. Derive: $\sim Q \supset \sim P$

1	$P \supset Q$	Assumption
2	$\mid\ \sim Q$	Assumption
3	$\mid\ \mid\ P$	Assumption
4	$\mid\ \mid\ Q$	1, 3 $\supset$E
5	$\mid\ \mid\ \sim Q$	2 R
6	$\mid\ \sim P$	3–5 $\sim$I
7	$\sim Q \supset \sim P$	2–6 $\supset$I

c. Derive: $H \equiv M$

1	$H \supset M$	Assumption
2	$\sim H \supset \sim M$	Assumption
3	$\mid\ H$	Assumption
4	$\mid\ M$	1, 3 $\supset$E
5	$\mid\ M$	Assumption
6	$\mid\ \mid\ \sim H$	Assumption
7	$\mid\ \mid\ \sim M$	2, 6 $\supset$E
8	$\mid\ \mid\ M$	5 R
9	$\mid\ H$	6–8 $\sim$E
10	$H \equiv M$	3–4, 5–9 $\equiv$I

e. Derive: $\sim I$

1	$\sim (F \supset G)$	Assumption
2	$\sim (G \supset H)$	Assumption
3	$\mid\ I$	Assumption
4	$\mid\ \sim (G \supset H)$	2 R
5	$\mid\ \mid\ G$	Assumption
6	$\mid\ \mid\ \mid\ \sim H$	Assumption
7	$\mid\ \mid\ \mid\ \sim (F \supset G)$	1 R
8	$\mid\ \mid\ \mid\ \mid\ F$	Assumption
9	$\mid\ \mid\ \mid\ \mid\ G$	5 R
10	$\mid\ \mid\ \mid\ F \supset G$	8–9 $\supset$I
11	$\mid\ \mid\ H$	6–10 $\sim$E
12	$\mid\ G \supset H$	5–11 $\supset$I
13	$\sim I$	3–12 $\sim$I

g. Derive: C

1	$L \equiv {\sim}(Z \equiv {\sim}C)$	Assumption
2	${\sim}(L \vee Z)$	Assumption
3	$\vert\ {\sim}C$	Assumption
4	$\vert\ \vert\ Z \equiv {\sim}C$	Assumption
5	$\vert\ \vert\ Z$	3, 4 ≡E
6	$\vert\ \vert\ L \vee Z$	5 ∨I
7	$\vert\ \vert\ {\sim}(L \vee Z)$	2 R
8	$\vert\ {\sim}(Z \equiv {\sim}C)$	4–7 ~I
9	$\vert\ L$	1, 8 ≡E
10	$\vert\ L \vee Z$	9 ∨I
11	$\vert\ {\sim}(L \vee Z)$	2 R
12	C	3–11 ~E

i. Derive: K

1	${\sim}(Y \supset X)$	Assumption
2	${\sim}(X \supset H)$	Assumption
3	$\vert\ {\sim}K$	Assumption
4	$\vert\ {\sim}(X \supset H)$	2 R
5	$\vert\ \vert\ X$	Assumption
6	$\vert\ \vert\ \vert\ {\sim}H$	Assumption
7	$\vert\ \vert\ \vert\ {\sim}(Y \supset X)$	1 R
8	$\vert\ \vert\ \vert\ \vert\ Y$	Assumption
9	$\vert\ \vert\ \vert\ \vert\ X$	5 R
10	$\vert\ \vert\ \vert\ Y \supset X$	8–9 ⊃I
11	$\vert\ \vert\ H$	6–10 ~E
12	$\vert\ X \supset H$	5–11 ⊃I
13	K	3–12 ~E

k. Derive: $(J \supset (E \,\&\, {\sim} F)) \supset Z$

1	$(L \supset X) \vee B$	Assumption
2	$({\sim}(L \supset X) \,\&\, {\sim} B) \equiv (J \supset (E \,\&\, {\sim} F))$	Assumption
3	$\quad J \supset (E \,\&\, {\sim} F)$	Assumption
4	$\quad\quad {\sim} Z$	Assumption
5	$\quad\quad {\sim}(L \supset X) \,\&\, {\sim} B$	2, 3 ≡E
6	$\quad\quad {\sim}(L \supset X)$	5 &E
7	$\quad\quad\quad (L \supset X)$	Assumption
8	$\quad\quad\quad (L \supset X)$	7 R
9	$\quad\quad\quad B$	Assumption
10	$\quad\quad\quad\quad {\sim}(L \supset X)$	Assumption
11	$\quad\quad\quad\quad B$	9 R
12	$\quad\quad\quad\quad {\sim} B$	5 &E
13	$\quad\quad\quad (L \supset X)$	10–12 ~E
14	$\quad\quad (L \supset X)$	1, 7–8, 9–13 ∨E
15	$\quad Z$	4–14 ~E
16	$(J \supset (E \,\&\, {\sim} F)) \supset Z$	3–15 ⊃I

m. Derive: $(R \equiv P) \equiv (R \equiv Q)$

1	$P \equiv Q$	Assumption
2	$\quad R \equiv P$	Assumption
3	$\quad\quad R$	Assumption
4	$\quad\quad P$	2, 3 ≡E
5	$\quad\quad Q$	1, 4 ≡E
6	$\quad\quad Q$	Assumption
7	$\quad\quad P$	1, 6 ≡E
8	$\quad\quad R$	2, 7 ≡E
9	$\quad R \equiv Q$	3–5, 6–8 ≡I
10	$\quad R \equiv Q$	Assumption
11	$\quad\quad R$	Assumption
12	$\quad\quad Q$	10, 11 ≡E
13	$\quad\quad P$	1, 12 ≡E
14	$\quad\quad P$	Assumption
15	$\quad\quad Q$	1, 14 ≡E
16	$\quad\quad R$	10, 15 ≡E
17	$\quad R \equiv P$	11–13, 14–16 ≡I
18	$(R \equiv P) \equiv (R \equiv Q)$	2–9, 10–17 ≡I

o. Derive: (A ∨ B) ⊃ ~ C

1	A ⊃ (Q & B)	Assumption
2	(~ Q ≡ B) & (C ⊃ A)	Assumption
3	│ A ∨ B	Assumption
4	│ │ A	Assumption
5	│ │ │ C	Assumption
6	│ │ │ Q & B	1, 4 ⊃E
7	│ │ │ B	6 &E
8	│ │ │ ~ Q ≡ B	2 &E
9	│ │ │ Q	6 &E
10	│ │ │ ~ Q	7, 8 ≡E
11	│ │ ~ C	5–10 ~ I
12	│ │ B	Assumption
13	│ │ │ C	Assumption
14	│ │ │ C ⊃ A	2 &E
15	│ │ │ A	13, 14 ⊃E
16	│ │ │ Q & B	1, 15 ⊃E
17	│ │ │ ~ Q ≡ B	2 &E
18	│ │ │ Q	16 &E
19	│ │ │ ~ Q	12, 17 ≡E
20	│ │ ~ C	13–19 ~ I
21	│ ~ C	3, 4–11, 12–20 ∨E
22	(A ∨ B) ⊃ ~ C	3–21 ⊃I

8. Validity

a. Derive: H

1	(H & I) ∨ (H & S)	Assumption
2	│ H & I	Assumption
3	│ H	2 &E
4	│ H & S	Assumption
5	│ H	4 &E
6	H	1, 2–3, 4–5 ∨E

c. Derive: J ≡ ~ C

```
1   | B ≡ ~ B                       Assumption
    |---------
2   |  | ~ (J ≡ ~ C)                Assumption
    |  |---------
3   |  |  | B                       Assumption
    |  |  |------
4   |  |  | ~ B                     1, 3 ≡E
5   |  |  | B                       3 R
6   |  | ~ B                        3–5 ~ I
7   |  | B                          1, 6 ≡E
8   | J ≡ ~ C                       2–7 ~ E
```

e. Derive: B

```
1   | M ⊃ I                         Assumption
2   | ~ I & L                       Assumption
3   | M ∨ B                         Assumption
    |---------
4   |  | M                          Assumption
    |  |------
5   |  |  | ~ B                     Assumption
    |  |  |------
6   |  |  | I                       1, 4 ⊃E
7   |  |  | ~ I                     2 &E
8   |  | B                          5–7 ~ E
9   |  | B                          Assumption
    |  |------
10  |  | B                          9 R
11  | B                             3, 4–8, 9–10 ∨E
```

g. Derive: ~ D

```
1   | M ⊃ A                                   Assumption
2   | (M ≡ (A & M)) ⊃ (C & ~ (A & D))         Assumption
3   | ~ (A & D) ≡ (C & ~ D)                   Assumption
    |---------------------------------
4   |  | M                                    Assumption
    |  |------
5   |  | A                                    1, 4 ⊃E
6   |  | A & M                                4, 5 &I
7   |  | A & M                                Assumption
    |  |------
8   |  | M                                    7 &E
9   | M ≡ (A & M)                             4–6, 7–8 ≡I
10  | C & ~ (A & D)                           2, 9 ⊃E
11  | ~ (A & D)                               10 &E
12  | C & ~ D                                 3, 11 ≡E
13  | ~ D                                     12 &E
```

i. Derive ~ S ≡ ~ N

1	(J & Y) ⊃ ~ A	Assumption
2	S ⊃ (A & ~ A)	Assumption
3	N ⊃ (A & (J & Y))	Assumption
4	~ S	Assumption
5	N	Assumption
6	A & (J & Y)	3, 5 ⊃E
7	J & Y	6 &E
8	A	6 &E
9	~ A	1, 7 ⊃E
10	~ N	5–9 ~ I
11	~ N	Assumption
12	S	Assumption
13	A & ~ A	2, 12 ⊃E
14	A	13 &E
15	~ A	13 &E
16	~ S	12–15 ~ I
17	~ S ≡ ~ N	4–10, 11–16 ≡I

k. Derive: (H & I) ⊃ J

1	(~ H ∨ J) ∨ K	Assumption
2	K ⊃ ~ I	Assumption
3	H & I	Assumption
4	~ H ∨ J	Assumption
5	~ H	Assumption
6	~ J	Assumption
7	H	3 &E
8	~ H	5 R
9	J	6–8 ~ E
10	J	Assumption
11	J	10 R
12	J	4, 5–9, 10–11 ∨E
13	K	Assumption
14	~ J	Assumption
15	I	3 &E
16	~ I	2, 13 ⊃E
17	J	14–16 ~ E
18	J	1, 4–12, 13–17 ∨E
19	(H & I) ⊃ J	3–18 ⊃I

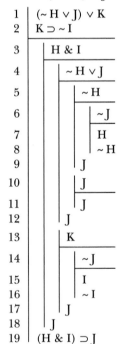

m. Derive: F

Line	Derivation	Subderivation	Subsubderivation	Justification
1	F ∨ H			Assumption
2	~ H ≡ (L ∨ G)			Assumption
3	(G & B) ∨ [G & (K ⊃ G)]			Assumption
4		G & B		Assumption
5		G		4 &E
6		G & (K ⊃ G)		Assumption
7		G		6 &E
8	G			3, 4–5, 6–7 ∨E
9	L ∨ G			8 ∨I
10	~ H			2, 9 ≡E
11		F		Assumption
12		F		11R
13		H		Assumption
14			~ F	Assumption
15			H	13 R
16			~ H	10 R
17		F		14–16 ~ E
18	F			1, 11–12, 13–17 ∨E

o. Derive: E ∨ F

```
 1  | (A ∨ B) & ~ C              Assumption
 2  | ~ C ⊃ (D & ~ A)            Assumption
 3  | B ⊃ (A ∨ E)                Assumption
    |-----------
 4  | ~ C                        1 &E
 5  | D & ~ A                    2, 4 ⊃E
 6  | A ∨ B                      1 &E
 7  | | A                        Assumption
    | |-----
 8  | | | ~ B                    Assumption
    | | |-----
 9  | | | A                      7 R
10  | | | ~ A                    5 &E
11  | | B                        8–10 ~ E
    |
12  | | B                        Assumption
    | |-----
13  | | B                        12 R
14  | B                          6, 7–11, 12–13 ∨E
15  | A ∨ E                      3, 14 ⊃E
16  | | A                        Assumption
    | |-----
17  | | | ~ E                    Assumption
    | | |-----
18  | | | A                      16 R
19  | | | ~ A                    5 &E
20  | | E                        17–19 ~ E
    |
21  | | E                        Assumption
    | |-----
22  | | E                        21 R
23  | E                          15, 16–20, 21–22 ∨E
24  | E ∨ F                      23 ∨I
```

9. Theorems

a. Derive: ~ [(A & B) & ~ (A & B)]

```
1  | | (A & B) & ~ (A & B)       Assumption
   | |-----------
2  | | A & B                     1 &E
3  | | ~ (A & B)                 1 &E
4  | ~ [(A & B) & ~ (A & B)]     1–3 ~ I
```

c. Derive: (A ≡ ~ A) ⊃ ~ (A ≡ ~ A)

```
 1  │ │ A ≡ ~ A                    Assumption
    │ ├─────────
 2  │ │ │ A                        Assumption
    │ │ ├─────
 3  │ │ │ ~ A                      1, 2 ≡E
 4  │ │ │ A                        2 R
 5  │ │ ~ A                        2–4 ~ I
 6  │ │ │ ~ A                      Assumption
    │ │ ├─────
 7  │ │ │ A                        1, 6 ≡E
 8  │ │ │ ~ A                      6 R
 9  │ │ A                          6–8 ~ E
10  │ ~ (A ≡ ~ A)                  1–9 ~ I
11  │ │ A ≡ ~ A                    Assumption
    │ ├─────────
12  │ │ ~ (A ≡ ~ A)                10 R
13  │ (A ≡ ~ A) ⊃ ~ (A ≡ ~ A)      11–12 ⊃I
```

e. Derive: (A ⊃ B) ∨ (B ⊃ A)

```
 1  │ │ ~ [(A ⊃ B) ∨ (B ⊃ A)]              Assumption
    │ ├─────────────────────
 2  │ │ │ A                                Assumption
    │ │ ├─────
 3  │ │ │ │ ~ B                            Assumption
    │ │ │ ├─────
 4  │ │ │ │ │ B                            Assumption
    │ │ │ │ ├─────
 5  │ │ │ │ │ A                            2 R
 6  │ │ │ │ B ⊃ A                          4–5 ⊃I
 7  │ │ │ │ (A ⊃ B) ∨ (B ⊃ A)              6 ∨I
 8  │ │ │ │ ~ [(A ⊃ B) ∨ (B ⊃ A)]          1 R
 9  │ │ │ B                                3–8 ~ E
10  │ │ A ⊃ B                              2–9 ⊃I
11  │ │ (A ⊃ B) ∨ (B ⊃ A)                  10 ∨I
12  │ │ ~ [(A ⊃ B) ∨ (B ⊃ A)]              1 R
13  │ (A ⊃ B) ∨ (B ⊃ A)                    1–12 ~ E
```

g. Derive: $[A \supset (B \supset C)] \equiv [(A \supset B) \supset (A \supset C)]$

1	$A \supset (B \supset C)$	Assumption
2	$A \supset B$	Assumption
3	A	Assumption
4	B	2, 3 $\supset$E
5	$B \supset C$	1, 3 $\supset$E
6	C	4, 5 $\supset$E
7	$A \supset C$	3–6 $\supset$I
8	$(A \supset B) \supset (A \supset C)$	2–7 $\supset$I
9	$(A \supset B) \supset (A \supset C)$	Assumption
10	A	Assumption
11	B	Assumption
12	A	Assumption
13	B	11 R
14	$A \supset B$	12–13 $\supset$I
15	$A \supset C$	9, 14 $\supset$E
16	C	10, 15 $\supset$E
17	$B \supset C$	11–16 $\supset$I
18	$A \supset (B \supset C)$	10–17 $\supset$I
19	$[A \supset (B \supset C)] \equiv [(A \supset B) \supset (A \supset C)]$	1–8, 9–18 $\equiv$I

i. Derive: $[(A \equiv B) \supset C] \supset [\sim (A \& B) \vee C]$

1	$(A \equiv B) \supset C$	Assumption
2	$\sim (\sim (A \& B) \vee C)$	Assumption
3	$A \& B$	Assumption
4	A	Assumption
5	B	3 &E
6	B	Assumption
7	A	3 &E
8	$A \equiv B$	4–5, 6–7 $\equiv$I
9	C	1, 8 $\supset$E
10	$\sim (A \& B) \vee C$	9 $\vee$I
11	$\sim (\sim (A \& B) \vee C)$	2 R
12	$\sim (A \& B)$	3–11 $\sim$I
13	$\sim (A \& B) \vee C$	12 $\vee$I
14	$\sim (\sim (A \& B) \vee C)$	2 R
15	$\sim (A \& B) \vee C$	2–14 $\sim$E
16	$[(A \equiv B) \supset C] \supset [\sim (A \& B) \vee C]$	1–15 $\supset$I

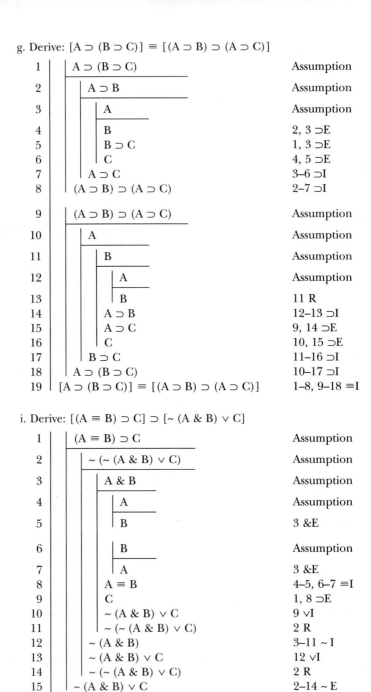

10. Equivalence

a. Derive: A ⊃ B

1	~ A ∨ B	Assumption
2	│ A	Assumption
3	│ │ ~ A	Assumption
4	│ │ │ ~ B	Assumption
5	│ │ │ A	2 R
6	│ │ │ ~ A	3 R
7	│ │ B	4–6 ~ E
8	│ │ B	Assumption
9	│ │ B	8 R
10	│ B	1, 3–7, 8–9 ∨E
11	A ⊃ B	2–10 ⊃I

Derive: ~ A ∨ B

1	A ⊃ B	Assumption
2	│ ~ (~ A ∨ B)	Assumption
3	│ │ ~ A	Assumption
4	│ │ ~ A ∨ B	3 ∨I
5	│ │ ~ (~ A ∨ B)	2 R
6	│ A	3–5 ~ E
7	│ B	1, 6 ⊃E
8	│ ~ A ∨ B	7 ∨I
9	│ ~ (~ A ∨ B)	2 R
10	~ A ∨ B	2–9 ~ E

c. Derive: A & ~ B

```
 1  | ~ (A ⊃ B)                        Assumption
    |----------
 2  |  | ~ A                           Assumption
    |  |------
 3  |  |  | A                          Assumption
    |  |  |----
 4  |  |  |  | ~ B                     Assumption
    |  |  |  |----
 5  |  |  |  | ~ A                     2 R
 6  |  |  |  | A                       3 R
 7  |  |  | B                          4–6 ~ E
 8  |  | A ⊃ B                         3–7 ⊃I
 9  |  | ~ (A ⊃ B)                     1 R
10  | A                                2–9 ~ E
11  |  | B                             Assumption
    |  |----
12  |  |  | A                          Assumption
    |  |  |----
13  |  |  | B                          11 R
14  |  | A ⊃ B                         12–13 ⊃I
15  |  | ~ (A ⊃ B)                     1 R
16  | ~ B                              11–15 ~ I
17  | A & ~ B                          10, 16 &I
```

Derive: ~ (A ⊃ B)

```
 1  | A & ~ B                          Assumption
    |----------
 2  |  | A ⊃ B                         Assumption
    |  |------
 3  |  | A                             1 &E
 4  |  | B                             2, 3 ⊃E
 5  |  | ~ B                           1 &E
 6  | ~ (A ⊃ B)                        2–5 ~ I
```

e. Derive: (A & B) ∨ (~ A & ~ B)

```
 1  | A ≡ B                                     Assumption
    |----------
 2  |  | ~ [(A & B) ∨ (~ A & ~ B)]              Assumption
    |  |------
 3  |  |  | A                                   Assumption
    |  |  |----
 4  |  |  | B                                   1, 3 ≡E
 5  |  |  | A & B                               3, 4 &I
 6  |  |  | (A & B) ∨ (~ A & ~ B)               5 ∨I
 7  |  |  | ~ [(A & B) ∨ (~ A & ~ B)]           2 R
 8  |  | ~ A                                    3–7 ~ I
 9  |  |  | B                                   Assumption
    |  |  |----
10  |  |  | A                                   1, 9 ≡E
11  |  |  | ~ A                                 8 R
12  |  | ~ B                                    9–11 ~ I
13  |  | ~ A & ~ B                              8, 12 &I
14  |  | (A & B) ∨ (~ A & ~ B)                  13 ∨I
15  |  | ~ [(A & B) ∨ (~ A & ~ B)]              2 R
16  | (A & B) ∨ (~ A & ~ B)                     2–15 ~ E
```

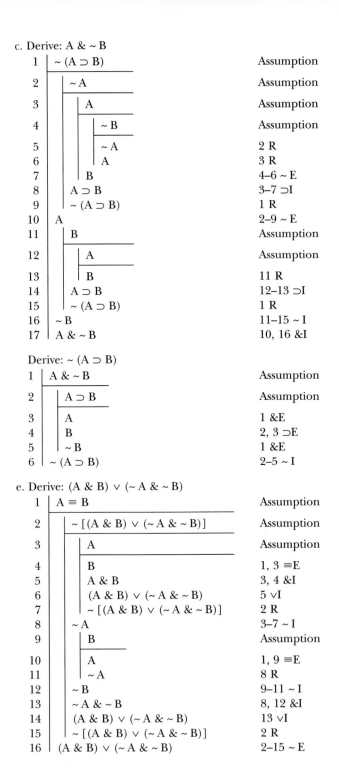

Derive: A ≡ B

1	(A & B) ∨ (~ A & ~ B)	Assumption
2	│ A & B	Assumption
3	│ │ A	Assumption
4	│ │ B	2 &E
5	│ │ B	Assumption
6	│ │ A	2 &E
7	│ A ≡ B	3–4, 5–6 ≡I
8	│ ~ A & ~ B	Assumption
9	│ │ A	Assumption
10	│ │ │ ~ B	Assumption
11	│ │ │ A	9 R
12	│ │ │ ~ A	8 &E
13	│ │ B	10–12 ~ E
14	│ │ B	Assumption
15	│ │ │ ~ A	Assumption
16	│ │ │ B	14 R
17	│ │ │ ~ B	8 &E
18	│ │ A	15–17 ~ E
19	│ A ≡ B	9–13, 14–18 ≡I
20	A ≡ B	1, 2–7, 8–19 ∨E

11. Inconsistency

a.

1	(A ⊃ B) & (A ⊃ ~ B)	Assumption
2	(C ⊃ A) & (~ C ⊃ A)	Assumption
3	A ⊃ B	1 &E
4	A ⊃ ~ B	1 &E
5	│ C	Assumption
6	│ C ⊃ A	2 &E
7	│ A	5, 6 ⊃E
8	│ B	3, 7 ⊃E
9	│ ~ B	4, 7 ⊃E
10	~ C	5–9 ~ I
11	~ C ⊃ A	2 &E
12	A	10, 11 ⊃E
13	B	3, 12 ⊃E
14	~ B	4, 12 ⊃E

c.	1	$W \vee (Z \supset Y)$	Assumption
	2	$\sim Y \,\&\, \sim (W \vee \sim Z)$	Assumption
	3	$\mid W$	Assumption
	4	$\mid \mid \sim Y$	Assumption
	5	$\mid \mid W \vee \sim Z$	3 ∨I
	6	$\mid \mid \sim (W \vee \sim Z)$	2 &E
	7	$\mid Y$	4–6 ~ E
	8	$\mid Z \supset Y$	Assumption
	10	$\mid \mid \sim Z$	Assumption
	11	$\mid \mid W \vee \sim Z$	10 ∨I
	12	$\mid \mid \sim (W \vee \sim Z)$	2 &E
	13	$\mid Z$	10–12 ~ E
	14	$\mid Y$	8, 13 ⊃E
	15	Y	1, 3–7, 8–14 ∨E
	16	$\sim Y$	2 &E

e.	1	$[(A \equiv B) \equiv (D \,\&\, \sim D)] \equiv B$	Assumption
	2	A	Assumption
	3	$\mid B$	Assumption
	4	$\mid (A \equiv B) \equiv (D \,\&\, \sim D)$	1, 3 ≡E
	5	$\mid \mid A$	Assumption
	6	$\mid \mid B$	3 R
	7	$\mid \mid B$	Assumption
	8	$\mid \mid A$	2 R
	9	$\mid A \equiv B$	5–6, 7–8 ≡I
	10	$\mid D \,\&\, \sim D$	4, 9 ≡E
	11	$\mid D$	10 &E
	12	$\mid \sim D$	10 &E
	13	$\sim B$	3–12 ~ I
	14	$\mid A \equiv B$	Assumption
	15	$\mid \mid \sim (D \,\&\, \sim D)$	Assumption
	16	$\mid \mid B$	2, 14 ≡E
	17	$\mid \mid \sim B$	13 R
	18	$\mid D \,\&\, \sim D$	15–17 ~ E
	19	$\mid D \,\&\, \sim D$	Assumption
	20	$\mid \mid \sim (A \equiv B)$	Assumption
	21	$\mid \mid D$	19 &E
	22	$\mid \mid \sim D$	19 &E
	23	$\mid A \equiv B$	20–22 ~ E
	24	$(A \equiv B) \equiv (D \,\&\, \sim D)$	14–18, 19–23 ≡I
	25	B	1, 24 ≡E

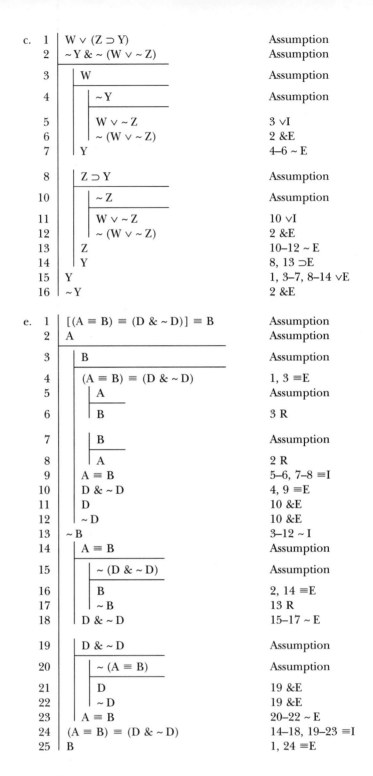

12. Validity

a. Derive: M

1	S & F	Assumption
2	F ⊃ B	Assumption
3	(B & ~ M) ⊃ ~ S	Assumption
4	– ~ M	Assumption
5	– F	1 &E
6	– B	2, 5 ⊃E
7	– B & ~ M	6, 4 &I
8	– ~ S	3, 7 ⊃E
9	– S	1 &E
10	M	4–9 ~ E

c. Derive: ~ J

1	(C ⊃ ~ R) & (R ⊃ L)	Assumption
2	C ≡ (C ∨ L)	Assumption
3	J ⊃ R	Assumption
4	– J	Assumption
5	– R	3, 4 ⊃E
6	– R ⊃ L	1 &E
7	– L	5, 6 ⊃E
8	– C ∨ L	7 ∨I
9	– C	2, 8 ≡E
10	– C ⊃ ~ R	1 &E
11	– ~ R	9, 10 ⊃E
12	~ J	4–11 ~ I

e. Derive: ~ M

1	~ (R ∨ W)	Assumption
2	(R ≡ M) ∨ [(M ∨ G) ⊃ (W ≡ M)]	Assumption
3	– M	Assumption
4	– – R ≡ M	Assumption
5	– – R	3, 4 ≡E
6	– – R ∨ W	5 ∨I
7	– – (M ∨ G) ⊃ (W ≡ M)	Assumption
8	– – M ∨ G	3 ∨I
9	– – W ≡ M	7, 8 ⊃E
10	– – W	3, 9 ≡E
11	– – R ∨ W	10 ∨I
12	– R ∨ W	2, 4–6, 7–11 ∨E
13	– ~ (R ∨ W)	1 R
14	~ M	3–13 ~ I

g. Derive: H ⊃ J

1	(H & T) ⊃ J	Assumption
2	(M ⊃ D) & (~ D ⊃ M)	Assumption
3	~ T ≡ (~ D & M)	Assumption
4	H	Assumption
5	~ J	Assumption
6	T	Assumption
7	H & T	4, 6 &I
8	J	1, 7 ⊃E
9	~ J	5 R
10	~ T	6–9 ~ I
11	~ D & M	3, 10 ≡E
12	M ⊃ D	2 &E
13	M	11 &E
14	D	12, 13 ⊃E
15	~ D	11 &E
16	J	5–15 ~ E
17	H ⊃ J	4–16 ⊃I

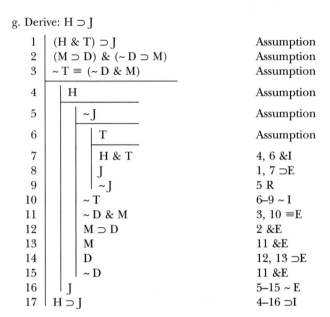

i. Derive: $L \supset T$

1	│ $L \supset (C \vee T)$	Assumption
2	│ $(\sim L \vee B) \ \&\ (\sim B \vee \sim C)$	Assumption
3	│ │ L	Assumption
4	│ │ $C \vee T$	1, 3 $\supset$E
5	│ │ │ C	Assumption
6	│ │ │ $\sim B \vee \sim C$	2 &E
7	│ │ │ │ $\sim B$	Assumption
8	│ │ │ │ $\sim L \vee B$	2 &E
9	│ │ │ │ │ $\sim L$	Assumption
10	│ │ │ │ │ │ $\sim T$	Assumption
11	│ │ │ │ │ │ L	3 R
12	│ │ │ │ │ │ $\sim L$	9 R
13	│ │ │ │ │ T	10–12 $\sim$E
14	│ │ │ │ │ B	Assumption
15	│ │ │ │ │ │ $\sim T$	Assumption
16	│ │ │ │ │ │ B	14 R
17	│ │ │ │ │ │ $\sim B$	7 R
18	│ │ │ │ │ T	15–17 $\sim$E
19	│ │ │ │ T	8, 9–13, 14–18 $\vee$E
20	│ │ │ │ $\sim C$	Assumption
21	│ │ │ │ │ $\sim T$	Assumption
22	│ │ │ │ │ $\sim C$	20 R
23	│ │ │ │ │ C	5 R
24	│ │ │ │ T	21–23 $\sim$E
25	│ │ │ T	6, 7–19, 20–24 $\vee$E
26	│ │ │ T	Assumption
27	│ │ │ T	26 R
28	│ │ T	4, 5–25, 26–27 $\vee$E
29	│ $L \supset T$	3–28 $\supset$ I

13. Inconsistency

a.

1	(M ⊃ B) & (B ⊃ P)	Assumption
2	M & ~ P	Assumption
3	M	2 &E
4	M ⊃ B	1 &E
5	B	3, 4 ⊃E
6	B ⊃ P	1 &E
7	P	5, 6 ⊃E
8	~ P	2 &E

c.

1	B ⊃ I	Assumption
2	(~ B & ~ I) ⊃ C	Assumption
3	~ C & ~ I	Assumption
4	B	Assumption
5	I	1, 4 ⊃E
6	~ I	3 &E
7	~ B	4–6 ~ I
8	~ I	3 &E
9	~ B & ~ I	7, 8 &I
10	C	2, 9 ⊃E
11	~ C	3 &E

e.

1	M ∨ (F ⊃ T)	Assumption
2	N ≡ ~ T	Assumption
3	(F & N) & ~ M	Assumption
4	M	Assumption
5	M	4 R
6	F ⊃ T	Assumption
7	~ M	Assumption
8	F & N	3 &E
9	F	8 &E
10	T	6, 9 ⊃E
11	N	8 &E
12	~ T	2, 11 ≡E
13	M	7–12 ~ E
14	M	1, 4–5, 6–13 ∨E
15	~ M	3 &E

14.a. We would not want to include this derivation rule because it is not truth-preserving. A sentence of *SL* of the form $\mathcal{P} \vee \mathcal{Q}$ can be true while $\mathcal{P}$ is false.

c. Suppose we are on line n of a derivation and a sentence $\mathscr{P}$ occurs on an earlier accessible line i. $\mathscr{P}$ can be derived without using the rule Reiteration as follows:

i	$\mathscr{P}$	
n	$\mathscr{P}$ & $\mathscr{P}$	i, i &I
$n + 1$	$\mathscr{P}$	n &E

e. Suppose an argument of *SL* has ~ $\mathscr{P}$ among its premises, where $\mathscr{P}$ is a theorem in *SD*. Consider a derivation that has the premises of the argument as its only primary assumptions and that has the negation of the conclusion as an auxiliary assumption immediately after the primary assumptions. Within the subderivation that has the negation of the conclusion as its assumption, ~ $\mathscr{P}$ can be derived by Reiteration, for ~ $\mathscr{P}$ occurs as one of the primary assumptions. Since $\mathscr{P}$ is a theorem in *SD*, it can also be derived within the subderivation without introducing any new assumptions that are not discharged. Consequently, Negation Elimination can be applied to discharge the negation of the conclusion yielding the (unnegated) conclusion. The conclusion is derivable from the set of premises; hence the argument is valid in *SD*.

15.a. Assume that some argument of *SL* is valid in *SD*. Then, by definition, the conclusion is derivable in *SD* from the set consisting of only premises. By the result (*), the conclusion is truth-functionally entailed by that set. So the argument is truth-functionally valid. Assume that some argument of *SL* is truth-functionally valid. Then the conclusion is truth-functionally entailed by the set consisting of the premises. By (*), the conclusion is derivable in *SD* from that set. So the argument is valid in *SD*.

c. Assume that sentences $\mathscr{P}$ and $\mathscr{Q}$ of *SL* are equivalent in *SD*. Then $\{\mathscr{P}\} \vdash \mathscr{Q}$ and $\{\mathscr{Q}\} \vdash \mathscr{P}$. By (*), it follows that $\{\mathscr{P}\} \vDash \mathscr{Q}$ and $\{\mathscr{Q}\} \vDash \mathscr{P}$. By Exercise 5.b in Section 3.5E, $\mathscr{P}$ and $\mathscr{Q}$ are truth-functionally equivalent. Assume that sentences $\mathscr{P}$ and $\mathscr{Q}$ of *SL* are truth-functionally equivalent. By Exercise 5.b in Section 3.5E, $\{\mathscr{P}\} \vDash \mathscr{Q}$ and $\{\mathscr{Q}\} \vDash \mathscr{P}$. By (*), then, $\{\mathscr{P}\} \vdash \mathscr{Q}$, and $\{\mathscr{Q}\} \vdash \mathscr{P}$. So $\mathscr{P}$ and $\mathscr{Q}$ are equivalent in *SL*.

Section 5.5E

1. Derivability

a. Derive: ~ D

1	D ⊃ E	Assumption
2	E ⊃ (Z & W)	Assumption
3	~ Z ∨ ~ W	Assumption
4	~ (Z & W)	3 DeM
5	~ E	2, 4 MT
6	~ D	1, 5 MT

c. Derive: K

1	$(W \supset S) \& \sim M$	Assumption
2	$(\sim W \supset H) \vee M$	Assumption
3	$(\sim S \supset H) \supset K$	Assumption
4	$W \supset S$	1 &E
5	$\sim S \supset \sim W$	4 Trans
6	$\sim M$	1 &E
7	$\sim W \supset H$	2, 6 DS
8	$\sim S \supset H$	5, 7 HS
9	K	3, 8 ⊃E

e. Derive: C

1	$(M \vee B) \vee (C \vee G)$	Assumption
2	$\sim B \& (\sim G \& \sim M)$	Assumption
3	$\sim B$	2 &E
4	$(B \vee M) \vee (C \vee G)$	1 Com
5	$B \vee [M \vee (C \vee G)]$	4 Assoc
6	$M \vee (C \vee G)$	3, 5 DS
7	$\sim G \& \sim M$	2 &E
8	$\sim G$	7 &E
9	$(M \vee C) \vee G$	6 Assoc
10	$M \vee C$	8, 9 DS
11	$\sim M$	7 &E
12	C	10, 11 DS

2. Validity

a. Derive: Y ≡ Z

1	$\sim Y \supset \sim Z$	Assumption
2	$\sim Z \supset \sim X$	Assumption
3	$\sim X \supset \sim Y$	Assumption
4	Y	Assumption
5	$\sim Z \supset \sim Y$	2, 3 HS
6	$Y \supset Z$	5 Trans
7	Z	4, 6 ⊃E
8	Z	Assumption
9	$Z \supset Y$	1 Trans
10	Y	8, 9 ⊃E
11	$Y \equiv Z$	4–7, 8–10 ≡I

c. Derive: I ⊃ ~ D

1	(F & G) ∨ (H & ~ I)	Assumption
2	I ⊃ ~ (F & D)	Assumption
3	│ I	Assumption
4	│ ~ (F & D)	2, 3 ⊃E
5	│ ~ F ∨ ~ D	4 DeM
6	│ ~ ~ I	3 DN
7	│ ~ H ∨ ~ ~ I	6 ∨I
8	│ ~ (H & ~ I)	7 DeM
9	│ F & G	1, 8 DS
10	│ F	9 &E
11	│ ~ ~ F	10 DN
12	│ ~ D	5, 11 DS
13	I ⊃ ~ D	3–12 ⊃I

e. Derive: I ∨ H

1	F ⊃ (G ⊃ H)	Assumption
2	~ I ⊃ (F ∨ H)	Assumption
3	F ⊃ G	Assumption
4	│ ~ I	Assumption
5	│ F ∨ H	2, 4 ⊃E
6	│ │ ~ H	Assumption
7	│ │ F	5, 6 DS
8	│ │ G	3, 7 ⊃E
9	│ │ G ⊃ H	1, 7 ⊃E
10	│ │ ~ G	6, 9 MT
11	│ H	6–10 ~ E
12	~ I ⊃ H	4–11 ⊃I
13	~ ~ I ∨ H	12 Impl
14	I ∨ H	13 DN

g. Derive: $X \equiv Y$

1	$[(X \& Z) \& Y] \vee (\sim X \supset \sim Y)$	Assumption
2	$X \supset Z$	Assumption
3	$Z \supset Y$	Assumption
4	X	Assumption
5	Z	2, 4 $\supset$E
6	Y	3, 5 $\supset$E
7	Y	Assumption
8	$(X \& Z) \& Y$	Assumption
9	$X \& Z$	8 &E
10	X	9 &E
11	$\sim X \supset \sim Y$	Assumption
12	$Y \supset X$	11 Trans
13	X	7, 12 $\supset$E
14	X	1, 8–10, 11–13 $\vee$E
15	$X \equiv Y$	4–6, 7–14 $\equiv$I

3. Theorems

a. Derive: $A \vee \sim A$

1	$\sim (A \vee \sim A)$	Assumption
2	$\sim A \& \sim\sim A$	1 DeM
3	$\sim A$	2 &E
4	$\sim\sim A$	2 &E
5	$A \vee \sim A$	1–4 $\sim$E

c. Derive: $A \vee [(\sim A \vee B) \& (\sim A \vee C)]$

1	$\sim A$	Assumption
2	$\sim A \vee (B \& C)$	1 $\vee$I
3	$(\sim A \vee B) \& (\sim A \vee C)$	2 Dist
4	$\sim A \supset [(\sim A \vee B) \& (\sim A \vee C)]$	1–3 $\supset$I
5	$\sim\sim A \vee [(\sim A \vee B) \& (\sim A \vee C)]$	4 Impl
6	$A \vee [(\sim A \vee B) \& (\sim A \vee C)]$	5 DN

e. Derive: $[A \supset (B \& C)] \equiv [(\sim B \vee \sim C) \supset \sim A]$

1	$A \supset (B \& C)$	Assumption
2	$\sim (B \& C) \supset \sim A$	1 Trans
3	$(\sim B \vee \sim C) \supset \sim A$	2 DeM
4	$(\sim B \vee \sim C) \supset \sim A$	Assumption
5	$\sim (B \& C) \supset \sim A$	4 DeM
6	$A \supset (B \& C)$	5 Trans
7	$[A \supset (B \& C)] \equiv [(\sim B \vee \sim C) \supset \sim A]$	1–3, 4–6 $\equiv$I

g. Derive: $[A \supset (B \equiv C)] \equiv (A \supset [(\sim B \vee C) \,\&\, (\sim C \vee B)])$

1	$A \supset (B \equiv C)$	Assumption
2	$A \supset [(B \supset C) \,\&\, (C \supset B)]$	1 Equiv
3	$A \supset [(\sim B \vee C) \,\&\, (C \supset B)]$	2 Impl
4	$A \supset [(\sim B \vee C) \,\&\, (\sim C \vee B)]$	3 Impl
5	$A \supset [(\sim B \vee C) \,\&\, (\sim C \vee B)]$	Assumption
6	$A \supset [(B \supset C) \,\&\, (\sim C \vee B)]$	5 Impl
7	$A \supset [(B \supset C) \,\&\, (C \supset B)]$	6 Impl
8	$A \supset (B \equiv C)$	7 Equiv
9	$[A \supset (B \equiv C)] \equiv (A \supset [(\sim B \vee C) \,\&\, (\sim C \vee B)])$	1–4, 5–8 $\equiv$I

i. Derive: $[\sim A \supset (\sim B \supset C)] \supset [(A \vee B) \vee (\sim\sim B \vee C)]$

1	$\sim A \supset (\sim B \supset C)$	Assumption
2	$\sim\sim A \vee (\sim B \supset C)$	1 Impl
3	$\sim\sim A \vee (\sim\sim B \vee C)$	2 Impl
4	$A \vee (\sim\sim B \vee C)$	3 DN
5	$A \vee [(\sim\sim B \vee \sim\sim B) \vee C]$	4 Idem
6	$A \vee [\sim\sim B \vee (\sim\sim B \vee C)]$	5 Assoc
7	$(A \vee \sim\sim B) \vee (\sim\sim B \vee C)$	6 Assoc
8	$(A \vee B) \vee (\sim\sim B \vee C)$	7 DN
9	$[\sim A \supset (\sim B \supset C)] \supset [(A \vee B) \vee (\sim\sim B \vee C)]$	1–8 $\supset$I

4. Equivalence

a. Derive: $\sim(\sim A \,\&\, \sim B)$

1	$A \vee B$	Assumption
2	$\sim\sim A \vee B$	1 DN
3	$\sim\sim A \vee \sim\sim B$	2 DN
4	$\sim(\sim A \,\&\, \sim B)$	3 DeM

Derive: $A \vee B$

1	$\sim(\sim A \,\&\, \sim B)$	Assumption
2	$\sim\sim A \vee \sim\sim B$	1 DeM
3	$A \vee \sim\sim B$	2 DN
4	$A \vee B$	3 DN

c. Derive: $\sim(A \supset C) \supset \sim B$

1	$(A \,\&\, B) \supset C$	Assumption
2	$(B \,\&\, A) \supset C$	1 Com
3	$B \supset (A \supset C)$	2 Exp
4	$\sim(A \supset C) \supset \sim B$	3 Trans

Derive: $(A \& B) \supset C$

1	$\sim(A \supset C) \supset \sim B$	Assumption
2	$B \supset (A \supset C)$	1 Trans
3	$(B \& A) \supset C$	2 Exp
4	$(A \& B) \supset C$	3 Com

e. Derive: $A \vee (\sim B \equiv \sim C)$

1	$A \vee (B \equiv C)$	Assumption
2	$A \vee [(B \supset C) \& (C \supset B)]$	1 Equiv
3	$A \vee [(\sim C \supset \sim B) \& (C \supset B)]$	2 Trans
4	$A \vee [(\sim C \supset \sim B) \& (\sim B \supset \sim C)]$	3 Trans
5	$A \vee [(\sim B \supset \sim C) \& (\sim C \supset \sim B)]$	4 Com
6	$A \vee (\sim B \equiv \sim C)$	5 Equiv

Derive: $A \vee (B \equiv C)$

1	$A \vee (\sim B \equiv \sim C)$	Assumption
2	$A \vee [(\sim B \supset \sim C) \& (\sim C \supset \sim B)]$	1 Equiv
3	$A \vee [(C \supset B) \& (\sim C \supset \sim B)]$	2 Trans
4	$A \vee [(C \supset B) \& (B \supset C)]$	3 Trans
5	$A \vee [(B \supset C) \& (C \supset B)]$	4 Com
6	$A \vee (B \equiv C)$	5 Equiv

5. Inconsistency

a.

1	$[(E \& F) \vee \sim\sim G] \supset M$	Assumption
2	$\sim[[(G \vee E) \& (F \vee G)] \supset (M \& M)]$	Assumption
3	$\sim([(G \vee E) \& (F \vee G)] \supset M)$	2 Idem
4	$\sim([(G \vee E) \& (G \vee F)] \supset M)$	3 Com
5	$\sim([G \vee (E \& F)] \supset M)$	4 Dist
6	$\sim([(E \& F) \vee G] \supset M)$	5 Com
7	$\sim([(E \& F) \vee \sim\sim G] \supset M)$	6 DN

c.

1	$M \& L$	Assumption
2	$[L \& (M \& \sim S)] \supset K$	Assumption
3	$\sim K \vee \sim S$	Assumption
4	$\sim(K \equiv \sim S)$	Assumption
5	$K \supset \sim S$	3 Impl
6	$[(L \& M) \& \sim S] \supset K$	2 Assoc
7	$(L \& M) \supset (\sim S \supset K)$	6 Exp
8	$L \& M$	1 Com
9	$\sim S \supset K$	7, 8 $\supset$E
10	$(K \supset \sim S) \& (\sim S \supset K)$	5, 9 &I
11	$K \equiv \sim S$	10 Equiv

e.

1	~ [W & (Z ∨ Y)]	Assumption
2	(Z ⊃ Y) ⊃ Z	Assumption
3	(Y ⊃ Z) ⊃ W	Assumption
4	~ W ∨ ~ (Z ∨ Y)	1 DeM
5	~ Z	Assumption
6	~ (Z ⊃ Y)	2, 5 MT
7	~ (~ Z ∨ Y)	6 Impl
8	~ ~ Z & ~ Y	7 DeM
9	~ ~ Z	8 &E
10	~ Z	5 R
11	Z	5–10 ~ E
12	Z ∨ Y	11 ∨I
13	~ ~ (Z ∨ Z)	12 DN
14	~ W	4, 13 DS
15	~ (Y ⊃ Z)	3, 14 MT
16	~ (~ Y ∨ Z)	15 Impl
17	~ ~ Y & ~ Z	16 DeM
18	~ Z	17 &E

6. Validity

a. Derive: ~ B

1	(R ⊃ C) ∨ (B ⊃ C)	Assumption
2	~ (E & A) ⊃ ~ (R ⊃ C)	Assumption
3	~ E & ~ C	Assumption
4	~ E	3 &E
5	~ E ∨ ~ A	4 ∨I
6	~ (E & A)	5 DeM
7	~ (R ⊃ C)	2, 6 ⊃E
8	B ⊃ C	1, 7 DS
9	~ C	3 &E
10	~ B	8, 9 MT

c. Derive: ~ W ⊃ ~ A

1	A ⊃ [W ∨ ~ (C ∨ R)]	Assumption
2	~ R ⊃ C	Assumption
3	~ W	Assumption
4	A	Assumption
5	W ∨ ~ (C ∨ R)	1, 4 ⊃E
6	~ (C ∨ R)	3, 5 DS
7	~ ~ R ∨ C	2 Impl
8	R ∨ C	7 DN
9	C ∨ R	8 Com
10	~ A	4–9 ~ I
11	~ W ⊃ ~ A	3–10 ⊃I

e. Derive: J ⊃ ~ (E ∨ ~ M)

1	~ (J & ~ H)	Assumption
2	~ H ∨ M	Assumption
3	E ⊃ ~ M	Assumption
4	J	Assumption
5	~ J ∨ ~ ~ H	1 DeM
6	~ ~ J	4 DN
7	~ ~ H	5, 6 DS
8	M	2, 7 DS
9	~ ~ M	8 DN
10	~ E	3, 9 MT
11	~ E & ~ ~ M	10, 9 &I
12	~ (E ∨ ~ M)	11 DeM
13	J ⊃ ~ (E ∨ ~ M)	4–12 ⊃I

g. Derive: ~ A ⊃ [H ⊃ (F & B)]

1	(H & ~ S) ⊃ A	Assumption
2	~ B ⊃ ~ S	Assumption
3	~ S ∨ C	Assumption
4	C ⊃ F	Assumption
5	~ A	Assumption
6	H	Assumption
7	H ⊃ (~ S ⊃ A)	1 Exp
8	~ S ⊃ A	6, 7 ⊃E
9	~ ~ S	5, 8 MT
10	C	3, 9 DS
11	F	4, 10 ⊃E
12	~ ~ B	2, 9 MT
13	B	12 DN
14	F & B	11, 13 &I
15	H ⊃ (F & B)	6–14 ⊃I
16	~ A ⊃ [H ⊃ (F & B)]	5–15 ⊃I

7. Inconsistency

a.

1	B ∨ ~ C	Assumption
2	(L ⊃ ~ G) ⊃ C	Assumption
3	(G ≡ ~ B) & (~ L ⊃ ~ B)	Assumption
4	~ L	Assumption
5	~ L ∨ ~ G	4 ∨I
6	L ⊃ ~ G	5 Impl
7	C	2, 6 ⊃E
8	~ L ⊃ ~ B	3 &E
9	~ B	4, 8 ⊃E
10	~ C	1, 9 DS

8.a. The rules of replacement are two-way rules. If we can derive $\mathcal{Q}$ from $\mathcal{P}$ by using only these rules, we can derive $\mathcal{P}$ from $\mathcal{Q}$ by using the rules in reverse order.

c. Suppose that before a current line n of a derivation, an accessible line i contains a sentence of the form $\mathcal{P} \supset \mathcal{Q}$. The sentence $\mathcal{P} \supset (\mathcal{P} \& \mathcal{Q})$ can be derived by using the following routine:

i	$\mathcal{P} \supset \mathcal{Q}$	
n	$\mathcal{P}$	Assumption
$n + 1$	$\mathcal{Q}$	i, n $\supset$E
$n + 2$	$\mathcal{P} \& \mathcal{Q}$	n, $n + 1$ &E
$n + 3$	$\mathcal{P} \supset (\mathcal{P} \& \mathcal{Q})$	$n - n+2$ $\supset$I

CHAPTER SIX

Section 6.1E

1.a. We shall prove that every sentence of *SL* that contains only binary connectives, if any, is true on every truth-value assignment on which all its atomic components are true. Hence every sentence of *SL* that contains only binary connectives is true on at least one truth-value assignment, and thus no such sentence can be truth-functionally false. We proceed by mathematical induction on the number of occurrences of connectives in such sentences. (Note that we need not consider *all* sentences of *SL* in our induction but only those with which the thesis is concerned.)

Basis clause: Every sentence with zero occurrences of a binary connective (and no occurrences of unary connectives) is true on every truth-value assignment on which all its atomic components are true.

Inductive step: If every sentence with k or fewer occurrences of binary connectives (and no occurrences of unary connectives) is true on every truth-value assignment on which all its atomic components are true, then every sentence with $k + 1$ occurrences of binary connectives (and no occurrences of unary connectives) is true on every truth-value assignment on which all its atomic components are true.

The proof of the basis clause is straightforward. A sentence with zero occurrences of a connective is an atomic sentence, and each atomic sentence is true on every truth-value assignment on which its atomic component (which is the sentence itself) is true.

The inductive step is also straightforward. Assume that the thesis holds for every sentence of *SL* with k or fewer occurrences of binary connectives and no unary connectives. Any sentence $\mathcal{P}$ with $k + 1$ occurrences of binary connectives and no unary connectives must be of one of the four forms $\mathcal{Q} \& \mathcal{R}$,

$\mathscr{Q} \vee \mathscr{R}$, $\mathscr{Q} \supset \mathscr{R}$, and $\mathscr{Q} \equiv \mathscr{R}$. In each case $\mathscr{Q}$ and $\mathscr{R}$ contain k or fewer occurrences of binary connectives, so the inductive hypothesis holds for both $\mathscr{Q}$ and $\mathscr{R}$. That is, both $\mathscr{Q}$ and $\mathscr{R}$ are true on every truth-value assignment on which all their atomic components are true. Since $\mathscr{P}$'s immediate components are $\mathscr{Q}$ and $\mathscr{R}$, its atomic components are just those of $\mathscr{Q}$ and $\mathscr{R}$. But conjunctions, disjunctions, conditionals, and biconditionals are true when both their immediate components are true. So $\mathscr{P}$ is also true on every truth-value assignment on which its atomic components are true, for both its immediate components are then true. This completes our proof. (Note that in this clause we ignored sentences of the form $\sim \mathscr{Q}$, for the thesis concerns only those sentences of *SL* that contain *no* occurrences of '~'.)

b. Every sentence $\mathscr{P}$ that contains no binary connectives either contains no connectives or contains at least one occurrence of '~'. We prove the thesis by mathematical induction on the number of occurrences of '~' in such sentences. The first case consists of the atomic sentences of *SL* since these contain zero occurrences of connectives.

Basis clause: Every atomic sentence is truth-functionally indeterminate.

Inductive step: If every sentence with k or fewer occurrences of '~' (and no binary connectives) is truth-functionally indeterminate, then every sentence with $k + 1$ occurrences of '~' (and no binary connectives) is truth-functionally indeterminate.

The basis clause is obvious.

The inductive step is also obvious. Suppose $\mathscr{P}$ contains $k + 1$ occurrences of '~' and no binary connectives and that the thesis holds for every sentence with fewer than $k + 1$ occurrences of '~' and no binary connectives. $\mathscr{P}$ is a sentence of the form $\sim \mathscr{Q}$, where $\mathscr{Q}$ contains k occurrences of '~'; hence, by the inductive hypothesis, $\mathscr{Q}$ is truth-functionally indeterminate. The negation of a truth-functionally indeterminate sentence is also truth-functionally indeterminate. Hence $\sim \mathscr{Q}$, that is, $\mathscr{P}$, is truth-functionally indeterminate. This completes the induction.

c. The induction is on the number of occurrences of connectives in $\mathscr{P}$. The thesis to be proved is

> If two truth-value assignments $\mathscr{A}'$ and $\mathscr{A}''$ assign the same truth-values to the atomic components of a sentence $\mathscr{P}$, then $\mathscr{P}$ has the same truth-value on $\mathscr{A}'$ and $\mathscr{A}''$.

Basis clause: The thesis holds for every sentence with zero occurrences of connectives.

Inductive step: If the thesis holds for every sentence with k or fewer occurrences of connectives, then the thesis holds for every sentence with $k + 1$ occurrences of connectives.

The basis clause is obvious. If $\mathscr{P}$ contains zero occurrences of connectives, then $\mathscr{P}$ is an atomic sentence and its own only atomic component. $\mathscr{P}$ must have the same truth-value on $\mathscr{A}'$ and $\mathscr{A}''$ because *ex hypothesi* it is assigned the same truth-value on each assignment.

To prove the inductive step, we let $\mathscr{P}$ be a sentence with $k + 1$ occurrences of connectives and assume that the thesis holds for every sentence containing k or fewer occurrences of connectives. Then $\mathscr{P}$ is of the form $\sim \mathscr{Q}$, $\mathscr{Q} \,\&\, \mathscr{R}$, $\mathscr{Q} \vee \mathscr{R}$, $\mathscr{Q} \supset \mathscr{R}$, or $\mathscr{Q} \equiv \mathscr{R}$. In each case the immediate component(s) of $\mathscr{P}$ contain k or fewer occurrences of connectives and hence fall under the inductive hypothesis. So each immediate component of $\mathscr{P}$ has the same truth-value on $\mathscr{A}'$ and $\mathscr{A}''$. $\mathscr{P}$ therefore has the same truth-value on $\mathscr{A}'$ and $\mathscr{A}''$, as determined by the characteristic truth-tables.

d. We prove the thesis by mathematical induction on the number of conjuncts in an iterated conjunction of sentences $\mathscr{P}_1, \ldots, \mathscr{P}_n$ of *SL*.

Basis clause: Every iterated conjunction of just one sentence of *SL* is true on a truth-value assignment if and only if that one sentence is true on that assignment.

Inductive step: If every iterated conjunction of k or fewer sentences of *SL* is true on a truth-value assignment if and only if each of those conjuncts is true on that assignment, then every iterated conjunction of $k + 1$ sentences of *SL* is true on a truth-value assignment if and only if each of those conjuncts is true on that assignment.

The basis clause is trivial.

To prove the inductive step, we assume that the thesis holds for iterated conjunctions of k or fewer sentences of *SL*. Let $\mathscr{P}$ be an iterated conjunction of $k + 1$ sentences. Then $\mathscr{P}$ is $\mathscr{Q} \,\&\, \mathscr{R}$, where $\mathscr{Q}$ is an iterated conjunction of k sentences. $\mathscr{P}$ is therefore an iterated conjunction of all the sentences of which $\mathscr{Q}$ is an iterated conjunction, and $\mathscr{R}$. By the inductive hypothesis, the thesis holds of $\mathscr{Q}$; that is, $\mathscr{Q}$ is true on a truth-value assignment if and only if the sentences of which $\mathscr{Q}$ is an iterated conjunction are true on that assignment. Hence, whenever all the sentences of which $\mathscr{P}$ is an iterated conjunction are true, both $\mathscr{Q}$ and $\mathscr{R}$ are true, and thus $\mathscr{P}$ is true as well. Whenever at least one of those sentences is false, either $\mathscr{Q}$ is false or $\mathscr{R}$ is false, making $\mathscr{P}$ false as well. Hence $\mathscr{P}$ is true on a truth-value assignment if and only if all the sentences of which it is an iterated conjunction are true on that assignment.

e. We proceed by mathematical induction on the number of occurrences of connectives in $\mathscr{P}$. The argument is

> The thesis holds for every atomic sentence $\mathscr{P}$.
>
> If the thesis holds for every sentence $\mathscr{P}$ with k or fewer occurrences of connectives, then it holds for every sentence $\mathscr{P}$ with $k + 1$ occurrences of connectives.
>
> ---
>
> The thesis holds for every sentence $\mathscr{P}$ of *SL*.

The proof of the basis clause is fairly simple. If $\mathscr{P}$ is an atomic sentence and $\mathscr{Q}$ is a sentential component of $\mathscr{P}$, then $\mathscr{Q}$ must be identical with $\mathscr{P}$ (since each atomic sentence is its own only atomic component). For any sentence $\mathscr{Q}_1$, then,

$[\mathscr{P}](\mathscr{Q}_1//\mathscr{Q})$ is simply the sentence $\mathscr{Q}_1$. Here it is trivial that if $\mathscr{Q}$ and $\mathscr{Q}_1$ are truth-functionally equivalent, so are $\mathscr{P}$ (which is just $\mathscr{Q}$) and $[\mathscr{P}](\mathscr{Q}_1//\mathscr{Q})$ (which is just $\mathscr{Q}_1$).

In proving the inductive step, the following result will be useful:

6.1.1. If $\mathscr{Q}$ and $\mathscr{Q}_1$ are truth-functionally equivalent and $\mathscr{R}$ and $\mathscr{R}_1$ are truth-functionally equivalent, then each of the following pairs are pairs of truth-functionally equivalent sentences:

$\sim \mathscr{Q}$	$\sim \mathscr{Q}_1$
$\mathscr{Q} \,\&\, \mathscr{R}$	$\mathscr{Q}_1 \,\&\, \mathscr{R}_1$
$\mathscr{Q} \vee \mathscr{R}$	$\mathscr{Q}_1 \vee \mathscr{R}_1$
$\mathscr{Q} \supset \mathscr{R}$	$\mathscr{Q}_1 \supset \mathscr{R}_1$
$\mathscr{Q} \equiv \mathscr{R}$	$\mathscr{Q}_1 \equiv \mathscr{R}_1$

Proof: The truth-value of a molecular sentence is wholly determined by the truth-values of its immediate components. Hence, if there is a truth-value assignment on which some sentence in the left-hand column has a truth-value different from that of its partner in the right-hand column, then on that assignment either $\mathscr{Q}$ and $\mathscr{Q}_1$ have different truth-values or $\mathscr{R}$ and $\mathscr{R}_1$ have different truth-values. But this is impossible because *ex hypothesi* $\mathscr{Q}$ and $\mathscr{Q}_1$ are truth-functionally equivalent and $\mathscr{R}$ and $\mathscr{R}_1$ are truth-functionally equivalent.

To prove the inductive step of the thesis, we assume the inductive hypothesis: that the thesis holds for every sentence with k or fewer occurrences of connectives. Let $\mathscr{P}$ be a sentence of *SL* with $k + 1$ occurrences of connectives, let $\mathscr{Q}$ be a sentential component of $\mathscr{P}$, let $\mathscr{Q}_1$ be a sentence that is truth-functionally equivalent to $\mathscr{Q}$, and let $[\mathscr{P}](\mathscr{Q}_1//\mathscr{Q})$ be a sentence that results from replacing one or more occurrences of $\mathscr{Q}$ in $\mathscr{P}$ with $\mathscr{Q}_1$. Suppose, first, that $\mathscr{Q}$ is identical with $\mathscr{P}$. Then, by the reasoning in the proof of the basis clause, it follows trivially that $\mathscr{P}$ and $[\mathscr{P}](\mathscr{Q}_1//\mathscr{Q})$ are truth-functionally equivalent. Now suppose that $\mathscr{Q}$ is a sentential component of $\mathscr{P}$ that is *not* identical with $\mathscr{P}$ (in which case we say that $\mathscr{Q}$ is a *proper* sentential component of $\mathscr{P}$). Either $\mathscr{P}$ is of the form $\sim \mathscr{R}$ or $\mathscr{P}$ has a binary connective as its main connective and is of one of the four forms $\mathscr{R} \,\&\, \mathscr{S}$, $\mathscr{R} \vee \mathscr{S}$, $\mathscr{R} \supset \mathscr{S}$, and $\mathscr{R} \equiv \mathscr{S}$. We shall consider the two cases separately.

i. $\mathscr{P}$ is of the form $\sim \mathscr{R}$. Since $\mathscr{Q}$ is a proper sentential component of $\mathscr{P}$, $\mathscr{Q}$ must be a sentential component of $\mathscr{R}$. Hence $[\mathscr{P}](\mathscr{Q}_1//\mathscr{Q})$ is a sentence $\sim [\mathscr{R}](\mathscr{Q}_1//\mathscr{Q})$. But $\mathscr{R}$ has k occurrences of connectives, so by the inductive hypothesis, $\mathscr{R}$ is truth-functionally equivalent to $[\mathscr{R}](\mathscr{Q}_1//\mathscr{Q})$. It follows from 6.1.1 that $\sim \mathscr{R}$ is truth-functionally equivalent to $\sim [\mathscr{R}](\mathscr{Q}_1//\mathscr{Q})$; that is, $\mathscr{P}$ is truth-functionally equivalent to $[\mathscr{P}](\mathscr{Q}_1//\mathscr{Q})$.

ii. $\mathscr{P}$ is of the form $\mathscr{R} \,\&\, \mathscr{S}$, $\mathscr{R} \vee \mathscr{S}$, $\mathscr{R} \supset \mathscr{S}$, or $\mathscr{R} \equiv \mathscr{S}$. Since $\mathscr{Q}$ is a proper component of $\mathscr{P}$, $[\mathscr{P}](\mathscr{Q}_1//\mathscr{Q})$ must be $\mathscr{P}$ with its left immediate component replaced by a sentence $[\mathscr{R}](\mathscr{Q}_1//\mathscr{Q})$, $\mathscr{P}$ with its right immediate component replaced with a sentence $[\mathscr{S}](\mathscr{Q}_1//\mathscr{Q})$, or $\mathscr{P}$ with both replacements made. Both $\mathscr{R}$ and $\mathscr{S}$ have fewer than $k + 1$ occurrences of connectives, and so the inductive hypothesis holds for both $\mathscr{R}$ and $\mathscr{S}$. Hence $\mathscr{R}$ is truth-functionally equivalent to $[\mathscr{R}](\mathscr{Q}_1//\mathscr{Q})$, and $\mathscr{S}$ is truth-functionally equivalent to $[\mathscr{S}](\mathscr{Q}_1//\mathscr{Q})$. And $\mathscr{R}$ is truth-functionally equivalent to $\mathscr{R}$ and $\mathscr{S}$ is truth-functionally equivalent to $\mathscr{S}$. Whatever replacements are made in $\mathscr{P}$, it follows by 6.1.1 that $\mathscr{P}$ is truth-functionally equivalent to $[\mathscr{P}](\mathscr{Q}_1//\mathscr{Q})$.

This completes the proof of the inductive step and thus the proof of our thesis.

2. An example of a sentence that contains only binary connectives and is truth-functionally true is 'A ⊃ A'. An attempted proof would break down in the proof of the inductive step (since no atomic sentence is truth-functionally true, the basis clause will go through).

Section 6.2E

1. Suppose that we have constructed, in accordance with the algorithm, a sentence for a row of a truth-function schema that defines a truth-function of n arguments. We proved in Exercise 1.d in Section 6.1E the result that an iterated conjunction $(\ldots(\mathscr{P}_1 \;\&\; \mathscr{P}_2) \;\&\; \ldots \;\&\; \mathscr{P}_n)$ is true on a truth-value assignment if and only if $\mathscr{P}_1, \ldots, \mathscr{P}_n$ are all true on that truth-value assignment. We have constructed the present iterated conjunction of atomic sentences and negations of atomic sentences in such a way that each conjunct is true when the atomic components have the truth-values represented in that row. Hence for that assignment the sentence constructed is true. For any other assignments to the atomic components of the sentence, at least one of the conjuncts is false; hence the conjunction is also false.

2.a. (A & ~ B) ∨ (~ A & ~ B)
b. A & ~ A
d. ([(A & B) & C] ∨ [(A & B) & ~ C]) ∨ [(~ A & ~ B) & C]

3. Suppose that the table defines a truth-function of n arguments. We first construct an iterated disjunction of n disjuncts such that the ith disjunct is the negation of the ith atomic sentence of *SL* if the ith truth-value in the row is **T**, and the ith disjunct is the ith atomic sentence of *SL* if the ith truth-value in the row is **F**. Note that this iterated disjunction is *false* exactly when its atomic components have the truth-values displayed in that row. We then negate the iterated disjunction, to obtain a sentence that is *true* for those truth-values and false for all other truth-values that may be assigned to its atomic components.

4. To prove that {'~', '&'} is truth-functionally complete, it will suffice to show that for each sentence of *SL* containing only '~', '∨', and '&', there is a truth-functionally equivalent sentence of *SL* that contains the same atomic components and in which the only connectives are '~' and '&'. For it will then follow, from the fact that {'~', '∨', '&'} is truth-functionally complete, that {'~', '&'} is also truth-functionally complete. But every sentence of the form

$$\mathscr{P} \vee \mathscr{Q}$$

is truth-functionally equivalent to

$$\sim (\sim \mathscr{P} \,\&\, \sim \mathscr{Q})$$

So by repeated substitutions, we can obtain, from sentences containing '~', '∨', and '&', truth-functionally equivalent sentences that contain only '~' and '&'.

To show that {'~', '⊃'} is truth-functionally complete, it suffices to point out that every sentence of the form

$$\mathscr{P} \,\&\, \mathscr{Q}$$

is truth-functionally equivalent to the corresponding sentence

$$\sim (\mathscr{P} \supset \sim \mathscr{Q})$$

and that every sentence of the form

$$\mathscr{P} \vee \mathscr{Q}$$

is truth-functionally equivalent to the corresponding sentence

$$\sim \mathscr{P} \supset \mathscr{Q}$$

For then we can find, for each sentence containing only '~', '∨', and '&', a truth-functionally equivalent sentence with the same atomic components containing only '~' and '⊃'. It follows that {'~', '⊃'} is truth-functionally complete, since {'~', '∨', '&'} is.

5. To show this, we need only note that the negation and disjunction truth-functions can be expressed using only the dagger. The truth-table for 'A ↓ A' is

A	A	↓	A
T	**T**	**F**	**T**
F	**F**	**T**	**F**

The sentence 'A ↓ A' expresses the negation truth-function, for the column under the dagger is identical with the column to the right of the vertical line in the characteristic truth-table for negation.

The disjunction truth-function is expressed by '(A ↓ B) ↓ (A ↓ B)', as the following truth-table shows:

A	B	(A	↓	B)	↓	(A	↓	B)
T	**T**	**T**	**F**	**T**	**T**	**T**	**F**	**T**
T	**F**	**T**	**F**	**F**	**T**	**T**	**F**	**F**
F	**T**	**F**	**F**	**T**	**T**	**F**	**F**	**T**
F	**F**	**F**	**T**	**F**	**F**	**F**	**T**	**F**

This table shows that '(A ↓ B) ↓ (A ↓ B)' is true on every truth-value assignment on which at least one of 'A' and 'B' is true. Hence that sentence expresses the disjunction truth-function.

Thus any truth-function that is expressed by a sentence of *SL* containing only the connectives '~' and '∨' can be expressed by a sentence containing only '↓' as a connective. To form such a sentence, we convert the sentence of *SL* containing just '~' and '∨' that expresses the truth-function in question as follows. Repeatedly replace components of the form $\sim \mathscr{P}$ with $\mathscr{P} \downarrow \mathscr{P}$ and components of the form $\mathscr{P} \vee \mathscr{Q}$ with $(\mathscr{P} \downarrow \mathscr{Q}) \downarrow (\mathscr{P} \downarrow \mathscr{Q})$ until a sentence containing '↓' as the only connective is obtained. Since {'∨', '~'} is truth-functionally complete, so is {'↓'}.

7. The set {'~'} is not truth-functionally complete because every sentence containing only '~' is truth-functionally indeterminate. Hence truth-functions expressed in *SL* by truth-functionally true sentences and truth-functions expressed in *SL* truth-functionally false sentences cannot be expressed by a sentence that contains only '~'.

The set {'&', '∨', '⊃', '≡'} is not truth-functionally complete because no sentence that contains only binary connectives (if any) is truth-functionally false. Hence no truth-function that is expressed in *SL* by a truth-functionally false sentence can be expressed by a sentence containing only binary connectives of *SL*.

8. We shall prove by mathematical induction that in the truth-table for a sentence $\mathscr{P}$ containing only the connectives '~' and '≡' and two atomic components, the column under the main connective of $\mathscr{P}$ has an even number of **T**s and an even number of **F**s. For then we shall know that no sentence containing only those connectives can express, for example, the truth-function defined as follows (the material conditional truth-function):

T	**T**	**T**
T	**F**	**F**
F	**T**	**T**
F	**F**	**T**

In the induction remember that any sentence of *SL* that contains two atomic components has a four-row truth-table. Our induction will proceed on the number of occurrences of connectives in $\mathscr{P}$. However, the first case, that considered in the basis clause, is the case where $\mathscr{P}$ contains *one* occurrence of a connective. This is because every sentence that contains zero occurrences of connectives is an atomic sentence and thus cannot contain more than one atomic component. *Basis clause:* The thesis holds for every sentence of *SL* with exactly two atomic components and one occurrence of (one of) the connectives '~' and '≡'.

In this case $\mathscr{P}$ cannot be of the form $\sim \mathscr{Q}$, for if the initial '~' is the only connective in $\mathscr{P}$, then $\mathscr{Q}$ is atomic, and hence $\mathscr{P}$ does not contain two atomic components. So $\mathscr{P}$ is of the form $\mathscr{Q} \equiv \mathscr{R}$, where $\mathscr{Q}$ and $\mathscr{R}$ are atomic sentences.

$\mathscr{Q} \equiv \mathscr{R}$ will have to be true on assignments that assign the same truth-values to $\mathscr{Q}$ and $\mathscr{R}$ and false on other assignments. Hence the thesis holds in this case.
Inductive step: If the thesis holds for every sentence of *SL* that contains k or fewer occurrences of the connectives '~' and '≡' (and no other connectives) and two atomic components, then the thesis holds for every sentence of *SL* that contains two atomic components and $k + 1$ occurrences of the connectives '~' and '≡' (and no other connectives).

Let $\mathscr{P}$ be a sentence of *SL* that contains exactly two atomic components and $k + 1$ occurrences of the connectives '~' and '≡' (and no other connectives). There are two cases to consider.

i. $\mathscr{P}$ is of the form ~ $\mathscr{Q}$. Then $\mathscr{Q}$ falls under the inductive hypothesis; hence in the truth-table for $\mathscr{Q}$ the column under the main connective contains an even number of **T**s and an even number of **F**s. The column for the sentence s~ $\mathscr{Q}$ simply reverses the **T**s and **F**s, so it also contains an even number of **T**s and an even number of **F**s.

ii. $\mathscr{P}$ is of the form $\mathscr{Q} \equiv \mathscr{R}$. Then $\mathscr{Q}$ and $\mathscr{R}$ each contain fewer occurrences of connectives. If, in addition, $\mathscr{Q}$ and $\mathscr{R}$ each contain both of the atomic components of $\mathscr{P}$, then they fall under the inductive hypothesis—$\mathscr{Q}$ has an even number of **T**s and an even number of **F**s in its truth-table column, and so does $\mathscr{R}$. On the other hand, if $\mathscr{Q}$ or $\mathscr{R}$ (or both) only contains one of the atomic components of $\mathscr{P}$ (e.g., if $\mathscr{P}$ is '~ A ≡ (B ≡ A)' then $\mathscr{Q}$ is '~ A'), then $\mathscr{Q}$ or $\mathscr{R}$ (or both) fails to fall under the inductive hypothesis. However, in this case the component in question also has an even number of **T**s and an even number of **F**s in its column in the truth-table for $\mathscr{P}$. This is because (a) two rows assign **T** to the single atomic component of $\mathscr{Q}$ and, by the result in Exercise 1.c, $\mathscr{Q}$ has the same truth-value in these two rows; and (b) two rows assign **F** to the single atomic component of $\mathscr{Q}$ and so, by the same result, $\mathscr{Q}$ has the same truth-value in these two rows.

We will now show that if $\mathscr{Q}$ and $\mathscr{R}$ each have an even number of **T**s and an even number of **F**s in their truth-table columns, then so must $\mathscr{P}$. Let us assume the contrary, that is, we shall suppose that $\mathscr{P}$ has an odd number of **T**s and an odd number of **F**s in its truth-table column. There are then two possibilities.

a. There are 3 **T**s and 1 **F** in $\mathscr{P}$'s truth-table column. Then in three rows of their truth-table columns, $\mathscr{Q}$ and $\mathscr{R}$ have the same truth-value, and in one row they have different truth-values. So either $\mathscr{Q}$ has one more **T** in its truth-table column than does $\mathscr{R}$, or vice-versa. Either way, since the sum of an even number plus 1 is odd, it follows that either $\mathscr{Q}$ has an odd number of **T**s in its truth-table column or $\mathscr{R}$ has an odd number of **T**s in its truth-table column. This contradicts our inductive hypothesis, so we conclude that $\mathscr{P}$ cannot have 3 **T**s and 1 **F** in its truth-table column.

b. There are 3 **F**s and 1 **T** in $\mathscr{P}$'s truth-table column. By reasoning similar to that just given, it is easily shown that this is impossible, given the inductive hypothesis.

Therefore $\mathcal{P}$ must have an even number of **Ts** and **Fs** in its truth-table column.

9. First, a binary connective whose unit set is truth-functionally complete must be such that a sentence of which it is the main connective is false whenever all its immediate components are true. Otherwise, every sentence containing only that connective would be true whenever its atomic components were. And then, for example, the negation truth-function would not be expressible using that connective. Similar reasoning shows that the main column of the characteristic truth-table must contain **T** in the last row. Otherwise, no sentence containing that connective could be truth-functionally true.

Second, the column in the characteristic truth-table must contain an odd number of **Ts** and an odd number of **Fs**. For otherwise, as the induction in Exercise 8 shows, any sentence containing two atomic components and only this connective would have an even number of **Ts** and an even number of **Fs** in its truth-table column. The disjunction truth-function, for example, would then not be expressible.

Combining these two results, it is easily verified that there are only two possible characteristic truth-tables for a binary connective whose unit set is truth-functionally complete—that for '↓' and that for '|'.

Section 6.3E

1.a. {A ⊃ B, C ⊃ D}, {A ⊃ B}, {C ⊃ D}, ∅

b. {C ⊃ ~ D, ~ D ⊃ C, C ∨ C}, {C ∨ ~ D, ~ D ∨ C}, {C ∨ ~ D, C ∨ C}, {~ D ∨ C, C∨ C}, {C ∨ ~ D}, {~ D ∨ C}, {C ∨ C}, ∅

c. {(B & A) ≡ K}, ∅

d. ∅

2. a, b, d, e.

4.a. To prove that *SD** is sound, it suffices to add a clause for the new rule to the induction in the proof of Metatheorem 6.2.

xiii. If $\mathcal{Q}_{k+1}$ at position $k+1$ is justified by ~ ≡I, then $\mathcal{Q}_{k+1}$ is a negated biconditional.

h	$\mathcal{P}$	
j	$\sim \mathcal{Q}$	
$k + 1$	$\sim (\mathcal{P} \equiv \mathcal{Q})$	$h, j \sim \equiv$I

By the inductive hypothesis, $\Gamma_h \vDash \mathcal{P}$ and $\Gamma_j \vDash \sim \mathcal{Q}$. Since $\mathcal{P}$ and $\sim \mathcal{Q}$ are accessible at position $k+1$, every member of Γ_h is a member of Γ_{k+1}, and every member of Γ_j is a member of Γ_{k+1}. Hence, by 6.3.1, $\Gamma_{k+1} \vDash \mathcal{P}$ and $\Gamma_{k+1} \vDash \sim \mathcal{Q}$. But $\sim (\mathcal{P} \equiv \mathcal{Q})$ is true whenever $\mathcal{P}$ and $\sim \mathcal{Q}$ are both true. So $\Gamma_{k+1} \vDash \sim (\mathcal{P} \equiv \mathcal{Q})$ as well.

c. To show that *SD** is not sound, it suffices to give an example of a derivation in *SD** of a sentence $\mathcal{P}$ from a set Γ of sentences such that $\mathcal{P}$ is *not* truth-functionally entailed by Γ. That is, we show that for some Γ and $\mathcal{P}$, $\Gamma \vdash \mathcal{P}$ in *SD**, but $\Gamma \nvDash \mathcal{P}$. Here is an example:

1	A	Assumption
2	A ∨ B	Assumption
3	B	1, 2 C∨E

It is easily verified that {A, A ∨ B} does not truth-functionally entail 'B'.

e. Yes. In proving Metatheorem 6.2, we showed that each rule of *SD* is truth-preserving. It follows that if every rule of *SD** is a rule of *SD,* then every rule of *SD** is truth-preserving. Of course, as we saw in Exercise 4.c, *adding* a rule produces a system that is not sound if the rule is not truth-preserving.

5. No. In *SD* we can derive $\mathscr{Q}$ from a sentence $\mathscr{P}$ & $\mathscr{Q}$ by &E. But, if '&' had the suggested truth-table, then {$\mathscr{P}$ & $\mathscr{Q}$} would *not* truth-functionally entail $\mathscr{Q}$, for (by the second row of the table) $\mathscr{P}$ & $\mathscr{Q}$ would be true when $\mathscr{P}$ is true and $\mathscr{Q}$ is false. Hence it would be the case that {$\mathscr{P}$ & $\mathscr{Q}$} $\vdash$ $\mathscr{Q}$ in *SD* but not the case that {$\mathscr{P}$ & $\mathscr{Q}$} $\vDash$ $\mathscr{Q}$.

6. To prove that *SD*+ is sound for sentential logic, we must show that the rules of *SD*+ that are not rules of *SD* are truth-preserving. (By Metatheorem 6.2, the rules of *SD* have been shown to be truth-preserving.) The three additional rules of inference in *SD*+ are Modus Tollens, Hypothetical Syllogism, and Disjunctive Syllogism. We introduced each of these rules in Chapter 5 as a *derived* rule. For example, we showed that Modus Tollens is eliminable, that anything that can be derived using this rule can be derived without it, using just the smaller set of rules in *SD.* It follows that each of these three rules is truth-preserving. For if use of one of these rules can lead from true sentences to false ones, then we can construct a derivation in *SD* (without using the derived rule) in which the sentence derived is not truth-functionally entailed by the set consisting of the undischarged assumptions. But Metatheorem 6.2 shows that this is impossible. Hence each of the derived rules is truth-preserving.

All that remains to be shown, in proving that *SD*+ is sound, is that the rules of replacement are also truth-preserving. We can incorporate this as a thirteenth case in the proof of the inductive step for Metatheorem 6.2:

xiii. If $\mathscr{Q}_{k+1}$ at position $k + 1$ is justified by a rule of replacement, then $\mathscr{Q}_{k+1}$ is derived as follows:

h	$\mathscr{P}$	
$k + 1$	$[\mathscr{P}](\mathscr{Q}_1//\mathscr{Q})$	h RR

where RR is some rule of replacement, sentence $\mathscr{P}$ at position h is accessible at position $k + 1$, and $[\mathscr{P}](\mathscr{Q}_1//\mathscr{Q})$ is a sentence that is the result of replacing a component $\mathscr{Q}$ of $\mathscr{P}$ with a component $\mathscr{Q}_1$ in accordance with one of the rules of replacement. That the sentence $\mathscr{Q}$ is truth-functionally equivalent to $\mathscr{Q}_1$, no matter what the rule of replacement is, is easily verified. So, by Exercise 1.e in Section

6.1E, $[\mathscr{P}](\mathscr{Q}_1//\mathscr{Q})$ is truth-functionally equivalent to $\mathscr{P}$. By the inductive hypothesis, $\Gamma_h \vDash \mathscr{P}$; and since $\mathscr{P}$ at h is accessible at position $k + 1$, it follows that $\Gamma_{k+1} \vDash \mathscr{P}$. But $[\mathscr{P}](\mathscr{Q}_1//\mathscr{Q})$ is true whenever $\mathscr{P}$ is true (since they are truth-functionally equivalent), so $\Gamma_{k+1} \vDash [\mathscr{P}](\mathscr{Q}_1//\mathscr{Q})$; that is, $\Gamma_{k+1} \vDash \mathscr{Q}_{k+1}$.

Section 6.4E

1. Proof of 6.4.2. Assume that $\Gamma \vdash \mathscr{P}$ in *SD*. Then there is a derivation in *SD* of the following sort

$$
\begin{array}{r|l}
1 & \mathscr{P}_1 \\
\cdot & \cdot \\
n & \mathscr{P}_n \\
\hline
\cdot & \cdot \\
m & \mathscr{P}
\end{array}
$$

(where $\mathscr{P}_1, \mathscr{P}_2, \ldots, \mathscr{P}_n$ are members of Γ). To show that $\Gamma \cup \{\sim \mathscr{P}\}$ is inconsistent in *SD*, we need only produce a derivation of some sentence $\mathscr{Q}$ and $\sim \mathscr{Q}$ from members of $\Gamma \cup \{\sim \mathscr{P}\}$. This is easy. Start with the derivation of $\mathscr{P}$ from Γ and add $\sim \mathscr{P}$ as a new primary assumption at line $n + 1$, renumbering subsequent lines as is appropriate. As a new last line, enter $\sim \mathscr{P}$ by Reiteration. The result is a derivation of the sort

$$
\begin{array}{r|ll}
1 & \mathscr{P}_1 & \\
\cdot & \cdot & \\
n & \mathscr{P}_n & \\
n + 1 & \sim \mathscr{P} & \\
\hline
\cdot & \cdot & \\
m + 1 & \mathscr{P} & \\
m + 2 & \sim \mathscr{P} & \quad n + 1 \;\; \text{R}
\end{array}
$$

So if $\Gamma \vdash \mathscr{P}$, then $\Gamma \cup \{\sim \mathscr{P}\}$ is inconsistent in *SD*.

Now assume that $\Gamma \cup \{\sim \mathscr{P}\}$ is inconsistent in *SD*. Then there is a derivation in *SD* of the sort

$$
\begin{array}{r|l}
1 & \mathscr{P}_1 \\
\cdot & \cdot \\
n & \mathscr{P}_n \\
n + 1 & \sim \mathscr{P} \\
\hline
\cdot & \cdot \\
m & \mathscr{Q} \\
\cdot & \cdot \\
p & \sim \mathscr{Q}
\end{array}
$$

(where $\mathscr{P}_1, \mathscr{P}_2, \ldots, \mathscr{P}_n$ all members of Γ). To show that $\Gamma \vdash \mathscr{P}$, we need only produce a derivation in which the primary assumptions are members of Γ and the last line is $\mathscr{P}$. This is easy. Start with this derivation, but make $\sim \mathscr{P}$ an auxiliary assumption rather than a primary assumption. Enter $\mathscr{P}$ as a new last line, justified by Negation Elimination. The result is a derivation of the sort

1	$\mathscr{P}_1$	
.	.	
n	$\mathscr{P}_n$	
$n + 1$	$\sim \mathscr{P}$	
.	.	
m	$\mathscr{Q}$	
.	.	
p	$\sim \mathscr{Q}$	
$p + 1$	$\mathscr{P}$	$n + 1 - p$ $\sim$E

Proof of 6.4.6. Assume $\Gamma \cup \{\mathscr{P}\}$ is inconsistent in *SD*. Then there is a derivation in *SD* of the sort

1	$\mathscr{P}_1$
.	
n	$\mathscr{P}_n$
$n + 1$	$\mathscr{P}$
.	.
m	$\mathscr{Q}$
.	.
p	$\sim \mathscr{Q}$

(where $\mathscr{P}_1, \mathscr{P}_2, \ldots, \mathscr{P}_n$ are members of Γ). But then there is also a derivation of the following sort

1	$\mathscr{P}_1$	
.	.	
n	$\mathscr{P}_n$	
$n + 1$	$\mathscr{P}$	
	.	
m	$\mathscr{Q}$	
p	$\sim \mathscr{Q}$	
$p + 1$	$\sim \mathscr{P}$	$n + 1 - p$ $\sim$I

This shows that if $\Gamma \cup \{\mathscr{P}\}$ is inconsistent in *SD*, then $\Gamma \vdash \sim \mathscr{P}$ in *SD*.

4. Since every rule of *SD* is a rule of *SD+*, every derivation in *SD* is a derivation in *SD+*. So if $\Gamma \vDash \mathscr{P}$, then $\Gamma \vdash \mathscr{P}$ in *SD*, by Metatheorem 6.3, and therefore $\Gamma \vdash \mathscr{P}$ in *SD+*. That is, *SD+* is complete for sentential logic.

7.a. Since we already know that *SD* is complete, we need only show that wherever Reiteration is used in a derivation in *SD*, it can be eliminated in favor of some combination of the remaining rules of *SD*. This was proved in Exercise 13.c in Section 5.4E. Hence *SD** is complete as well.

8. We used the fact that Conjunction Elimination is a rule of *SD* in proving (b) for 6.4.7, where we showed that if a sentence $\mathcal{P}$ & $\mathcal{Q}$ is a member of a set Γ^* that is maximally consistent in *SD*, then both $\mathcal{P}$ and $\mathcal{Q}$ are members of Γ^*.

9. First assume that some set Γ is truth-functionally consistent. Then obviously every finite subset of Γ is truth-functionally consistent as well, for all members of a finite subset of Γ are members of Γ, hence all are true on at least one truth-value assignment.

Now assume that some set Γ is truth-functionally inconsistent. If Γ is finite, then obviously at least one finite subset of Γ (namely, Γ itself) is truth-functionally inconsistent. If Γ is infinite, then, by Lemma 6.1, Γ is inconsistent in *SD*, and, by 6.4.3, some finite subset Γ' of Γ is inconsistent in *SD*—that is, for some sentence $\mathcal{P}$, $\Gamma' \vdash \mathcal{P}$ and $\Gamma' \vdash \sim \mathcal{P}$. Hence, by Metatheorem 6.2, $\Gamma' \vDash \mathcal{P}$ and $\Gamma' \vDash \sim \mathcal{P}$, so (by 6.3.3) Γ' is truth-functionally inconsistent; hence not every finite subset of Γ is truth-functionally consistent.

CHAPTER SEVEN

Section 7.2E

1.a. 'The President' is a singular term, 'Democrat' is not
x is a Democrat
('w' or 'y' or 'z' may be used in place of 'x')

c. 'Sarah' and 'Smith College' are the singular terms
x attends Smith College
Sarah attends x
x attends y

e. The singular terms are 'Charles' and 'Rita'
w and Rita are brother and sister
Charles and w are brother and sister
w and z are brother and sister

g. The singular terms are '2', '4', and '8'
x times 4 is 8
2 times x is 8
2 times 4 is y
x times y is 8
x times 4 is y
2 times x is y
x times y is z

i. The singular terms are ‘0’, ‘0’, and ‘0’

z plus 0 is 0
0 plus z is 0
0 plus 0 is z
w plus y is 0
w plus 0 is y
0 plus w is y
w plus y is z

Section 7.3E

1.a. Bai
c. Bbn
e. Beh
g. (Aph & Ahn) & Ank
i. Aih ≡ Aip
k. ([(Lap & Lbp) & (Lcp & Ldp)] & Lep) & ~ ([(Bap ∨ Bbp) ∨ (Bcp ∨ Bdp)] ∨ Bep)
m. (Tda & Tdb) & (Tdc & Tde)
o. ~ ([(Tab ∨ Tac) ∨ (Tad ∨ Tae)] ∨ Taa) & [(Lab & Lac) & (Lad & Lae)]

2.a. (Ba & Ia) & ~ Ra
c. (Bd & Rd) & Id
e. Ib ⊃ (Id & Ia)
g. Lab & Dac
i. ~ (Lca ∨ Dca) & (Lcd & Dcd)
k. Acb ≡ (Sbc & Rb)
m. (Sdc & Sca) ⊃ Sda
o. (Lcb & Lba) ⊃ (Dca & Sca)
q. (Rd & ~ Ra) & (~ Rb & ~ Rc)

3.a. One appropriate symbolization key is

UD:	Margaret, Todd, Charles, and Sarah
Gx:	x is good at skateboarding
Lx:	x likes skateboarding
Hx:	x wears headgear
Kx:	x wears knee pads
Rxy:	x is more reckless than y (at skateboarding)
Sxy:	x is more skillful than y (at skateboarding)
c:	Charles
m:	Margaret
s:	Sarah
t:	Todd

(Lm & Lt) & ~ (Gm ∨ Gt)
Gc & ~ Lc
Gs & Ls
[(Hm & Ht) & (Hc & Hs)] & [(Kc & Ks) & ~ (Km ∨ Kt)]
[(Rsm & Rst) & Rsc] & [(Scs & Scm) & Sct]

Note: it may be tempting to use a two-place predicate to symbolize being good at skateboarding, for example, 'Gxy', and another two-place predicate to symbolize liking skateboarding. So too we might use two-place predicates to symbolize wearing headgear and wearing kneepads. Doing so would require including skateboarding, headgear, and knee pads in the universe of discourse. But things are now a little murky. Skateboarding is more of an activity than a thing (although activities are often the "topics of conversation" as when we say that some people like, for example, hiking, skiing, and canoeing while others don't). And while we might include all headgear and kneepads in our universe of discourse, we do not know which ones the characters in our passage wear, so we would be hard pressed to name the favored items.

Moreover, here there is no need to invoke these two-place predicates because here we are not asked to investigate logical relations that can only be expressed with two-place predicates. The case would be different if the passage included the sentence 'If Sarah is good at anything she is good at sailing' and we were asked to show that it follows from the passage that Sarah is good at sailing. (On the revised scenario we are told that Sarah is good at skateboarding, and that if she is good at anything—she is, skateboarding—she is good at sailing. So she is good at sailing. Here we are treating skateboarding as *something,* something Sarah is good at. But we will leave these complexities until we have fully developed the language *PL.*)

c. One appropriate symbolization key is

UD: Andrew, Christopher, Amanda
Hz: z is a hiker
Mz: z is a mountain climber
Kz: z is a kayaker
Sz: z is a swimmer
Lzw: z likes w
Nzw: z is nuts about w
a: Andrew
c: Christopher
m: Amanda

(Ha & Hc) & ~ (Ma ∨ Mc)
(Hm & Mm) & Km
(Ka ∨ Kc) & ~ (Ka & Kc)
~ [(Sa ∨ Sc) ∨ Sm]

((Lac & Lca) & [(Lam & Lma) & (Lmc & Lcm)]) & (Nma & Nam)

Section 7.4E

1.a. (∀z)Bz
c. ~ (∃x)Bx
e. (∃x)Bx & (∃x)Rx
g. (∃z)Rz ⊃ (∃z)Bz
i. (∀y)By ≡ ~ (∃y)Ry

2.a. Pj ⊃ (∀x)Px
c. (∃y)Py ⊃ (Pj & Pr)
e. ~ Pr ⊃ ~ (∃x)Px
g. (Pj ⊃ Pr) & (Pr ⊃ (∀x)Px)
i. (∀y)Sy & ~ (∀y)Py
k. (∀x)Sx ⊃ (∃y)Py

Section 7.5E

1.a. A formula but not a sentence (an open sentence): the 'z' in 'Zz' is free.

c. A formula and a sentence.

e. A formula but not a sentence (an open sentence): the 'x' in 'Fxz' is free.

g. A formula and a sentence.

i. Not a formula. '~ (∃x)' is an expression of *SL*, but '(~ ∃x)' is not.

k. Not a formula. Since there is no 'y' in 'Lxx', '(∃y)Lxx' is not a formula. Hence, neither is '(∃x)(∃y)Lxx'.

m. A formula and a sentence.

o. A formula but not a sentence (an open sentence): 'w' in 'Fw' is free.

2.a. A sentence. The subformulas are

(∃x)(∀y)Byx	(∃x)
(∀y)Byx	(∀y)
Byx	None

c. Not a sentence. The 'x' in '(Bg ⊃ Fx)' is free. The subformulas are

(∀x)(~ Fx & Gx) ≡ (Bg ⊃ Fx)	≡
(∀x)(~ Fx & Gx)	(∀x)
Bg ⊃ Fx	⊃
~ Fx & Gx	&
~ Fx	~
Gx	None
Bg	None
Fx	None

e. Sentence. The subformulas are

$\sim (\exists x)Px \ \& \ Rab$	&
$\sim (\exists x)Px$	$\sim$
Rab	None
$(\exists x)Px$	$(\exists x)$
Px	None

g. Sentence. The subformulas are

$\sim [\sim (\forall x)Fx \equiv (\exists w) \sim Gw] \supset Maa$	$\supset$
$\sim [\sim (\forall x)Fx \equiv (\exists w) \sim Gw]$	$\sim$
Maa	None
$\sim (\forall x)Fx \equiv (\exists w) \sim Gw$	$\equiv$
$\sim (\forall x)Fx$	$\sim$
$(\exists w) \sim Gw$	$(\exists w)$
$(\forall x)Fx$	$(\forall x)$
Fx	None
$\sim Gw$	$\sim$
Gw	None

i. Sentence. The subformulas are

$\sim \sim \sim (\exists x)(\forall z)(Gxaz \vee \sim Hazb)$	$\sim$
$\sim \sim (\exists x)(\forall z)(Gxaz \vee \sim Hazb)$	$\sim$
$\sim (\exists x)(\forall z)(Gxaz \vee \sim Hazb)$	$\sim$
$(\exists x)(\forall z)(Gxaz \vee \sim Hazb)$	$(\exists x)$
$(\forall z)(Gxaz \vee \sim Hazb)$	$(\forall z)$
$Gxaz \vee \sim Hazb$	$\vee$
Gxaz	None
$\sim Hazb$	$\sim$
Hazb	None

k. Sentence. The subformulas are

$(\exists x)[Fx \supset (\forall w)(\sim Gx \supset \sim Hwx)]$	$(\exists x)$
$Fx \supset (\forall w)(\sim Gx \supset \sim Hwx)$	$\supset$
Fx	None
$(\forall w)(\sim Gx \supset \sim Hwx)$	$(\forall w)$
$\sim Gx \supset \sim Hwx$	$\supset$
$\sim Gx$	$\sim$
$\sim Hwx$	$\sim$
Gx	None
Hwx	None

m. A sentence. The subformulas are

(Hb ∨ Fa) ≡ (∃z)(~ Fz & Gza)	≡
Hb ∨ Fa	∨
(∃z)(~ Fz & Gza)	(∃z)
Hb	None
Fa	None
~ Fz & Gza	&
~ Fz	~
Gza	None
Fz	None

3.a. (∀x)(Fx ⊃ Ga)	Quantified
c. ~ (∀x)(Fx ⊃ Ga)	Truth-functional
e. ~ (∃x)Hx	Truth-functional
g. (∀x)(Fx ≡ (∃w)Gw)	Quantified
i. (∃w)(Pw ⊃ (∀y)(Hy ≡ ~ Kyw))	Quantified
k. ~ [(∃w)(Jw ∨ Nw) ∨ (∃w)(Mw ∨ Lw)]	Truth-functional
m. (∀z)Gza ⊃ (∃z)Fz	Truth-functional
o. (∃z) ~ Hza	Quantified
q. (∀x) ~ Fx ≡ (∀z) ~ Hza	Truth-functional

4.a. Maa & Fa
c. ~ (Ca ≡ ~ Ca)
e. (Fa & ~ Gb) ⊃ (Bab ∨ Bba)
g. ~ (∃z)Naz ≡ (∀w)(Mww & Naw)
i. Fab ≡ Gba
k. ~ (∃y)(Hay & Hya)
m. (∀y)[(Hay & Hya) ⊃ (∃z)Gza]

5.a. (∀y)Ray ⊃ Byy	No
c. (∀y)(Rwy ⊃ Byy)	No
e. (∀y)(Ryy ⊃ Byy)	No
g. (Ray ⊃ Byy)	No
i. Rab ⊃ Bbb	No

6.a. (∀y) ~ Ray ≡ Paa	Yes
c. (∀y) ~ Ray ≡ Pba	No
e. (∀y) (~ Ryy ≡ Paa)	No
g. (∀y) ~ Raw ≡ Paa	No

Section 7.6E

1.a. A-sentence	(∀y)(Py ⊃ Cy)
c. O-sentence	(∃w)(Dw & ~ Sw)
e. I-sentence	(∃z)(Nz & Bz)

g. E-sentence $(\forall x)(Px \supset {\sim} Sx)$
i. A-sentence $(\forall w)(Pw \supset Mw)$
k. A-sentence $(\forall y)(Sy \supset Cy)$
m. E-sentence $(\forall y)(Ky \supset {\sim} Sy)$
o. E-sentence $(\forall y)(Qy \supset {\sim} Zy)$

2.a. $(\forall y)(By \supset Ly)$
c. $(\forall z)(Rz \supset {\sim} Lz)$
e. $(\exists x)Bx \ \& \ (\exists x)Rx$
g. $[(\exists z)Bz \ \& \ (\exists z)Rz] \ \& \ {\sim} (\exists z)(Bz \ \& \ Rz)$
i. $(\exists y)By \ \& \ [(\exists y)Sy \ \& \ (\exists y)Ly]$
k. $(\forall w)(Cw \supset Rw) \ \& \ {\sim} (\forall w)(Rw \supset Cw)$
m. $(\forall y)Ry \vee [(\forall y)By \vee (\forall y)Gy]$
o. $(\exists w)(Rw \ \& \ Sw) \ \& \ (\exists w)(Rw \ \& \ {\sim} Sw)$
q. $(\exists x)Ox \ \& \ (\forall y)(Ly \supset {\sim} Oy)$

3.a. An I-sentence and the corresponding O-sentence of *PL* can both be true. Consider the English sentences ‘Some positive integers are even’ and ‘Some positive integers are not even’. Where the UD is positive integers and ‘Ex’ is interpreted as ‘x is even’, these can be symbolized as ‘$(\exists x)Ex$’ and ‘$(\exists x) \sim Ex$’, respectively, and both sentences of *PL* are true.

An I-sentence and an O-sentence can also both be false. Consider ‘Some tiggers are fast’ and ‘Some tiggers are not fast’. Where the UD is mammals, ‘Tx’ is interpreted as ‘x is a tigger’ and ‘Fx’ as ‘x is fast’, these become, respectively, ‘$(\exists x)(Tx \ \& \ Fx)$’ and ‘$(\exists x)(Tx \ \& \sim Fx)$’. As there are no tiggers, both sentences of *PL* are false. Note, however, that there cannot be an I-sentence and a corresponding O-sentence of the sorts $(\exists x)\mathscr{A}$ and $(\exists x) \sim \mathscr{A}$, where $\mathscr{A}$ is an atomic formula and both the I-sentence and the O-sentence are false. For however $\mathscr{A}$ is interpreted, either there is something that satisfies it, or there is not. In the first instance $(\exists x)\mathscr{A}$ is true, in the second $(\exists x) \sim \mathscr{A}$.

Section 7.7E

1.a. $(\forall z)(Pz \supset Hz)$
c. $(\exists z)(Pz \ \& \ Hz)$
e. $(\forall w)[(Hw \ \& \ Pw) \supset {\sim} Iw]$
g. ${\sim} (\forall x)[(Px \vee Ix) \supset Hx]$
i. $(\forall y)[(Iy \ \& \ Hy) \supset Ry]$
k. $(\exists z)Iz \supset Ih$
m. $(\exists w)Iw \supset (\forall x)(Rx \supset Ix)$
o. ${\sim} (\exists y)[Hy \ \& \ (Py \ \& \ Iy)]$
q. $(\forall z)(Pz \supset Iz) \supset {\sim} (\exists z)(Pz \ \& \ Hz)$
s. $(\forall w)(Rw \supset [(Lw \ \& \ Iw) \ \& \ {\sim} Hw])$

2.a. $(\forall w)(Lw \supset Aw)$
c. $(\forall x)(Lx \supset Fx) \ \& \ (\forall x)(Tx \supset \sim Fx)$
e. $(\exists y)[(Fy \ \& \ Ly) \ \& \ Cdy]$
g. $(\forall z)[(Lz \lor Tz) \supset Fz]$
i. $(\exists w)(Tw \ \& \ Fw) \ \& \sim (\forall w)(Tw \supset Fw)$
k. $(\forall x)[(Lx \ \& \ Cbx) \supset (Ax \ \& \sim Fx)]$
m. $(\exists z)(Lz \ \& \ Fz) \supset (\forall w)(Tw \supset Fw)$
o. $\sim Fb \ \& \ Bb$

3.a. $(\forall x)(Ex \supset Yx)$
c. $(\exists y)(Ey \ \& \ Yy) \ \& \sim (\forall y)(Ey \supset Yy)$
e. $(\exists z)(Ez \ \& \ Yz) \supset (\forall x)(Lx \supset Yx)$
g. $(\forall w)[(Ew \ \& \ Sw) \supset Yw]$
i. $(\forall w)[(Lw \ \& \ Ew) \supset (Yw \ \& \ Rw)]$
k. $(\forall x)[(Ex \lor Lx) \supset (Yx \supset Rx)]$
m. $\sim (\exists z)[(Pz \ \& \sim Rz) \ \& \ Yz]$
o. $(\forall x)[(Ex \ \& \ Sxx) \supset Yx]$
q. $(\forall x)([Ex \lor Lx) \ \& \ (Rx \lor Yx)] \supset Sxx)$
s. $(\forall z)([Yz \ \& \ (Lz \ \& \ Ez)] \supset Szz)$

4.a. $(\forall x)[Px \supset (Ux \ \& \ Ox)]$
c. $(\forall z)[Az \supset \sim (Oz \lor Uz)]$
e. $(\forall w)(Ow \equiv Uw)$
g. $(\exists y)(Py \ \& \ Uy) \ \& \ (\forall y)[(Py \ \& \ Ay) \supset \sim Uy]$
i. $(\exists z)[Pz \ \& \ (Oz \ \& \ Uz)] \ \& \ (\forall x)[Sx \supset (Ox \ \& \ Ux)]$
k. $((\exists x)(Sx \ \& \ Ux) \ \& \ (\exists x)(Px \ \& \ Ux)) \ \& \sim (\exists x)(Ax \ \& \ Ux)$

Section 7.8E

1.a. $(\exists y)[Sy \ \& \ (Cy \ \& \ Ly)]$
c. $\sim (\forall w)[(Sw \ \& \ Lw) \supset Cw]$
e. $\sim (\forall x)[(\exists y)(Sy \ \& \ Sxy) \supset Sx]$
g. $\sim (\forall x)[(\exists y)(Sy \ \& \ (Dxy \lor Sxy)) \supset Sx]$
i. $(\forall z)[(Sz \ \& \ (\exists w)(Swz \lor Dwz)) \supset Lz]$
k. $Sr \lor (\exists y)(Sy \ \& \ Dry)$
m. $(Sr \ \& \ (\forall z)[(Dzr \lor Szr) \supset Sz]) \lor (Sj \ \& \ (\forall z)[(Dzj \lor Szj) \supset Sz])$
2.a. $(\forall x)[Ax \supset (\exists y)(Fy \ \& \ Exy)] \ \& \ (\forall x)[Fx \supset (\exists y)(Ay \ \& \ Exy)]$
c. $\sim (\exists y)(Fy \ \& \ Eyp)$
e. $\sim (\exists y)(Fy \ \& \ Eyp) \ \& \ (\exists y)(Cy \ \& \ Eyp)$
g. $\sim (\exists w)(Aw \ \& \ Uw) \ \& \ (\exists w)(Aw \ \& \ Fw)$
i. $(\exists w)[(Aw \ \& \sim Fw) \ \& \ (\forall y)[(Fy \ \& \ Ay) \supset Ewy]]$
k. $(\exists z)[Fz \ \& \ (\forall y)(Ay \supset Dzy)] \ \& \ (\exists z)[Az \ \& \ (\forall y)(Fy \supset Dzy)]$
m. $(\forall x)[(\forall y)Dxy \supset (Px \lor (Ax \lor Ox))]$

3.a. $(\forall x)[Px \supset (\exists y)(Syx \ \& \ Bxy)]$
c. $(\forall y)[(Py \ \& \ (\forall z)Bzy) \supset (\forall w)(Swy \supset Byw)]$
e. $(\forall w)(\forall x)[(Pw \ \& \ Sxw) \supset Bwx] \supset (\forall z)(Pz \supset Wz)$

g. $(\forall x)(\forall y)([(Px \mathbin{\&} Syx) \mathbin{\&} Bxy] \supset (\sim Uxy \mathbin{\&} \sim Lyx))$
i. $(\exists y)[Py \mathbin{\&} (\forall z)(Pz \supset Byz)]$
k. $(\forall z)((Pz \mathbin{\&} Uz) \supset [(\forall w)(Swz \supset Bzw) \vee (\forall w)(Swz \supset Gzw)])$
m. $(\forall w)(\forall x)([(Pw \mathbin{\&} Sxw) \mathbin{\&} (Bwx \mathbin{\&} Bxw)] \supset (Ww \mathbin{\&} Wx))$
o. $(\exists x)(\exists y)[(Px \mathbin{\&} Syx) \mathbin{\&} \sim Uxty]$
q. $(\forall y)(\forall z)([(Py \mathbin{\&} Szy) \mathbin{\&} \sim Lzy] \supset (\sim Uzy \mathbin{\&} Bzy))$

4.a. Hildegard sometimes loves Manfred.
c. Manfred sometimes loves Hildegard and Manfred always loves Siegfried.
e. If Manfred ever loves himself, then he does so whenever Hildegard loves him.
g. There is someone no one ever loves.
i. There is a time at which someone loves everyone.
k. There is always someone who loves everyone.
m. No one loves anyone all the time.
o. Everyone loves, at some time, himself or herself.

Section 7.9E

1.a. $(\forall x)[(Wx \mathbin{\&} \sim x = d) \supset Sx]$
c. $(\forall x)[(Wx \mathbin{\&} \sim x = d) \supset [Sx \vee (\exists y)[Sy \mathbin{\&} (Dxy \vee Sxy)]]]$
e. $[Sdj \mathbin{\&} (\forall x)(Sxj \supset x = d)] \mathbin{\&} \sim (\exists x)Dxj$
g. $(\exists x)[(Sxr \mathbin{\&} Sxj) \mathbin{\&} (\forall y)[(Syr \vee Syj) \supset y = x]]$
i. $(\exists x)(\exists y)[((Dxr \mathbin{\&} Dyr) \mathbin{\&} (Sx \mathbin{\&} Sy)) \mathbin{\&} \sim x = y]$
k. $(\exists x)[(Sxj \mathbin{\&} Sx) \mathbin{\&} (\forall y)(Syj \supset y = x)] \mathbin{\&} (\exists x)(\exists y)(([(Sx \mathbin{\&} Sy) \mathbin{\&} (Dxj \mathbin{\&} Dyj)] \mathbin{\&} \sim x = y) \mathbin{\&} (\forall z)[Dzj \supset (z = x \vee z = y)])$

2.a. Every positive integer is less than some positive integer [or] There is no largest positive integer.
c. There is positive integer than which no integer is less.
e. 2 is even and prime, and it is the only positive integer that is both even and prime.
g. The product of any pair of odd positive integers is itself odd.
i. If either of a pair of positive integers is even, their product is even.
k. There is exactly one prime that is greater than 5 and less than 9.

3.a. $(\forall x)(\forall y)(Nxy \supset Nyx)$	Symmetric only
c.	Neither reflexive, nor symmetric, nor transitive
e. $(\forall x)(\forall y)(Rxy \supset Ryx)$ $(\forall x)(\forall y)(\forall z)[(Rxy \mathbin{\&} Ryz) \supset Rxz]$	Symmetric and transitive
g. $(\forall x)Txx$ $(\forall x)(\forall y)(\forall z)[(Txy \mathbin{\&} Tyz) \supset Txz]$	Transitive and reflexive (in UD: Physical objects)
i. $(\forall x)(\forall y)(Exy \supset Eyx)$ $(\forall x)Exx$	Symmetric and reflexive (in UD: People)

k. $(\forall x)Wxx$
$(\forall x)(\forall y)(Wxy \supset Wyx)$
$(\forall x)(\forall y)(\forall z)[(Wxy \& Wyz) \supset Wxz]$
Symmetric, transitive, and reflexive (in UD: Physical objects)

m. $(\forall x)(\forall y)(\forall z)[(Axy \& Ayz) \supset Axz]$
Transitive only

o. $(\forall x)Lxx$
$(\forall x)(\forall y)(Lxy \supset Lyx)$
$(\forall x)(\forall y)(\forall z)[(Lxy \& Lyz) \supset Lxz]$
Symmetric, transitive, and reflexive (in UD: People)

4.a. Sjc
c. $Sjc \& (\forall x)[(Sxc \& \sim x = j) \supset Ojx]$
e. $(\exists x)[(Dxd \& (\forall y)[(Dyd \& \sim y = x) \supset Oxy]) \& Px]$
g. $Dcd \& (\forall x)[(Dxd \& \sim x = c) \supset Ocx]$
i. $(\exists x)[(Sxh \& (\forall y)[(Syh \& \sim y = x) \supset Txy]) \& Mcx]$
k. $(\exists x)[(Bx \& (\forall y)(By \supset y = x)) \&$
$(\exists w)((Mx \& (\forall z)(Mz \supset z = w)) \& x = w)]$
m. $(\exists x)[(Mxc \& Bxj) \& (\forall w)(Bwj \supset x = w)]$

CHAPTER EIGHT

Section 8.1E

1.a. **F**
c. **T**
e. **F**
g. **T**

2.a. **T**
c. **T**
e. **F**
g. **F**

3.a. One interpretation is

UD: Set of people
Nxy: x is the mother of y
a: Jane Doe
d: Jay Doe

c. One interpretation is

UD: Set of U.S. cities
Lx: x is in California
Cxy: x is to the north of y
h: San Francisco
m: Los Angeles

e. One interpretation is

UD: Set of positive integers
Mx: x is odd
Nx: x is even
a: 1
b: 2

4.a. One interpretation is

UD: Set of positive integers
Cxy: x equals y squared
r: 2
s: 3

c. One interpretation is

UD: Set of people
Lx: x is a lion
i: Igor Stravinsky
j: Jesse Winchester
m: Margaret Mead

e. One interpretation is

UD: Set of positive integers
Jx: x is even
a: 1
b: 2
c: 3
d: 4

5.a. One interpretation is

UD: Set of people
Fxy: x is the mother of y
a: Liza Minelli
b: Judy Garland (Liza Minelli's mother)

On this interpretation, 'Fab ⊃ Fba' is true, and 'Fba ⊃ Fab' is false.

c. One interpretation is

UD: Set of planets
Cxyz: the orbit of x is between the orbit of y and the orbit of z
Mx: x is inhabited by human life
a: Earth
p: Venus
q: Pluto
r: Mars

On this interpretation, '~ Ma ∨ Cpqr' is false, and 'Capq ∨ ~ Mr' is true.

e. One interpretation is

UD:	Set of positive integers
Lxy:	x is less than y
Mxy:	x equals y
j:	1
k:	1

On this interpretation the first sentence is true and the second false.

6.a. Suppose that 'Ba' is true on some interpretation. Then 'Ba ∨ ~ Ba' is true on that interpretation. Suppose that 'Ba' is false on some interpretation. Then '~ Ba' is true on that interpretation, and so is 'Ba ∨ ~ Ba'. Since on any interpretation 'Ba' is either true or false, we have shown that 'Ba ∨ ~ Ba' is true on every interpretation.

7.a. False. For consider any person w who is over 40 years old. It is true that that person is over 40 years old but false that some person is her own sister. So that person w is *not* such that if w is over 40 years old then some person is her own sister.

c. False. The sentence says that there is at least one person x such that every person y is either a child or a brother of x, which is obviously false.

e. True. The antecedent, '(∃x)Cx', is true. At least one person is over 40 years old. And the consequent, '((∃x)(∃y)Fxy ⊃ (∃y)By)', is also true: '(∃x)(∃y)Fxy' is true, and '(∃y)By' is true.

g. True. The antecedent, '(∀x)Bx', is false, so the conditional sentence is true.

i. True. The sentence says that there is at least one person x such that either x is over 40 years old or x and some person y are sisters and y is over 40 years old. Both conditions are true.

8.a. True. Every U.S. President held office after George Washington's first term. Note that for the sentence to be true, George Washington too must have held office after George Washington's first term of office. He did—he was in office for two terms.

c. True. George Washington was the first U.S. President, and at least one U.S. President y held office after Washington.

e. True. Each U.S. President y is such that if y is a U.S. citizen (which y is) then at least one U.S. President held office before or after y's first term.

g. False. Every U.S. President x held office after George Washington's first term, but, for any such President x, no non-U.S. citizen has held office before x (because every U.S. President *is* a U.S. citizen).

i. True (in 1996!). The sentence says that a disjunction is not the case and therefore that each disjunct is false. The first disjunct, 'Bg', is false—George Washington was not a female. The second disjunct, which says that there is a U.S. President who held office after every U.S. President's first term of office, is false (there is no one yet who has held office after Bill Clinton's first term).

9.a. True. The first conjunct, 'Bb', is true. The second conjunct is also true since no positive integer that is greater than 2 is equal to 2.

c. True. No positive integer x is equal to any number than which it is greater.

e. True. The antecedent is true since it is not the case that every positive integer is greater than every positive integer. But 'Mcba' is also true: 3 − 2 = 1.

g. True. No positive integer z that is even is such that the result of subtracting 1 from z is also even.

i. False. Not every positive integer (in fact, *no* positive integer) is such that it equals itself if and only if there are not two positive integers of which it is the difference. Every positive integer equals itself, but every positive integer is also the difference between two positive integers.

Section 8.2E

1.a. The sentence is false on the following interpretation:

UD: Set of positive integers
Fx: x is divisible by 4
Gx: x is even

Every positive integer that is divisible by 4 is even, but not every positive integer is even.

c. The sentence is false on the following interpretation:

UD: Set of positive integers
Bxy: x is less than y

Every positive integer is less than at least one positive integer, but there is no single positive integer that every positive integer is less than.

e. The sentence is false on the following interpretation:

UD: Set of positive integers
Fx: x is odd
Gx: x is prime

The antecedent, '(∀x)Fx ⊃ (∀w)Gw', is true since *its* antecedent, '(∀x)Fx', is false. But the consequent, '(∀z)(Fz ⊃ Gz)', is false since at least one odd positive integer is not prime (the integer 9, for example).

g. The sentence is false on the following interpretation:

UD: Set of positive integers
Gx: x is negative
Fxy: x equals y

No positive integer is negative, but not every positive integer is such that <u>if</u> it equals itself (which everyone does) <u>then</u> it is negative.

2.a. The sentence is true on the following interpretation:

UD: Set of positive integers
Bxy: x equals y

The sentence to the left of '≡' is true since it is not the case that all positive integers equal one another; and the sentence to the right of '≡' is true since each positive integer is equal to itself.

c. The sentence is true on the following interpretation:

UD: Set of positive integers
Fx: x is odd
Gx: x is even

At least one positive integer is odd, and at least one positive integer is even, but no positive integer is both odd and even.

e. The sentence is true on the following interpretation:

UD: Set of positive integers
Fx: x is negative
Gx: x is odd

Trivially, every negative positive integer is odd since no positive integer is negative; and every positive integer that is odd is not negative.

g. The sentence is true on the following interpretation:

UD: Set of positive integers
Bx: x is prime
Hx: x is odd

The antecedent is false—not every positive integer is such that it is prime if and only if it is odd, and the consequent is true—at least one positive integer is both prime and odd.

i. The sentence is true on the following interpretation:

UD: Set of positive integers
Bxy: x is less than y

The less-than relation is transitive, making the first conjunct true; for every positive integer there is a greater one, making the second conjunct true; and the less-than relation is irreflexive, making the third conjunct true.

3.a. The sentence is true on the following interpretation:

UD: Set of positive integers
Fx: x is odd
Gx: x is prime

At least one positive integer is both odd and prime, but also at least one positive integer is neither odd nor prime.

The sentence is false on the following interpretation:

UD: Set of positive integers

Fx: x is positive
Gx: x is prime

At least one positive integer is both positive and prime, but no positive integer is neither positive nor prime.

c. The sentence is true on the following interpretation:

UD: Set of positive integers
Bxy: x is evenly divisible by y
n: the number 9

The antecedent, '(∀x)Bnx', is false on this interpretation; 9 is not evenly divisible by every positive integer.

The sentence is false on the following interpretation:

UD: Set of positive integers
Bxy: x is less than or equal to y
n: the number 1

The number 1 is less than or equal to every positive integer, so the antecedent is true and the consequent false.

e. The sentence is true on the following interpretation:

UD: Set of positive integers
Nxy: x equals y

Each positive integer x is such that each positive integer w that is equal to x is equal to itself.

The sentence is false on the following interpretation:

UD: Set of positive integers
Nxy: x is greater than y

No positive integer x is such that every positive integer w that is greater or smaller than x is greater than itself.

g. The sentence is true on the following interpretation:

UD: Set of positive integers
Cx: x is greater than 0
Dx: x is prime

Every positive integer is either greater than 0 or prime (because every positive integer is greater than 0), and at least one positive integer is both greater than 0 and prime. The biconditional is therefore true on this interpretation.

The sentence is false on the following interpretation:

UD: Set of positive integers
Cx: x is even
Dx: x is odd

Every positive integer is either even or odd, but no positive integer is both. The biconditional is therefore false on this interpretation.

4.a. If the antecedent is true on an interpretation, then at least one member x of the UD, let's assume a, stands in the relation B to every member y of the UD. But then it follows that for every member y of the UD, there is at least one member x that stands in the relation B to y—namely, a. So the consequent is also true. If the antecedent is false on an interpretation, then the conditional is trivially true. So the sentence is true on every interpretation.

c. If 'Fa' is true on an interpretation, then 'Fa ∨ [(∀x)Fx ⊃ Ga]' is true. If 'Fa' is false on an interpretation, then '(∀x)Fx' is false, making '(∀x)Fx ⊃ Ga' true. Either way, the disjunction is true.

e. If '(∃x)Hx' is true on an interpretation, then the disjunction is true on that interpretation. If '(∃x)Hx' is false on an interpretation, then no member of the UD is H. In this case, every member of the UD is such that if it is H (which it is not) then it is J, and so the second disjunct is true, making the disjunction true as well. Either way, then, the disjunction is true.

5.a. No member of any UD is such that it is in the extension of 'B' if and only if it isn't in the extension of 'B'. So the existentially quantified sentence is false on every interpretation.

c. The second conjunct is true on an interpretation if and only if no member of the UD is G and no member of the UD is not F—that is, every member of the UD *is* F. But then the first conjunct must be false, because its antecedent is true but its consequent is false. Thus there is no interpretation on which the entire conjunction is true; it is quantificationally false.

Section 8.3E

1.a. The first sentence is false and the second true on the following interpretation:

UD: Set of positive integers
Fx: x is odd
Gx: x is prime
a: the number 4

Some positive integer is odd and the number 4 is not prime, so '(∃x)Fx ⊃ Ga' is false. But any even positive integer is such that if that integer is odd (which it is not) then the number 4 is prime; so '(∃x)(Fx ⊃ Ga)' is true.

c. The first sentence is false and the second true on the following interpretation:

UD: Set of integers
Fx: x is a multiple of 2
Gx: x is an odd number

It is false that either every integer is a multiple of 2 or every integer is odd, but it is true that every integer is either a multiple of 2 or odd.

e. The first sentence is false and the second true on the following interpretation:

UD: Set of positive integers
Fx: x is odd
Gx: x is prime

An odd prime (e.g., the number 3) is not such that it is even if and only if it is prime. But '(∃x)Fx ≡ (∃x)Gx' is true since '(∃x)Fx' and '(∃x)Gx' are both true.

g. The first sentence is true and the second false on the following interpretation:

UD: Set of positive integers
Bx: x is less than 5
Dxy: x is divisible by y without remainder

The number 1 is less than 5 and divides every positive integer without remainder. But '(∀x)(Bx ⊃ (∀y)Dyx)' is false, for 2 is less than 5 but does not divide any odd number without remainder.

i. The first sentence is false and the second true on the following interpretation:

UD: set of positive integers
Fx: x is odd
Kxy: x is smaller than y

The number 1 does not satisfy the condition that <u>if</u> it is odd (which it is) <u>then</u> there is a positive integer that is smaller than it. But at least one positive integer does satisfy the condition—in fact, all other positive integers do.

2.a. Suppose that '(∀x)Fx ⊃ Ga' is true on an interpretation. Then either '(∀x)Fx' is false or 'Ga' is true. If '(∀x)Fx' is false, then some member of the UD is not in the extension of 'F'. But then that object is trivially such that <u>if</u> it is F (which it is not) <u>then</u> a is G. So '(∃x)(Fx ⊃ Ga)' is true. If 'Ga' is true, then trivially every member x of the UD is such that <u>if</u> x is F <u>then</u> a is G; so '(∃x)(Fx ⊃ Ga)' is true in this case as well.

Now suppose that '(∀x)Fx ⊃ Ga' is false on some interpretation. Then '(∀x)Fx' is true, and 'Ga' is false. Every object in the UD is then in the extension of 'F'; hence no member x is such that <u>if</u> it is F (which it is) <u>then</u> a is G (which is false). So '(∃x)(Fx ⊃ Ga)' is false as well.

c. Suppose that '(∃x)(Fx ∨ Gx)' is true on an interpretation. Then at least one member of the UD is either in the extension of 'F' or in the extension of 'G'. This individual therefore does not satisfy '~ Fy & ~ Gy', and so '(∀y)(~ Fy & ~ Gy)' is false and its negation true.

Now suppose that '(∃x)(Fx ∨ Gx)' is false on an interpretation. Then no member of the UD satisfies 'Fx ∨ Gx'—no member of the UD is in the extension of 'F' or in the extension of 'G'. In this case, every member of the UD satisfies '~ Fy & ~ Gy'; so '(∀y)(~ Fy & ~ Gy)' is true and its negation false.

3.a. All the set members are true on the following interpretation:

UD: Set of positive integers
Bx: x is odd
Cx: x is prime

At least one positive integer is odd, and at least one positive integer is prime, and some positive integers are neither odd nor prime.

c. All the set members are true on the following interpretation:

UD: Set of positive integers
Fx: x is greater than 10
Gx: x is greater than 5
Nx: x is smaller than 3
Mx: x is smaller than 5

Every positive integer that is greater than 10 is greater than 5, every positive integer that is smaller than 3 is smaller than 5, and no positive integer that is greater than 5 is also smaller than 5.

e. All the set members are true on the following interpretation:

UD: Set of positive integers
Nx: x is negative
Mx: x equals 0
Cxy: x is greater than 7

The two sentences are trivially true, the first because no positive integer is negative and the second because no positive integer equals 0.

g. All the set members are true on the following interpretation:

UD: Set of positive integers
Nx: x is prime
Mx: x is an even number

The first sentence is true because 3 is prime but not even. Hence not all primes are even numbers. The second is true because any nonprime integer is such that if it is prime (which it is not) then it is even. Hence it is false that all positive integers fail to satisfy this condition.

i. All the set members are true on the following interpretation:

UD: Set of positive integers
Fxy: x evenly divides y
Gxy: x is greater than y
a: 1

At least one positive integer is evenly divisible by 1, at least one positive integer is such that 1 is not greater than that integer, and every positive integer is either evenly divisible by 1 or such that 1 is greater than it.

4.a. If the set is quantificationally consistent, then there is an interpretation on which both set members are true. But if '(∃x) (Bx & Cx)' is true on an interpretation, then at least one member x of the UD is in the extensions of both 'B' and 'C'. That member is *not* neither B nor C, so, if '(∃x) (Bx & Cx)' is true, then '(∀x) ~ (Bx ∨ Cx)' is false. There is no interpretation on which both set members are true.

c. If the first set member is true on an interpretation, then every pair x and y of members of the UD is such that either x stands in the relation B to y or y stands in the relation B to x. In particular, each pair consisting of a member of the UD and itself must satisfy the condition and so must stand in the relation B to itself. This being so, the second set member is false on such an interpretation. Thus there can be no interpretation on which both set members are true.

5. Suppose that $\mathscr{P}$ and $\mathscr{Q}$ are quantificationally equivalent. Then on every interpretation $\mathscr{P}$ and $\mathscr{Q}$ have the same truth-value. Thus the biconditional $\mathscr{P} \equiv \mathscr{Q}$ is true on every interpretation (since a biconditional is true when its immediate components have the same truth-value); hence it is quantificationally true.

Suppose that $\mathscr{P} \equiv \mathscr{Q}$ is quantificationally true. Therefore it is true on every interpretation. Then $\mathscr{P}$ and $\mathscr{Q}$ have the same truth-value on every interpretation (since a biconditional is true only if its immediate components have the same truth-value) and are quantificationally equivalent.

Section 8.4E

1.a. The set members are true and '(∃x) (Hx & Fx)' false on the following interpretation:

UD: Set of positive integers
Fx: x is evenly divisible by 2
Hx: x is odd
Gx: x is greater than or equal to 1

Every positive integer that is evenly divisible by 2 is greater than or equal to 1, every odd positive integer is greater than or equal to 1, but no positive integer is both evenly divisible by 2 and odd.

c. The set member is true and 'Fa' is false on the following interpretation:

UD: Set of positive integers
Fx: x is even
a: the number 1

At least one positive integer is even, but the number 1 is not even.

e. The set members are true and '(∃x)Bx' is false on the following interpretation:

UD: Set of positive integers
Bx: x is negative
Cx: x is prime

Every positive integer is trivially such that if it is negative then it is prime, for no positive integer is negative; and at least one positive integer is prime. But no positive integer is negative.

g. The set member is true and '$(\forall x) \sim Lxx$' is false on the following interpretation:

UD: Set of positive integers
Lxy: x is greater than or equal to y

Every positive integer x is such that for some positive integer y, x is not greater than or equal to y. But it is false that every positive integer is not greater than or equal to itself.

2.a. The premises are true and the conclusion false on the following interpretation:

UD: Set of positive integers
Fx: x is positive
Gx: x is negative
Nx: x equals 0

The first premise is true since its antecedent is false. The second premise is trivially true because no positive integer equals 0. The conclusion is false for no positive integer satisfies the condition of being either not positive or negative.

c. The premises are true and the conclusion false on the following interpretation:

UD: Set of positive integers
Fx: x is prime
Gx: x is even
Hx: x is odd

There is an even prime positive integer (the number 2), and at least one positive integer is odd and prime, but no positive integer is both even and odd.

e. The premises are true and the conclusion false on the following interpretation:

UD: Set of positive integers
Fx: x is negative
Gx: x is odd

The first premise is trivially true, for no positive integer is negative. For the same reason, the second premise is true. But at least one positive integer is odd, and so the conclusion is false.

g. The premises are true and the conclusion false on the following interpretation:

UD: Set of positive integers
Gx: x is prime
Dxy: x equals y

Some positive integer is prime, and every prime number equals itself, but there is no prime number that is equal to every positive integer.

i. The premises are true and the conclusion false on the following interpretation:

UD: Set of positive integers
Fx: x is odd
Gx: x is positive
Hx: x is prime

Every odd positive integer is positive, and every prime positive integer is positive, but not every positive integer is odd or prime.

3.a. A symbolization of the first argument is

$$\frac{(\forall x)Bx}{(\exists x)Bx}$$

To see that this argument is quantificationally valid, assume that '(∀x)Bx' is true on some interpretation. Then every member of the UD is B. Since every UD is nonempty, it follows that there is at least one member that is B. So '(∃x)Bx' is true as well.

A symbolization of the second argument is

$$\frac{(\forall x)(Px \supset Bx)}{(\exists x)(Px \,\&\, Bx)}$$

The premise is true and the conclusion false on the following interpretation:

UD: Set of positive integers
Px: x is negative
Bx: x is prime

c. One symbolization of the first argument is

$$\frac{(\exists x)(\forall y)Lxy}{(\forall y)(\exists x)Lxy}$$

To see that the argument is quantificationally valid, assume that the premise is true on some interpretation. Then some member x of the UD—let's call it a—stands in the relation L to every member of the UD. Thus for each member y of the UD, there is some member—namely, a—that stands in the relation L to y. So the conclusion is true as well.

A symbolization of the second argument is

$$\frac{(\forall x)(\exists y)Lyx}{(\exists y)(\forall x)Lyx}$$

The following interpretation makes the premise true and the conclusion false:

UD: Set of positive integers
Lxy: x is larger than y

For each positive integer, there is a larger one, but no positive integer is the largest.

e. A symbolization of the first argument is

$$\frac{(\exists x)(Tx \mathbin{\&} Sx) \mathbin{\&} (\exists x)(Tx \mathbin{\&} \sim Hx)}{(\exists x)(Tx \mathbin{\&} (Sx \vee \sim Hx))}$$

To see that this argument is quantificationally valid, assume that the premise is true on some interpretation. Then at least one member of the UD—let's call it a—is both T and S and at least one member of the UD is both T and not H. a satisfies the condition of being both T and either S or H, and so the conclusion is true as well.

A symbolization of the second argument is

$$\frac{(\forall x)(Tx \supset Sx) \mathbin{\&} \sim (\exists x)(Tx \mathbin{\&} Hx)}{(\exists x)(Tx \mathbin{\&} (Sx \vee \sim Hx))}$$

The following interpretation makes the premise true and the conclusion false:

UD: Set of positive integers
Tx: x is negative
Sx: x is odd
Hx: x is prime

Every negative positive integer (there are none) is odd, and there is no positive integer that is negative and prime. But it is false that some positive integer is both negative and either odd or not prime.

g. A symbolization of the first argument is

$$\frac{(\forall x)(Ax \supset Cx) \mathbin{\&} (\forall x)(Cx \supset Sx)}{(\forall x)(Ax \supset Sx)}$$

To see that the argument is quantificationally valid, assume that the premise is true on some interpretation. Then every member of the UD that is A is also C, and every member of the UD that is C is also S. So if a member of the UD is A, it is C and therefore S as well, which is what the conclusion says.

A symbolization of the second argument is

$$\frac{(\forall x)(Sx \supset Cx)\ \&\ (\forall x)(Cx \supset Ax)}{(\forall x)(Ax \supset Sx)}$$

The premise is true and the conclusion false on the following interpretation:

UD: Set of positive integers
Ax: x is positive
Cx: x is greater than 1
Sx: x is even

Every even positive integer is greater than 1, and every positive integer that is greater than 1 is positive. But not every positive integer that is positive is even—some positive integers are odd.

Section 8.5E

1.a. Ca ⊃ Daa
c. Ba ∨ Faa
e. Ca ⊃ (N ⊃ Ba)
g. Ba ⊃ Ca
i. Ca ∨ (Daa ∨ Ca)

2. Remember that, in expanding a sentence containing the individual constant 'g', we must use that constant.
a. Dag & Dgg
c. [Aa & (Daa ∨ Dba)] ∨ [Ab & (Dab ∨ Dbb)]
e. [Ua ⊃ ((Daa ∨ Daa) ∨ (Dab ∨ Dba))]
& [Ub ⊃ ((Dba ∨ Dab) ∨ (Dbb ∨ Dbb))]
g. [Dag ⊃ ((~ Ua & Daa) ∨ (~ Ug & Dag))]
& [Dgg ⊃ ((~ Ua & Dga) ∨ (~ Ug & Dgg))]
i. ~ (K ∨ ((Daa & Dab) ∨ (Dba & Dbb)))

3. Remember that if any individual constants occur in a sentence, those constants must be used in the expansion of the sentence.
a. Bb & [(Gab ⊃ ~ Eab) & (Gbb ⊃ ~ Ebb)]
c. [(Gaa ⊃ ~ Eaa) & (Gab ⊃ ~ Eab)] & [(Gba ⊃ ~ Eba) & (Gbb ⊃ ~ Ebb)]
e. Impossible! This sentence contains three individual constants, 'a', 'b', and 'c'; so it can be expanded only for sets of at least three constants.
g. [Ba ⊃ ~ ((Ba & Maaa) ∨ (Bb & Maab))]
& [Bb ⊃ ~ ((Ba & Mbaa) ∨ (Bb & Mbab))]
i. [Eaa ≡ ~ ((Maaa ∨ Maba) ∨ (Mbaa ∨ Mbba))]
& [Ebb ≡ ~ ((Maab ∨ Mabb) ∨ (Mbab ∨ Mbbb))]

4.a. [(Ga ⊃ Naa) & (Gb ⊃ Nbb)] & (Gc ⊃ Ncc)
c. ((Na ≡ Ba) ∨ (Na ≡ Bb)) ∨ (Na ≡ Bc)

5. The truth-table for an expansion for the set {'a'} is

Fa	(Fa	&	~ Fa)	↓ ⊃	~ Fa
T	**T**	**F**	**F T**	**T**	**F T**
F	**F**	**F**	**T F**	**T**	**T F**

This truth-table shows that the the sentence

((∃x)Fx & (∃y) ~ Fy) ⊃ (∀x) ~ Fx

is true on every interpretation with a one-member UD. The truth-table for an expansion for the set {'a', 'b'} is

Fa	Fb	[(Fa	∨	Fb)	&	(~ Fa	∨	~ Fb)]	↓ ⊃	(~ Fa	&	~ Fb)
T	**T**	**T**	**T**	**T**	**F**	**F T**	**F**	**F T**	**T**	**F T**	**F**	**F T**
T	**F**	**T**	**T**	**F**	**T**	**F T**	**T**	**T F**	**F**	**F T**	**F**	**T F**
F	**T**	**F**	**T**	**T**	**T**	**T F**	**T**	**F T**	**F**	**T F**	**F**	**F T**
F	**F**	**F**	**F**	**F**	**F**	**T F**	**T**	**T F**	**T**	**T F**	**T**	**T F**

This truth-table shows that the sentence

((∃x)Fx & (∃y) ~ Fy) ⊃ (∀x) ~ Fx

is true on at least one interpretation with a two-member UD and false on at least one interpretation with a two-member UD.

6.a. One assignment to its atomic components for which the expansion

[Naa ∨ (Naa ∨ Nan)] & [Nnn ∨ (Nna ∨ Nnn)]

is true is

Naa	Nan	Nna	Nnn	[Naa	∨	(Naa	∨	Nan)]	↓ &	[Nnn	∨	(Nna	∨	Nnn)]
T	**T**	**T**	**T**	**T**	**T**	**T**	**T**	**T**	**T**	**T**	**T**	**T**	**T**	**T**

Using this information, we shall construct an interpretation with a two-member UD such that the relation N holds between each two members of the UD:

UD: The set {1, 2}
Nxy: x is less than, equal to, or greater than y

Every member of the UD is less than, equal to, or greater than both itself and the other member of the UD, and so '(∀x)(Nxx ∨ (∃y)Nxy)' is true on this interpretation.

c. There is only one assignment to its atomic components for which the expansion 'Saan & Snnn' is true.

			↓	
Saan	Snnn	Saan	&	Snnn
T	T	T	T	T

Using this information, we construct an interpretation with a two-member UD:

UD: The set {1, 2}
Sxyz: x equals y times z
n: 1

Because 1 = 1 × 1 and 2 = 2 × 1, '(∀y)Syyn' is true on this interpretation.

7.a.

			↓			
Fa	Ga	(Fa	⊃	Ga)	⊃	Ga
F	F	F	T	F	F	F

c.

											↓							
Baa	Bab	Bba	Bbb	[(Baa	∨	Bab)	&	(Bba	∨	Bbb)]	⊃	[(Baa	&	Bba)	∨	(Bab	&	Bbb)]
T	F	F	T	T	T	F	T	F	T	T	F	T	F	F	F	F	F	T

e.

											↓							
Fa	Ga	Fb	Gb	[(Fa	&	Fb)	⊃	(Ga	&	Gb)]	⊃	[(Fa	⊃	Ga)	&	(Fb	⊃	Gb)]
T	F	F	T	T	F	F	T	F	F	T	F	T	F	F	F	F	T	T

g.

				↓			
Faa	Ga	~	Ga	⊃	(Faa	⊃	Ga)
T	F	T	F	F	T	F	F

8.a.

												↓			
Baa	Bab	Bba	Bbb	~	[(Baa	&	Bab)	&	(Bba	&	Bbb)]	≡	(Baa	&	Bbb)
T	F	F	T	T	T	F	F	F	F	F	T	T	T	T	T

c.

Fa	Fb	Ga	Gb	[(Fa	$\vee$	Fb)	&	(Ga	$\vee$	Gb)]
T	**F**	**F**	**T**	**T**	**T**	**F**	**T**	**F**	**T**	**T**

↓ &	~	[(Fa	&	Ga)	$\vee$	(Fb	&	Gb)]
T	**T**	**T**	**F**	**F**	**F**	**F**	**F**	**T**

e.

Fa	Ga	(Fa	$\supset$	Ga)	↓ &	(Ga	$\supset$	~	Fa)
F	**T**	**F**	**T**	**T**	**T**	**T**	**T**	**T**	**F**

g.

Ba	Ha	(Ba	$\equiv$	Ha)	↓ $\supset$	(Ba	&	Ha)
T	**T**	**T**	**T**	**T**	**T**	**T**	**T**	**T**

i. Sneaky. This one can't be done because, as pointed out in Section 8.2, the sentence is false on all interpretations with finite UDs.

9.a.

Fa	Fb	Ga	Gb	((Fa	&	Ga)	$\vee$	(Fb	&	Gb))
T	**T**	**F**	**F**	**T**	**F**	**F**	**F**	**T**	**F**	**F**

↓ $\supset$	(~	(Fa	$\vee$	Ga)	$\vee$	~	(Fb	$\vee$	Gb))
T	**F**	**T**	**T**	**F**	**F**	**F**	**T**	**T**	**F**

Fa	Fb	Ga	Gb	((Fa	&	Ga)	$\vee$	(Fb	&	Gb))
T	**F**	**T**	**T**	**T**	**T**	**T**	**T**	**F**	**F**	**T**

↓ $\supset$	(~	(Fa	$\vee$	Ga)	$\vee$	~	(Fb	$\vee$	Gb))
F	**F**	**T**	**T**	**T**	**F**	**F**	**F**	**T**	**T**

c.

		↓		
Bnn	Bnn	⊃	~	Bnn
F	F	T	T	F

		↓		
Bnn	Bnn	⊃	~	Bnn
T	T	F	F	T

e.

				↓	
Naa	(Naa	∨	Naa)	⊃	Naa
T	T	T	T	T	T

Naa	Nab	Nba	Nbb	[[(Naa	∨	Naa)	⊃	Naa]
T	T	T	F	T	T	T	T	T

						↓					
&	[(Nba	∨	Nab)	⊃	Nbb]]	&	[[(Nab	∨	Nba)	⊃	Naa]
F	T	T	T	F	F	F	T	T	T	T	T

&	[(Nbb	∨	Nbb)	⊃	Nbb]]
T	F	F	F	T	F

g.

					↓			
Ca	Da	(Ca	∨	Da)	≡	(Ca	&	Da)
T	T	T	T	T	T	T	T	T

					↓			
Ca	Da	(Ca	∨	Da)	≡	(Ca	&	Da)
T	F	T	T	F	F	T	F	F

11. The expanded sentence 'Ga & ~ Ga' is a truth-functional compound. It is false on every truth-value assignment, so it is quantificationally false. But the fact that this sentence is quantificationally false only shows that '(∃y)Gy & (∃y) ~ Gy' is not true on any interpretation that has a one-member UD—for it is an expansion using only one constant. The sentence is in fact not quantificationally false, for it is true on some interpretations with larger universes of discourse. We may expand the sentence for the set {'a', 'b'} to show this:

					↓					
Ga	Gb	(Ga	∨	Gb)	&	(~	Ga	∨	~	Gb)
T	F	T	T	F	T	F	T	T	T	F

12.a.

						↓					↓			
Fa	Fb	Ga	(Fa	∨	Fb)	⊃	Ga	(Fa	⊃	Ga)	∨	(Fb	⊃	Ga)
T	**F**	**F**	**T**	**T**	**F**	**F**	**F**	**T**	**F**	**F**	**T**	**F**	**T**	**F**

c.

							↓							↓			
Fa	Fb	Ga	Gb	(Fa	&	Fb)	∨	(Ga	&	Gb)	(Fa	∨	Ga)	&	(Fb	∨	Gb)
T	**F**	**F**	**T**	**T**	**F**	**F**	**F**	**F**	**F**	**T**	**T**	**T**	**F**	**T**	**F**	**T**	**T**

e.

							↓							↓			
Fa	Fb	Ga	Gb	(Fa	≡	Ga)	&	(Fb	≡	Gb)	(Fa	∨	Fb)	≡	(Ga	∨	Gb)
T	**F**	**F**	**T**	**T**	**F**	**F**	**F**	**F**	**F**	**T**	**T**	**T**	**F**	**T**	**F**	**T**	**T**

g.

											↓					
Ba	Bb	Daa	Dab	Dba	Dbb	(Ba	&	(Daa	&	Dba))	∨	(Bb	&	(Dab	&	Dbb))
F	**F**	**T**	**T**	**T**	**T**	**F**	**F**	**T**	**T**	**T**	**F**	**F**	**F**	**T**	**T**	**T**

					↓					
(Ba	⊃	(Daa	&	Dba))	&	(Bb	⊃	(Dab	&	Dbb))
F	**T**	**T**	**T**	**T**	**T**	**F**	**T**	**T**	**T**	**T**

i.

													↓							
Fa	Fb	Kaa	Kab	Kba	Kbb	((Fa	⊃	Kaa)	∨	(Fa	⊃	Kba))	&	((Fb	⊃	Kab)	∨	(Fb	⊃	Kbb))
T	**T**	**F**	**T**	**F**	**T**	**T**	**F**	**F**	**F**	**T**	**F**	**F**	**F**	**T**	**T**	**T**	**T**	**T**	**T**	**T**

							↓							
((Fa	⊃	Kaa)	∨	(Fa	⊃	Kba))	∨	((Fb	⊃	Kab)	∨	(Fb	⊃	Kbb))
T	**F**	**F**	**F**	**T**	**F**	**F**	**T**	**T**	**T**	**T**	**T**	**T**	**T**	**T**

13.a.

					↓			↓		↓							
Ba	Bb	Ca	Cb	Ba	∨	Bb	Ca	∨	Cb	~	[(Ba	∨	Ca)	&	(Bb	∨	Cb)]
T	**F**	**T**	**F**	**T**	**T**	**F**	**T**	**T**	**F**	**T**	**T**	**T**	**T**	**F**	**F**	**F**	**F**

c.

					↓			↓			↓		
Fa	Ga	Ma	Na	Fa	⊃	Ga	Na	⊃	Ma	Ga	⊃	~	Ma
F	**F**	**F**	**F**	**F**	**T**	**F**	**F**	**T**	**F**	**F**	**T**	**T**	**F**

e.

				↓					↓		
Caa	Ma	Na	Na	⊃	(Ma	&	Caa)	Ma	⊃	~	Caa
T	**F**	**F**	**F**	**T**	**F**	**F**	**T**	**F**	**T**	**F**	**T**

g.

				↓							
Ma	Mb	Na	Nb	~	[(Na	⊃	Ma)	&	(Nb	⊃	Mb)]
F	**T**	**T**	**T**	**T**	**T**	**F**	**F**	**F**	**T**	**T**	**T**

↓									
~	[~	(Na	⊃	Ma)	&	~	(Nb	⊃	Mb)]
T	**T**	**T**	**F**	**F**	**F**	**F**	**T**	**T**	**T**

i.

		↓	↓			↓	
Faa	Gaa	Faa	~	Gaa	Faa	∨	Gaa
T	**F**	**T**	**T**	**F**	**T**	**T**	**F**

15.a.

						↓			↓			↓	
Fa	Ga	Na	(Fa	⊃	Ga)	⊃	Na	Na	⊃	Ga	~Fa	∨	Ga
T	**F**	**F**	**T**	**F**	**F**	**T**	**F**	**F**	**T**	**F**	**F T**	**F**	**F**

c.

									↓			
Fa	Fb	Ga	Gb	Ha	Hb	(Fa	&	Ga)	∨	(Fb	&	Gb)
T	**T**	**T**	**F**	**F**	**T**	**T**	**T**	**T**	**T**	**T**	**F**	**F**

			↓							↓			
(Fa	&	Ha)	∨	(Fb	&	Hb)	(Ga	&	Ha)	∨	(Gb	&	Hb)
T	**F**	**F**	**T**	**T**	**T**	**T**	**T**	**F**	**F**	**F**	**F**	**F**	**T**

e.

			↓		↓		↓	
Fa	Ga	Fa	⊃	Ga	~	Fa	~	Ga
F	**T**	**F**	**T**	**T**	**T**	**F**	**F**	**T**

g.

							↓					↓			
Daa	Dab	Dba	Dbb	Ga	Gb	Ga	∨	Gb	(Ga	⊃	Daa)	&	(Gb	⊃	Dbb)
T	**F**	**F**	**T**	**F**	**T**	**F**	**T**	**T**	**F**	**T**	**T**	**T**	**T**	**T**	**T**

							↓							
[(Ga	&	Daa)	&	(Ga	&	Dab)]	∨	[(Gb	&	Dba)	&	(Gb	&	Dbb)]
F	**F**	**T**	**F**	**F**	**F**	**F**	**F**	**T**	**F**	**F**	**F**	**T**	**T**	**T**

i.

				↓			↓			↓	
Fa	Ga	Ha	Fa	⊃	Ga	Ha	⊃	Ga	Fa	∨	Ha
F	**F**	**F**	**F**	**T**	**F**	**F**	**T**	**F**	**F**	**F**	**F**

Section 8.6E

1.a. **F**
c. **T**
e. **T**
g. **F**
i. **F**

2.a. The sentence is false on the following interpretation:

UD: Set of positive integers

There is no positive integer that is identical to every positive integer.

c. The sentence is false on the following interpretation:

UD: The set {1, 2, 3}

It is not true that for any three members of the UD, at least two are identical.

e. The sentence is false on the following interpretation:

UD: The set {1}
Gxy: x is greater than y

It is not true that there is a pair of members of the UD such that either the members of the pair are not identical or one member is greater than the other. The only pair of members of the UD consists of 1 and 1.

3.a. Consider any interpretation and any members x, y, and z of its UD. If x and y are not the same member or if y and z are not the same member, then these members do not satisfy the condition specified by '(x = y & y = z)', and so they do satisfy '[(x = y & y = z) ⊃ x = z]'. On the other hand, if x and y are the same and y and z are the same, then x and z must be the same, satisfying the consequent 'x = z'. In this case as well, then, x, y, and z satisfy '[(x = y & y = z) ⊃ x = z]'. Therefore the universal claim is true on every interpretation.

c. Consider any interpretation and any members x and y of its UD. If x and y are not the same, they do not satisfy 'x = y' and so do satisfy '[x = y ⊃ (Gxy ≡ Gyx)]'. If x and y are the same, and hence satisfy 'x = y', they must satisfy '(Gxy ≡ Gyx)' as well—the pair consisting of the one object and itself is either in the extension or not. Therefore the universal claim must be true on every interpretation.

4.a. The first sentence is true and the second false on the following interpretation:

UD: Set of positive integers

Every positive integer is identical to at least one positive integer (itself), but not even one positive integer is identical to every positive integer.

c. The first sentence is false and the second is true on the following interpretation:

UD: Set of positive integers
a: 1
b: 1
c: 2
d: 3

5.a. The sentences are all true on the following interpretation:

UD: Set of positive integers
a: 1
b: 1
c: 1
d: 2

c. The sentences are all true on the following interpretation:

UD: Set of positive integers

The first sentence is true because there are at least two positive integers. The second sentence is true because for any positive integer x, we can find a pair of positive integers z and w such that either x is identical to z or x is identical to w—just let one of the pair be x itself.

6.a. The following interpretation shows that the entailment does not hold:

UD: The set {1, 2}

It is true that for any x, y, and z in the UD, at least two of x, y, and z must be identical. But it is not true that for any x and y in the UD, x and y must be identical.

c. The following interpretation shows that the entailment does not hold:

UD: The set {1, 2}
Gxy: x is greater than or equal to y

At least one member of the UD (the number 2) is greater than or equal to every member of the UD, and at least one member of the UD (the number 1) is not greater than or equal to any member of the UD other than itself. But no member of the UD is not greater than or equal to itself.

7.a. The argument can be symbolized as

$$(\forall x)[Mx \supset (\exists y)(\sim y = x \,\&\, Lxy)] \,\&\, (\forall x)[Mx \supset (\forall y)(Pxy \supset Lxy)]$$

$$(\forall x)(Mx \supset \sim Pxx)$$

The argument is quantificationally invalid, as the following interpretation shows:

UD: Set of positive integers
Mx: x is odd
Lxy: x is less than or equal to y
Pxy: x squared equals y

For every odd positive integer, there is at least one other positive integer that it is less than or equal to, and every odd positive integer is such that it is less than or equal to its square(s). However, the conclusion, which says that no odd positive integer is its own square, is false because the square of 1 is 1.

c. The argument can be symbolized as

$$\frac{(\forall x)[(Fx \mathbin{\&} (\exists y)(Pxy \mathbin{\&} Lxy)) \supset Lxx]}{(\forall x)[Fx \supset (\exists y)(\exists z)((Lxy \mathbin{\&} Lxz) \mathbin{\&} {\sim} y = z)]}$$

The argument is quantificationally invalid, as the following interpretation shows:

UD: Set of positive integers
Fx: x is odd
Lxy: x is greater than y
Pxy: x is less than y

Trivially, every odd positive integer that is both less than and greater than some positive integer (there are none) is less than itself. But not all odd positive integers are greater than at least two positive integers—the number 1 is not.

e. The argument may be symbolized as

$$(\forall x) \sim (\exists y)(\exists z)(\exists w)([[Pyz \mathbin{\&} Pzx) \mathbin{\&} Pwx]$$
$$\mathbin{\&} [({\sim} y = z \mathbin{\&} {\sim} z = w) \mathbin{\&} {\sim} w = y]]$$
$$\mathbin{\&} (\forall x_1)[Px_1x \supset ((x_1 = y \vee x_1 = z) \vee x_1 = w)])$$
$$\frac{(\forall x)(\exists y)(\exists z)[(Pyx \mathbin{\&} Pzx) \mathbin{\&} {\sim} y = z)]}{(\forall x)(\exists y)(\exists z)[((Pyx \mathbin{\&} Pzx) \mathbin{\&} {\sim} y = z) \mathbin{\&} (\forall w)(Pwx \supset (w = y \vee w = z))]}$$

The argument is quantificationally invalid, as the following interpretation shows:

UD: Set of positive integers
Pxy: x is greater than y

No positive integer is less than exactly three positive integers (for any positive integer, there are infinitely many positive integers that are greater). Every positive integer is less than at least two positive integers. But no positive integer is less than exactly two positive integers.

8.a.

	↓
a = a	~ a = a
T	F T

	↓
a = a a = b b = a b = b	(~ a = a ∨ ~ b = a) ∨ (~ a = b ∨ ~ b = b)
T F F T	F T T T F T T F T F T

c.

	↓ ↓
a = a Gaa	(Gaa ∨ Gaa) ∨ a = a Gaa
T F	F F F T T F

e.

	↓ ↓
a = a a = b b = a b = b	a = a & b = b (~ a = a ∨ ~ a = b) ∨ (~ b = a ∨ ~ b = b)
T F F T	T T T F T T T F T T F T F T

↓
(~ a = a & ~ a = b) ∨ (~ b = a & ~ b = b)
F T F T F F T F F F T

Section 8.7E

1.a. Let **d** be a variable assignment for this interpretation. **d** satisfies the antecedent '~ (∀x)Ex' just in case it fails to satisfy '(∀x)Ex'. **d** fails to satisfy '(∀x)Ex' just in case there is at least one member **u** of the UD such that **d**[**u**/x] fails to satisfy 'Ex'. The number 1 is such a member: **d**[1/x] fails to satisfy 'Ex' because ⟨**d**[1/x](x)⟩, which is ⟨1⟩, is not a member of **I**(E), the set of 1-tuples of even positive integers. So **d** satisfies '~ (∀x)Ex'.

d satisfies the consequent '(∃y)Lyo' when there is at least one member **u** of the UD such that **d**[**u**/y] satisfies 'Lyo', that is, just in case there is at least one member **u** such that ⟨**d**[**u**/y](y), **I**(o)⟩, which is ⟨**u**, 1⟩, is in **I**(L). There is no such member, for there is no positive integer that is less than 1. Therefore **d** does not satisfy '(∃y)Lyo' and consequently **d** does not satisfy the conditional '~ (∀x)Ex ⊃ (∃y)Lyo'. The sentence is false on this interpretation.

c. Let **d** be a variable assignment for this interpretation. **d** satisfies '(∃x)(Ko ∨ Ex)' just in case there is some member **u** of the UD such that **d**[**u**/x] satisfies 'Ko ∨ Ex'. There is such a member—take 2 as an example. **d**[2/x] satisfies 'Ko ∨ Ex' because **d**[2/x] satisfies the second disjunct. **d**[2/x] satisfies 'Ex' because ⟨**d**[2/x](x)⟩, which is ⟨2⟩, is a member of **I**(E)—2 is even. Therefore **d** satisfies '(∃x)(Ko ∨ Ex)'. The sentence is true on this interpretation.

e. Let **d** be a variable assignment for this interpretation. **d** satisfies '(Ko ≡ (∀x)Ex) ⊃ (∃y)(∃z)Lyz' if and only if either **d** fails to satisfy the antecedent or **d** does satisfy the consequent. **d** satisfies the antecedent because it fails to satisfy both 'Ko' (no satisfaction assignment satisfies this formula) and '(∀x)Ex'. **d** does not satisfy the latter because not every member **u** of the UD is such that **d**[**u**/x] satisfies 'Ex'—no odd number is in the extension of 'E'.

d also satisfies the consequent '(∃y)(∃z)Lyz' because, for example, **d**[1/y] satisfies '(∃z)Lyz'. The latter is the case because, for example, **d**[1/y, 2/z] satisfies 'Lyz'; ⟨1, 2⟩ is in the extension of 'L'. The sentence is true on this interpretation.

2.a. Let **d** be a variable assignment for this interpretation. **d** satisfies '(∃x)(Ex ⊃ (∀y)Ey)' just in case there is at least one member **u** of the UD such that **d**[**u**/x] satisfies 'Ex ⊃ (∀y)Ey'. There is such a member; take 1 as an example. **d**[1/x] satisfies 'Ex ⊃ (∀y)Ey' because it fails to satisfy 'Ex'. **d**[1/x] fails to satisfy 'Ex' because ⟨**d**[1/x](x)⟩, which is ⟨1⟩, is not a member of **I**(E)—1 is not even. So **d** satisfies '(∃x)(Ex ⊃ (∀y)Ey)'. The sentence is true on this interpretation.

c. Let **d** be a variable assignment for this interpretation. **d** satisfies '(∀x)(Tx ⊃ (∃y)Gyx)' just in case every member **u** of the UD is such that **d**[**u**/x] satisfies 'Tx ⊃ (∃y)Gyx', that is, just in case both **d**[1/x] and **d**[3/x] satisfy 'Tx ⊃ (∃y)Gyx'. **d**[1/x] satisfies 'Tx ⊃ (∃y)Gyx' because it satisfies '(∃y)Gyx'. **d**[1/x] satisfies '(∃y)Gyx' because there is at least one member **u** of the UD such that **d**[1/x, **u**/y] satisfies 'Gyx'—3 is such a member. **d**[1/x, 3/y] satisfies 'Gyx' because ⟨**d**[1/x, 3/y](y), **d**[1/x, 3/y](x)⟩, which is ⟨3, 1⟩, is a member of **I**(G)—3 is greater than 1.

d[3/x] satisfies 'Tx ⊃ (∃y)Gyx' because **d**[3/x] does not satisfy 'Tx'. **d**[3/x] does not satisfy 'Tx' because ⟨**d**[3/x](x)⟩, which is ⟨3⟩, is not a member of **I**(T)—3 is not less than 2. So both **d**[1/x] and **d**[3/x] satisfy 'Tx ⊃ (∃y)Gyx' and therefore **d** satisfies '(∀x)(Tx ⊃ (∃y)Gyx)'. The sentence is true on this interpretation.

e. Let **d** be a variable assignment for this interpretation. **d** satisfies this sentence just in case for every member **u** of the UD, **d**[**u**/x] satisfies '(∀y)Gxy ∨ (∃y)Gxy'. However, the number 1 is *not* such that **d**[1/x] satisfies the formula. **d**[1/x] does not satisfy '(∀y)Gxy', because there is not even one member **u** of the UD such that **d**[1/x, **u**/y] satisfies 'Gxy'—no 2-tuple ⟨1, **u**⟩ is in the extension of 'G'. **d**[1/x] also does not satisfy '(∃y)Gxy', for the same reason. Because **d**[1/x] does not satisfy '(∀y)Gxy ∨ (∃y)Gxy', **d** does not satisfy the universally quantified sentence. The sentence is false on this interpretation.

3.a. Let **d** be a variable assignment for this interpretation. **d** satisfies 'Mooo ≡ Pooo' just in case either **d** satisfies both 'Mooo' and 'Pooo' or **d** satisfies neither of 'Mooo' and 'Pooo'. **d** does not satisfy 'Mooo' because ⟨**I**(o), **I**(o), **I**(o)⟩, which is ⟨1, 1, 1⟩, is not a member of **I**(M)—$1 - 1 \neq 1$. **d** does not satisfy 'Pooo' because ⟨**I**(o), **I**(o), **I**(o)⟩, which again is ⟨1, 1, 1⟩, is not a member of **I**(P)—$1 + 1 \neq 1$. So **d** satisfies neither immediate component and therefore does satisfy 'Mooo ≡ Pooo'. The sentence is true on this interpretation.

c. Let **d** be a variable assignment for this interpretation. **d** satisfies

'(∀x)(∀y)(∀z)(Mxyz ≡ Pxyz)' just in case every member **u** of the UD is such that **d**[**u**/x] satisfies '(∀y)(∀z)(Mxyz ≡ Pxyz)'. **d**[**u**/x] satisfies '(∀y)(∀z)(Mxyz ≡ Pxyz)' just in case every member $\mathbf{u}_1$ of the UD is such that **d**[**u**/x, $\mathbf{u}_1$/y] satisfies '(∀z)(Mxyz ≡ Pxyz)'. **d**[**u**/x, $\mathbf{u}_1$/y] satisfies '(∀z)(Mxyz ≡ Pxyz)' just in case every member $\mathbf{u}_2$ of the UD is such that **d**[**u**/x, $\mathbf{u}_1$/y, $\mathbf{u}_2$/z] satisfies 'Mxyz ≡ Pxyz'. So **d** satisfies '(∀x)(∀y)(∀z)(Mxyz ≡ Pxyz) just in case for any members **u**, $\mathbf{u}_1$, and $\mathbf{u}_2$ of the UD, **d**[**u**/x, $\mathbf{u}_1$/y, $\mathbf{u}_2$/z] satisfies 'Mxyz ≡ Pxyz'. But this is not the case. For example, **d**[1/x, 2/y, 3/z] does not satisfy 'Mxyz', because ⟨**d**[1/x, 2/y, 3/z](x), **d**[1/x, 2/y, 3/z](y), **d**[1/x, 2/y, 3/z](z)⟩, which is ⟨1, 2, 3⟩, is not a member of **I**(M)—$1 - 2 \neq 3$. On the other hand, **d**[1/x, 2/y, 3/z] does satisfy 'Pxyz', because ⟨**d**[1/x, 2/y, 3/z](x), **d**[1/x, 2/y, 3/z](y), **d**[1/x, 2/y, 3/z](z)⟩, which again is ⟨1, 2, 3⟩, is a member of **I**(P)—$1 + 2 = 3$. The assignment **d**[1/x, 2/y, 3/z] therefore does not satisfy 'Mxyz ≡ Pxyz', and so **d** does not satisfy '(∀x)(∀y)(∀z)(Mxyz ≡ Pxyz)'. The sentence is false on this interpretation.

e. Let **d** be a variable assignment for this interpretation. **d** satisfies this sentence if and only if for every member **u** of the UD, **d**[**u**/y] satisfies '(∃z)(Pyoz ⊃ Pooo)'. The latter is the case for a member **u** of the UD if and only if there is a member $\mathbf{u}_1$ of the UD such that **d**[**u**/y, $\mathbf{u}_1$/z] satisfies 'Pyoz ⊃ Pooo'. No variable assignment can satisfy 'Pooo', for ⟨1, 1, 1⟩ is not in the extension of 'P'. But for any member **u** of the UD we can find a member $\mathbf{u}_1$ such that ⟨**u**, 1, $\mathbf{u}_1$⟩, is not in the extension of 'P'; pick any number other than the number that is the successor of **u**. The sentence is true on this interpretation.

5. We shall show that the sentence is true on every interpretation. Let **I** be any interpretation. '(∀x)((∀y)Fy ⊃ Fx)' is true on **I** if and only if every variable assignment satisfies the sentence. A variable assignment **d** satisfies '(∀x)((∀y)Fy ⊃ Fx)' if and only if every member **u** of the UD is such that **d**[**u**/x] satisfies '(∀y)Fy ⊃ Fx'. Consider any member **u** of the UD. If ⟨**u**⟩ is a member of **I**(**F**), then **d**[**u**/x] satisfies 'Fx' and hence also satisfies '(∀y)Fy ⊃ Fx'. If ⟨**u**⟩ is not a member of **I**(F), then **d**[**u**/x] does not satisfy '(∀y)Fy'. This is because **u** is such that **d**[**u**/x, **u**/y] does not satisfy 'Fy'—⟨**d**[**u**/x, **u**/y](y)⟩, which is ⟨**u**⟩, is not a member of **I**(F). So if ⟨**u**⟩ is not a member of **I**(F), then **d**[**u**/x] satisfies '(∀y)Fy ⊃ Fx' because it fails to satisfy the antecedent. Each member **u** of the UD is such that either ⟨**u**⟩ is a member of **I**(F) or it isn't, so each member **u** of the UD is such that **d**[**u**/x] satisfies '(∀y)Fy ⊃ Fx'. Therefore **d** must satisfy '(∀x)((∀y)Fy ⊃ Fx)'. The sentence is true on every interpretation.

7. Assume that 'Fa' is true on an interpretation. Then every variable assignment for this interpretation satisfies 'Fa'. So we know that ⟨**I**(a)⟩ is in the extension of 'F'. We shall now show that every variable assignment also satisfies '(∃x)Fx'. Let **d** be any such assignment. **d** satisfies '(∃x)Fx' if and only if there is some member **u** of the UD such that **d**[**u**/x] satisfies 'Fx'. We know that there is such a member, namely, **I**(a). **d**[**I**(a)/x] satisfies 'Fx' because ⟨**I**(a)⟩ is in the extension of 'F'. Therefore '(∃x)Fx' is true on the interpretation as well.

9.a. Let **d** be a variable assignment for this interpretation. Then **d** satisfies '(∀x)(∀y)[~ x = y ⊃ (Ex ⊃ Gxy)]' if and only if for every positive integer **u, d**[**u**/x] satisfies '(∀y)[~ x = y ⊃ (Ex ⊃ Gxy)]'. This will be the case if and only if for every pair of positive integers **u** and $\mathbf{u}_1$, **d**[**u**/x, $\mathbf{u}_1$/y] satisfies '~ x = y ⊃ (Ex ⊃ Gxy)'. But **d**[2/x, 3/y], for example, does not satisfy the open sentence. **d**[2/x, 3/y] does satisfy '~ x = y', for 2 and 3 are distinct members of the UD. **d**[2/x, 3/y] does not satisfy 'Ex ⊃ Gxy', for it satisfies the antecedent and fails to satisfy the consequent. **d**[2/x, 3/y] satisfies 'Ex' because ⟨**d**[2/x, 3/y](x)⟩, which is ⟨2⟩, is a member of **I**(E). **d**[2/x, 3/y] fails to satisfy 'Gxy' because ⟨**d**[2/x, 3/y](x), **d**[2/x, 3/y](y)⟩, which is ⟨2, 3⟩, is not a member of **I**(G)—2 is not greater than 3. We conclude that '(∀x)(∀y)[~ x = y ⊃ (Ex ⊃ Gxy)]' is false on this interpretation.

c. Let **d** be a variable assignment for this interpretation. Then **d** satisfies the sentence if and only if for every member **u** of the UD, **d**[**u**/x] satisfies 'Ex ⊃ (∃y)(~ x = y & ~ Gxy). Every odd positive integer **u** is such that **d**[**u**/x] satisfies the formula because every odd positive integer **u** is such that **d**[**u**/x] fails to satisfy 'Ex'. Every even positive integer **u** is such that **d**[**u**/x] satisfies the formula because every positive integer (odd or even) satisfies the consequent, '(∃y)(~ x = y & ~ Gxy)'. For every positive integer **u** there is a positive integer $\mathbf{u}_1$ such that **d**[**u**/x, $\mathbf{u}_1$/y] satisfies '~ x = y & ~ Gxy': Let $\mathbf{u}_1$ be any integer that is greater than **u**. In this case, **d**[**u**/x, $\mathbf{u}_1$/y] satisfies '~ x = y' because **u** and $\mathbf{u}_1$ are not identical, and the variant also satisfies '~ Gxy' because ⟨**u**, $\mathbf{u}_1$⟩ is not in the extension of 'G'. The sentence is therefore true on this interpretation.

10.a. A sentence of the form (∀*x*)*x* = *x* is true on an interpretation **I** if and only if every variable assignment satisfies the sentence on **I**. A variable assignment **d** satisfies (∀*x*)*x* = *x* if and only if for every member **u** of the UD, **d**[**u**/*x*] satisfies *x* = *x*—and this is the case if and only for every member **u** of the UD, **d**[**u**/*x*](*x*) is identical to **d**[**u**/*x*](*x*). Trivially, this is so. Therefore (∀*x*)*x* = *x* is satisfied by every variable assignment on every interpretation; it is quantificationally true.

CHAPTER NINE

Section 9.1E

a.	1.	(∃x)Fx✓	SM
	2.	(∃x) ~ Fx✓	SM
	3.	Fa	1 ∃D
	4.	~ Fb	2 ∃D

The tree is open.

c.	1.	(∃x)(Fx & ~ Gx) ✓		SM
	2.	(∀x)(Fx ⊃ Gx)		SM
	3.	Fa & ~ Ga ✓		1 ∃D
	4.	Fa		3 &D
	5.	~ Ga		3 &D
	6.	Fa ⊃ Ga ✓		2 ∀D
		/	\	
	7.	~ Fa	Ga	6 ⊃D
		×	×	

The tree is closed.

e.	1.	~ (∀x)(Fx ⊃ Gx) ✓	SM
	2.	~ (∃x)Fx ✓	SM
	3.	~ (∃x)Gx ✓	SM
	4.	(∃x) ~ (Fx ⊃ Gx) ✓	1 ~ ∀D
	5.	(∀x) ~ Fx	2 ~ ∃D
	6.	(∀x) ~ Gx	3 ~ ∃D
	7.	~ (Fa ⊃ Ga) ✓	4 ∃D
	8.	Fa	7 ~ ⊃D
	9.	~ Ga	7 ~ ⊃D
	10.	~ Fa	5 ∀D
		×	

g.	1.	(∃x)Fx ✓	SM
	2.	(∃y)Gy ✓	SM
	3.	(∃z)(Fz & Gz) ✓	SM
	4.	Fa	1 ∃D
	5.	Gb	2 ∃D
	6.	Fc & Gc ✓	3 ∃D
	7.	Fc	6 &D
	8.	Gc	6 &D

The tree is open.

i.	1.	(∀x)(∀y)(Fxy ⊃ Fyx)		SM
	2.	(∃x)(∃y)(Fxy & ~ Fyx) ✓		SM
	3.	(∃y)(Fay & ~ Fya) ✓		2 ∃D
	4.	Fab & ~ Fba ✓		3 ∃D
	5.	Fab		4 &D
	6.	~ Fba		4 &D
	7.	(∀y)(Fay ⊃ Fya)		1 ∀D
	8.	Fab ⊃ Fba ✓		7 ∀D
		/	\	
	9.	~ Fab	Fba	8 ⊃D
		×	×	

The tree is closed.

k.

1.	(∃x)Fx ⊃ (∀x)Fx ✓		SM
2.	~ (∀x)(Fx ⊃ (∀y)Fy) ✓		SM
3.	(∃x) ~ (Fx ⊃ (∀y)Fy) ✓		2 ~ ∀D
4.	~ (Fa ⊃ (∀y)Fy) ✓		3 ∃D
5.	Fa		4 ~ ⊃D
6.	~ (∀y)Fy ✓		4 ~ ⊃D
7.	(∃y) ~ Fy ✓		6 ~ ∀D
8.	~ Fb		7 ∃D
9.	~ (∃x)Fx ✓	(∀x)Fx	1 ⊃D
10.	(∀x) ~ Fx		9 ~ ∃D
11.	~ Fa		10 ∀D
12.	×	Fb	9 ∀D
		×	

The tree is closed.

m.

1.	(∀x)(Fx ⊃ (∃y)Gyx)		SM
2.	~ (∀x) ~ Fx ✓		SM
3.	(∀x)(∀y) ~ Gxy		SM
4.	(∃x) ~ ~ Fx ✓		2 ~ ∀D
5.	~ ~ Fa ✓		4 ∃D
6.	Fa		5 ~ ~ D
7.	Fa ⊃ (∃y)Gya ✓		1 ∀D
8.	~ Fa	(∃y)Gya ✓	7 ⊃D
9.	×	Gba	8 ∃D
10.		(∀y) ~ Gby	3 ∀D
11.		~ Gba	10 ∀D
		×	

The tree is closed.

o.

1.	(∃x)Lxx ✓		SM
2.	~ (∃x)(∃y)(Lxy & Lyx) ✓		SM
3.	(∀x) ~ (∃y)(Lxy & Lyx)		2 ~ ∃D
4.	Laa		1 ∃D
5.	~ (∃y)(Lay & Lya) ✓		3 ∀D
6.	(∀y) ~ (Lay & Lya)		5 ~ ∃D
7.	~ (Laa & Laa) ✓		6 ∀D
8.	~ Laa	~ Laa	7 ~ &D
	×	×	

The tree is closed.

q.

1.	(∃x)(Fx ∨ Gx) ✓		SM
2.	(∀x)(Fx ⊃ ~ Gx)		SM
3.	(∀x)(Gx ⊃ ~ Fx)		SM
4.	~ (∃x)(~ Fx ∨ ~ Gx) ✓		SM
5.	(∀x) ~ (~ Fx ∨ ~ Gx)		4 ~ ∃D
6.	Fa ∨ Ga		1 ∃D
7.	Fa ⊃ ~ Ga ✓		2 ∀D
8.	Ga ⊃ ~ Fa ✓		3 ∀D
9.	~ (~ Fa ∨ ~ Ga) ✓		5 ∀D
10.	~ ~ Fa ✓		9 ~ ∨D
11.	~ ~ Ga ✓		9 ~ ∨D
12.	Ga		11 ~ ~ D
13.	Fa		10 ~ ~ D
14.	~ Fa	~ Ga	7 ⊃D
	×	×	

The tree is closed.

Section 9.2E

Note: In these answers, whenever a tree is open we give a complete tree. This is because the strategems we have suggested do not uniquely determine the order of decomposition, and so the first open branch to be completed on your tree may not be the first such branch completed on our tree. In accordance with strategem 5, you should stop when your tree has one completed open branch.

a.

1.	(∀x)Fx ∨ (∃y)Gy ✓		SM
2.	(∃x)(Fx & Gb) ✓		SM
3.	Fa & Gb ✓		2 ∃D
4.	Fa		3 &D
5.	Gb		3 &D
6.	(∀x)Fx	(∃y)Gy ✓	1 ∨D
7.	Fa		6 ∀D
8.	Fb		6 ∀D
9.		Gc	6 ∃D

The tree is open (both branches are completed open branches). The set is quantificationally consistent.

c. 1.	(∀x)(Fx ⊃ Gxa)			SM
2.	(∃x)Fx ✓			SM
3.	(∀y) ~ Gya			SM
4.	Fb			2 ∃D
5.	Fb ⊃ Gba ✓			1 ∀D
6.	~ Fb		Gba	5 ⊃D
7.	×		~ Gba	3 ∀D
			×	

The tree is closed. The set is quantificationally inconsistent.

e. 1.	(∀x)(Fx ⊃ Gxa)				SM
2.	(∃x)Fx ✓				SM
3.	(∀y)Gya				SM
4.	Fb				2 ∃D
5.	Fb ⊃ Gba ✓				1 ∀D
6.	~ Fb	Gba			5 ⊃D
7.	×	Gba			3 ∀D
8.		Gaa			3 ∀D
9.		Fa ⊃ Gaa ✓			1 ∀D
10.			~ Fa	Gaa	9 ⊃D

The tree is open (the two right-hand branches are completed open branches). The set is quantificationally consistent.

g. 1.	(∀x)(Fx ∨ Gx)		SM
2.	~ (∃y)(Fy ∨ Gy) ✓		SM
3.	(∀y) ~ (Fy ∨ Gy)		2 ~ ∃D
4.	~ (Fa ∨ Ga) ✓		3 ∀D
5.	~ Fa		4 ~ ∨D
6.	~ Ga		4 ~ ∨D
7.	Fa ∨ Ga ✓		1 ∀D
8.	Fa	Ga	7 ∨D
	×	×	

The tree is closed. The set is quantificationally inconsistent.

i. 1.	(∀z)Hz		SM
2.	(∃x)Hx ⊃ (∀y)Fy ✓		SM
3.	Ha		1 ∀D
4.	~ (∃x)Hx ✓	(∀y)Fy	2 ⊃D
5.	(∀x) ~ Hx		4 ~ ∃D
6.	~ Ha		5 ∀D
7.	×	Fa	4 ∀D

The tree is open (the right-hand branch is a completed open branch). The set is quantificationally consistent.

k. 1.	(∀x)(∀y)Lxy		SM
2.	(∃z) ~ Lza ⊃ (∀z) ~ Lza ✓		SM
3.	(∀y)Lay		1 ∀D
4.	Laa		3 ∀D
5.	~ (∃z) ~ Lza ✓	(∀z) ~ Lza	2 ⊃D
6.		~ Laa	5 ∀D
7.	(∀z) ~ ~ Lza	×	5 ~ ∃D
8.	~ ~ Laa ✓		7 ∀D
9.	Laa		8 ~ ~ D

The tree is open (the left-hand branch is a completed open branch). The set is quantificationally consistent.

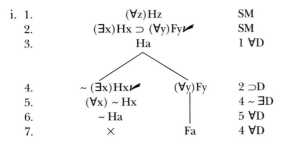

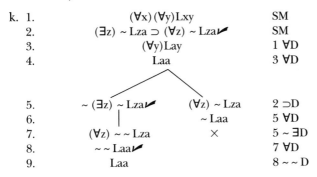

m.

1.	(∀x)(Rx ≡ ~ Hxa)					SM
2.	~ (∀y) ~ Hby✓					SM
3.	Ra					SM
4.	(∃y) ~ ~ Hby✓					2 ~ ∀D
5.	~ ~ Hbc✓					4 ∃D
6.	Hbc					5 ~ ~ D
7.	Ra ≡ ~ Haa✓					1 ∀D
8.	Rb ≡ ~ Hba✓					1 ∀D
9.	Rc ≡ ~ Hca✓					1 ∀D
10.	Ra				~ Ra	7 ≡D
11.	~ Haa				~ ~ Haa	7 ≡D
					×	
12.	Rb		~ Rb			8 ≡D
13.	~ Hba		~ ~ Hba✓			8 ≡D
14.	Rc	~ Rc	Rc	~ Rc		9 ≡D
15.	~ Hca	~ ~ Hca✓	~ Hca	~ ~ Hca✓		9 ≡D
16.		Hca			Hca	15 ~ ~ D
17.			Hba	Hba		13 ~ ~ D

The tree is open (all but the rightmost branch are completed open branches). The set is quantificationally consistent.

Section 9.3E

1.a.

1.	~ ((∃x)Fx ∨ ~ (∃x)Fx)✓	SM
2.	~ (∃x)Fx✓	1 ~ ∨D
3.	~ ~ (∃x)Fx✓	1 ~ ∨D
4.	(∀x) ~ Fx	2 ~ ∃D
5.	(∃x)Fx✓	3 ~ ~ D
6.	Fa	5 ∃D
7.	~ Fa	4 ∀D
	×	

The tree is closed. The sentence '(∃x)Fx ∨ ~ (∃x)Fx' is quantificationally true.

c.

1.	~ ((∀x)Fx ∨ (∀x) ~ Fx)✓	SM
2.	~ (∀x)Fx✓	1 ~ ∨D
3.	~ (∀x) ~ Fx✓	1 ~ ∨D
4.	(∃x) ~ Fx✓	2 ~ ∀D
5.	(∃x) ~ ~ Fx✓	3 ~ ∀D
6.	~ Fa	4 ∃D
7.	~ ~ Fb✓	5 ∃D
8.	Fb	7 ~ ~ D

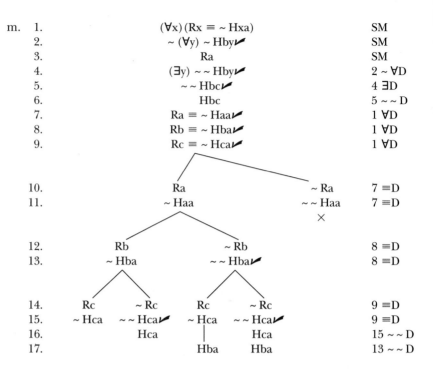

The tree is open. The sentence '(∀x)Fx ∨ (∀x) ~ Fx' is not quantificationally true.

e.

1.	~ ((∀x)Fx ∨ (∃x) ~ Fx)✓	SM
2.	~ (∀x)Fx✓	1 ~ ∨D
3.	~ (∃x) ~ Fx✓	1 ~ ∨D
4.	(∃x) ~ Fx✓	2 ~ ∀D
5.	(∀x) ~ ~ Fx	3 ~ ∃D
6.	~ Fa	4 ∃D
7.	~ ~ Fa✓	5 ∀D
8.	Fa	7 ~ ~ D
	×	

The tree is closed. The sentence '(∀x)Fx ∨ (∃x) ~ Fx' is quantificationally true.

g.

1.	~ ((∀x)(Fx ∨ Gx) ⊃ ((∃x) ~ Fx ⊃ (∃x)Gx))✓		SM
2.	(∀x)(Fx ∨ Gx)		1 ~ ⊃D
3.	~ ((∃x) ~ Fx ⊃ (∃x)Gx)✓		1 ~ ⊃D
4.	(∃x) ~ Fx✓		3 ~ ⊃D
5.	~ (∃x)Gx✓		3 ~ ⊃D
6.	(∀x) ~ Gx		5 ~ ∃D
7.	~ Fa		4 ∃D
8.	Fa ∨ Ga✓		2 ∀D
9.	Fa	Ga	8 ∨D
10.	×	~ Ga	6 ∀D
		×	

The tree is closed. The sentence '(∀x)(Fx ∨ Gx) ⊃ [(∃x) ~ Fx ⊃ (∃x)Gx]' is quantificationally true.

i.

1.	~ (((∀x)Fx ∨ (∀x)Gx) ⊃ (∀x)(Fx ∨ Gx))✓		SM
2.	(∀x)Fx ∨ (∀x)Gx✓		1 ~ ⊃D
3.	~ (∀x)(Fx ∨ Gx)✓		1 ~ ⊃D
4.	(uQx) ~ (Fx ∨ Gx)✓		3 ~ ∀D
5.	~ (Fa ∨ Ga)✓		4 ∃D
6.	~ Fa		5 ~ ∨D
7.	~ Ga		5 ~ ∨D
8.	(∀x)Fx	(∀x)Gx	2 ∨D
9.	Fa	Ga	8 ∀D
	×	×	

The tree is closed. The sentence '((∀x)Fx ∨ (∀x)Gx) ⊃ (∀x)(Fx ∨ Gx)' is quantificationally true.

k. 1.	~ ((∃x)(Fx & Gx) ⊃ ((∃x)Fx & (∃x)Gx)) ✓		SM
2.	(∃x)(Fx & Gx) ✓		1 ~ ⊃D
3.	~ ((∃x)Fx & (∃x)Gx) ✓		1 ~ ⊃D
4.	Fa & Ga ✓		2 ∃D
5.	Fa		4 &D
6.	Ga		4 &D
7.	~ (∃x)Fx ✓	~ (∃x)Gx ✓	3 ~ &D
8.	(∀x) ~ Fx	(∀x) ~ Gx	7 ~ ∃D
9.	~ Fa	~ Ga	8 ∀D
	×	×	

The tree is closed. The sentence '(∃x)(Fx & Gx) ⊃ ((∃x)Fx & (∃x)Gx)' is quantificationally true.

m. 1.	~ (~ (∃x)Fx ∨ (∀x) ~ Fx) ✓	SM
2.	~ ~ (∃x)Fx ✓	1 ~ ∨D
3.	~ (∀x) ~ Fx ✓	1 ~ ∨D
4.	(∃x)Fx ✓	2 ~ ~ D
5.	(∃x) ~ ~ Fx ✓	3 ~ ∀D
6.	Fa	4 ∃D
7.	~ ~ Fb ✓	5 ∃D
8.	Fb	7 ~ ~ D

The tree is open. The sentence '~ (∃x)Fx ∨ (∀x) ~ Fx' is not quantificationally true.

o. 1.	~ ((∀x)((Fx & Gx) ⊃ Hx) ⊃ (∀x)(Fx ⊃ (Gx & Hx))) ✓						SM
2.	(∀x)((Fx & Gx) ⊃ Hx)						1 ~ ⊃D
3.	~ (∀x)(Fx ⊃ (Gx & Hx)) ✓						1 ~ ⊃D
4.	(∃x) ~ (Fx ⊃ (Gx & Hx)) ✓						3 ~ ∀D
5.	~ (Fa ⊃ (Ga & Ha)) ✓						4 ∃D
6.	Fa						5 ~ ⊃D
7.	~ (Ga & Ha) ✓						5 ~ ⊃D
8.	(Fa & Ga) ⊃ Ha ✓						2 ∀D
9.	~ (Fa & Ga) ✓				Ha		8 ⊃D
10.	~ Ga		~ Ha		~ Ga	~ Ha	7 ~ &D
						×	
11.	~ Fa	~ Ga	~ Fa	~ Ga			9 ~ &D
	×		×				

The tree is open. The sentence '(∀x)[(Fx & Gx) ⊃ Hx] ⊃ (∀x)[Fx ⊃ (Gx & Hx)]' is not quantificationally true.

q.	1.	~ ((∀x)(Fx ⊃ Gx) ⊃ (∀x)(Fx ⊃ (∀y)Gy)) ✓	SM
	2.	(∀x)(Fx ⊃ Gx)	1 ~ ⊃D
	3.	~ (∀x)(Fx ⊃ (∀y)Gy) ✓	1 ~ ⊃D
	4.	(∃x) ~ (Fx ⊃ (∀y)Gy) ✓	3 ~ ∀D
	5.	~ (Fa ⊃ (∀y)Gy) ✓	4 ∃D
	6.	Fa	5 ~ ⊃D
	7.	~ (∀y)Gy ✓	5 ~ ⊃D
	8.	(∃y) ~ Gy ✓	7 ~ ∀D
	9.	~ Gb	8 ∃D
	10.	Fa ⊃ Ga ✓	2 ∀D
	11.	~ Fa Ga	10 ⊃D
	12.	× Fb ⊃ Gb ✓	2 ∀D
	13.	~ Fb Gb	12 ⊃D
		× (under Gb)	

The tree is open. The sentence '(∀x)(Fx ⊃ Gx) ⊃ (∀x)[Fx ⊃ (∀y)Gy]' is not quantificationally true.

s.	1.	~ ((∀x)Gxx ⊃ (∀x)(∀y)Gxy) ✓	SM
	2.	(∀x)Gxx	1 ~ ⊃D
	3.	~ (∀x)(∀y)Gxy ✓	1 ~ ⊃D
	4.	(∃x) ~ (∀y)Gxy ✓	3 ~ ∀D
	5.	~ (∀y)Gay ✓	4 ∃D
	6.	(∃y) ~ Gay ✓	5 ~ ∀D
	7.	~ Gab	6 ∃D
	8.	Gaa	2 ∀D
	9.	Gbb	2 ∀D

The tree is open. The sentence '(∀x)Gxx ⊃ (∀x)(∀y)Gxy' is not quantificationally true.

u.	1.	~ ((∃x)(∀y)Gxy ⊃ (∀x)(∃y)Gyx) ✓	SM
	2.	(∃x)(∀y)Gxy ✓	1 ~ ⊃D
	3.	~ (∀x)(∃y)Gyx ✓	1 ~ ⊃D
	4.	(∃x) ~ (∃y)Gyx ✓	3 ~ ∀D
	5.	(∀y)Gay	2 ∃D
	6.	~ (∃y)Gyb ✓	4 ∃D
	7.	(∀y) ~ Gyb	6 ~ ∃D
	8.	Gab	5 ∀D
	9.	~ Gab	7 ∀D
		×	

The tree is closed. The sentence '(∃x)(∀y)Gxy ⊃ (∀x)(∃y)Gyx' is quantificationally true.

w. 1.	~ (((∃x)Lxx ⊃ (∀y)Lyy) ⊃ (Laa ⊃ Lgg)) ✓		SM
2.	(∃x)Lxx ⊃ (∀y)Lyy ✓		1 ~ ⊃D
3.	~ (Laa ⊃ Lgg) ✓		1 ~ ⊃D
4.	Laa		3 ~ ⊃D
5.	~ Lgg		3 ~ ⊃D
6.	~ (∃x)Lxx ✓	(∀y)Lyy	2 ⊃D
7.	(∀x) ~ Lxx		6 ~ ∃D
8.	~ Laa		7 ∀D
9.	×	Lgg	6 ∀D
		×	

The tree is closed. The sentence '[(∃x)Lxx ⊃ (∀y)Lyy] ⊃ (Laa ⊃ Lgg)' is quantificationally true.

2.a. 1.	(∀x)Fx & (∃x) ~ Fx ✓	SM
2.	(∀x)Fx	1 &D
3.	(uQx) ~ Fx ✓	1 &D
4.	~ Fa	3 ∃D
5.	Fa	2 ∀D
	×	

The tree is closed. Therefore the sentence is quantificationally false.

c. 1.	(∃x)Fx & (∃x) ~ Fx ✓	SM
2.	(∃x)Fx ✓	1 &D
3.	(∃x) ~ Fx ✓	1 &D
4.	Fa	2 ∃D
5.	~ Fb	3 ∃D

The tree is open. Therefore the sentence is not quantificationally false.

e. 1.	(∀x)(Fx ⊃ (∀y) ~ Fy)		SM
2.	Fa ⊃ (∀y) ~ Fy ✓		1 ∀D
3.	~ Fa	(∀y) ~ Fy	2 ⊃D
4.		~ Fa	3 ∀D

The tree is open. Therefore the sentence is not quantificationally false.

g. 1.	(∀x)(Fx ≡ ~ Fx)		SM
2.	Fa ≡ ~ Fa ✓		1 ∀D
3.	Fa	~ Fa	2 ≡D
4.	~ Fa	~ ~ Fa ✓	2 ≡D
5.	×	Fa	4 ~ ~ D
		×	

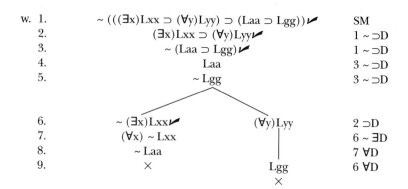

The tree is closed. Therefore the sentence is quantificationally false.

i.	1.	(∃x)(∃y)(Fxy & ~ Fyx) ✓	SM
	2.	(∃y)(Fay & ~ Fya) ✓	1 ∃D
	3.	Fab & ~ Fba ✓	2 ∃D
	4.	Fab	3 &D
	5.	~ Fba	3 &D

The tree is open. Therefore the sentence is not quantificationally false.

k.	1.	(∀x)(∀y)(Fxy ⊃ ~ Fyx)		SM
	2.	(∀y)(Fay ⊃ ~ Fya)		1 ∀D
	3.	Faa ⊃ ~ Faa ✓		2 ∀D
	4.	~ Faa	~ Faa	3 ⊃D

The tree is open. Therefore the sentence is not quantificationally false.

m.	1.	(∃x)(∀y)Gxy & ~ (∀y)(∃x)Gxy ✓	SM
	2.	(∃x)(∀y)Gxy ✓	1 &D
	3.	~ (∀y)(∃x)Gxy ✓	1 &D
	4.	(∃y) ~ (∃x)Gxy ✓	3 ~ ∀D
	5.	(∀y)Gay	2 ∃D
	6.	~ (∃x)Gxb ✓	4 ∃D
	7.	(∀x) ~ Gxb	6 ~ ∃D
	8.	Gab	5 ∀D
	9.	~ Gab	7 ∀D
		×	

The tree is closed. Therefore the sentence is quantificationally false.

3.a.	1.	~ ((∃x)Fxx ⊃ (∃x)(∃y)Fxy) ✓	SM
	2.	(∃x)Fxx ✓	1 ~ ⊃D
	3.	~ (∃x)(∃y)Fxy ✓	1 ~ ⊃D
	4.	(∀x) ~ (∃y)Fxy	3 ~ ∃D
	5.	Faa	2 ∃D
	6.	~ (∃y)Fay ✓	4 ∀D
	7.	(∀y) ~ Fay	6 ~ ∃D
	8.	~ Faa	7 ∀D
		×	

The tree for the negation of '(∃x)Fxx ⊃ (∃x)(∃y)Fxy' is closed. Therefore the latter sentence is quantificationally true.

c.	1.	~ ((∃x)(∀y)Lxy ⊃ (∃x)Lxx) ✓	SM
	2.	(∃x)(∀y)Lxy ✓	1 ~ ⊃D
	3.	~ (∃x)Lxx ✓	1 ~ ⊃D
	4.	(∀x) ~ Lxx	3 ~ ∃D
	5.	(∀y)Lay	2 ∃D
	6.	~ Laa	4 ∀D
	7.	Laa	5 ∀D
		×	

The tree for the negation of '(∃x) (∀y) Lxy ⊃ (∃x)Lxx' is closed. Therefore the latter sentence is quantificationally true.

e.	1.	~ ((∀x) (Fx ⊃ (∃y)Gya) ⊃ (Fb ⊃ (∃y)Gya)) ✓		SM
	2.	(∀x) (Fx ⊃ (∃y)Gya)		1 ~ ⊃D
	3.	~ (Fb ⊃ (∃y)Gya) ✓		1 ~ ⊃D
	4.	Fb		3 ~ ⊃D
	5.	~ (∃y)Gya ✓		3 ~ ⊃D
	6.	(∀y) ~ Gya		5 ~ ∃D
	7.	Fb ⊃ (∃y)Gya ✓		2 ∀D
	8.	~ Fb	(∃y)Gya ✓	7 ⊃D
	9.	×	Gca	8 ∃D
	10.		~ Gca	6 ∀D
			×	

The tree for the negation of '(∀x) (Fx ⊃ (∃y)Gya) ⊃ (Fb ⊃ (∃y)Gya)' is closed. Therefore the latter sentence is quantificationally true.

g.	1.	~ ((∀x) (Fx ⊃ (∀y)Gxy) ⊃ (∃x) (Fx ⊃ ~ (∀y)Gxy)) ✓		SM
	2.	(∀x) (Fx ⊃ (∀y)Gxy)		1 ~ ⊃D
	3.	~ (∃x) (Fx ⊃ ~ (∀y)Gxy) ✓		1 ~ ⊃D
	4.	(eQx) ~ (Fx ⊃ ~ (∀y)Gxy)		3 ~ ∃D
	5.	~ (Fa ⊃ ~ (∀y)Gay) ✓		4 ∀D
	6.	Fa		5 ~ ⊃D
	7.	~ ~ (∀y)Gay ✓		5 ~ ⊃D
	8.	(∀y)Gay		7 ~ ~ D
	9.	Fa ⊃ (∀y)Gay ✓		2 ∀D
	10.	~ Fa	(∀y)Gay	9 ⊃D
	11.	×	Gaa	10 ∀D
	12.		Gaa	8 ∀D

1.	(∀x) (Fx ⊃ (∀y)Gxy) ⊃ (∃x) (Fx ⊃ ~ (∀y)Gxy) ✓			SM
2.	~ (∀x) (Fx ⊃ (∀y)Gxy) ✓	(∃x) (Fx ⊃ ~ (∀y)Gxy) ✓		1 ⊃D
3.	(∃x) ~ (Fx ⊃ (∀y)Gxy) ✓			2 ~ ∀D
4.	~ (Fa ⊃ (∀y)Gay) ✓			3 ∃D
5.	Fa			4 ~ ⊃D
6.	~ (∀y)Gay ✓			4 ~ ⊃D
7.	(∃y) ~ Gay ✓			6 ~ ∀D
8.	~ Gab			7 ∃D
9.		Fa ⊃ ~ (∀y)Gay ✓		2 ∃D
10.		~ Fa	~ (∀y)Gay ✓	9 ⊃D
11.			(∃y) ~ Gay ✓	10 ~ ∀D
12.			~ Gab	11 ∃D

Both the tree for the given sentence and the tree for its negation are open. Therefore the given sentence is quantificationally indeterminate.

4.a.	1.	~ ((∀x)Mxx ≡ ~ (∃x) ~ Mxx)✓		SM
	2.	(∀x)Mxx	~ (∀x)Mxx✓	1 ~ ≡D
	3.	~ ~ (∃x) ~ Mxx✓	~ (∃x) ~ Mxx✓	1 ~ ≡D
	4.	(∃x) ~ Mxx✓		3 ~ ~ D
	5.	~ Maa		4 ∃D
	6.	Maa		2 ∀D
	7.	×	(∃x) ~ Mxx✓	2 ~ ∀D
	8.		(∀x) ~ ~ Mxx	3 ~ ∃D
	9.		~ Mbb	7 ∃D
	10.		~ ~ Mbb✓	8 ∀D
	11.		Mbb	10 ~ ~ D
			×	

The tree is closed. Therefore the sentences '(∀x)Mxx' and '~ (∃x) ~ Mxx' are quantificationally equivalent.

c.	1.	~ ((∀x)(Fa ⊃ Gx) ≡ (Fa ⊃ (∀x)Gx))✓				SM
	2.	(∀x)(Fa ⊃ Gx)		~ (∀x)(Fa ⊃ Gx)✓		1 ~ ≡D
	3.	~ (Fa ⊃ (∀x)Gx)✓		Fa ⊃ (∀x)Gx✓		1 ~ ≡D
	4.	Fa				3 ~ ⊃D
	5.	~ (∀x)Gx✓				3 ~ ⊃D
	6.	(∃x) ~ Gx✓				5 ~ ∀D
	7.	~ Gb				6 ∃D
	8.	Fa ⊃ Gb✓				2 ∀D
	9.	~ Fa	Gb			8 ⊃D
	10.	×	×	(∃x) ~ (Fa ⊃ Gx)✓		2 ~ ∀D
	11.			~ (Fa ⊃ Gc)✓		10 ∃D
	12.			Fa		11 ~ ⊃D
	13.			~ Gc		11 ~ ⊃D
	14.			~ Fa	(∀x)Gx	3 ⊃D
	15.			×	Gc	14 ∀D
					×	

The tree is closed. Therefore the sentences '(∀x)(Fa ⊃ Gx)' and 'Fa ⊃ (∀x)Gx' are quantificationally equivalent.

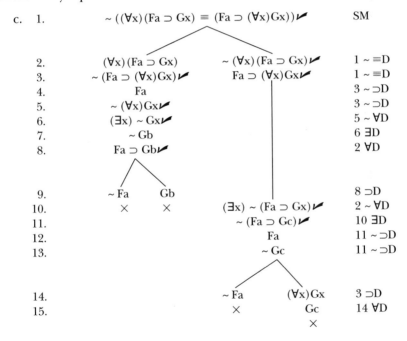

e.

Line	Branch 1	Branch 2	Branch 3	Branch 4	
1.	$\sim(((\exists x)Fx \supset Ga) \equiv (\exists x)(Fx \supset Ga))$✓				SM
2.	$(\exists x)Fx \supset Ga$✓		$\sim((\exists x)Fx \supset Ga)$✓		$1 \sim\equiv D$
3.	$\sim(\exists x)(Fx \supset Ga)$✓		$(\exists x)(Fx \supset Ga)$✓		$1 \sim\equiv D$
4.	$(\forall x) \sim (Fx \supset Ga)$				$3 \sim\exists D$
5.	$\sim(\exists x)Fx$✓	Ga			$2 \supset D$
6.	$(\forall x) \sim Fx$				$5 \sim\exists D$
7.	$\sim(Fa \supset Ga)$✓	$\sim(Fa \supset Ga)$✓			$4\ \forall D$
8.	Fa	Fa			$7 \sim\supset D$
9.	$\sim Ga$	$\sim Ga$			$7 \supset D$
10.	$\sim Fa$	×			$6\ \forall D$
11.	×		$(\exists x)Fx$✓		$2 \sim\supset D$
12.			$\sim Ga$		$2 \sim\supset D$
13.			$Fb \supset Ga$✓		$3\ \exists D$
14.			Fc		$11\ \exists D$
15.			$\sim Fb$	Ga	$13 \supset D$
				×	

The tree is open. Therefore the sentences '$(\exists x)Fx \supset Ga$' and '$(\exists x)(Fx \supset Ga)$' are not quantificationally equivalent.

g.

Line	Branch 1	Branch 2	Branch 3	Branch 4	
1.	$\sim(((\forall x)Fx \supset Ga) \equiv (\exists x)(Fx \supset Ga))$✓				SM
2.	$(\forall x)Fx \supset Ga$✓		$\sim((\forall x)Fx \supset Ga)$✓		$1 \sim\equiv D$
3.	$\sim(\exists x)(Fx \supset Ga)$✓		$(\exists x)(Fx \supset Ga)$✓		$1 \sim\equiv D$
4.	$(\forall x) \sim (Fx \supset Ga)$				$3 \sim\exists D$
5.	$\sim(\forall x)Fx$✓	Ga			$2 \supset D$
6.	$(\exists x) \sim Fx$✓				$5 \sim\forall D$
7.	$\sim Fb$				$6\ \exists D$
8.	$\sim(Fb \supset Ga)$✓	$\sim(Fa \supset Ga)$✓			$4\ \forall D$
9.	Fb	Fa			$8 \sim\supset D$
10.	$\sim Ga$	$\sim Ga$			$8 \sim\supset D$
11.	×	×	$(\forall x)Fx$		$2 \sim\supset D$
12.			$\sim Ga$		$2 \sim\supset D$
13.			$Fc \supset Ga$✓		$3\ \exists D$
14.			$\sim Fc$	Ga	$13 \supset D$
15.			Fc	×	$11\ \forall D$
			×		

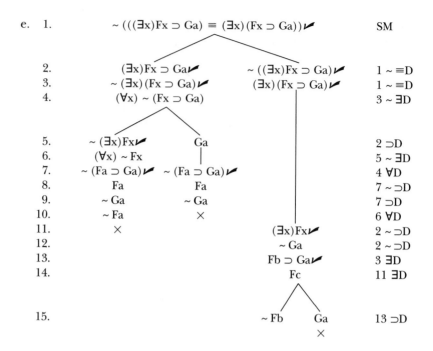

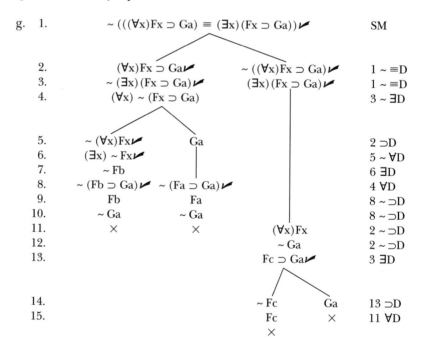

The tree is closed. Therefore the sentences '(∀x)Fx ⊃ Ga' and '(∃x)(Fx ⊃ Ga)' are quantificationally equivalent.

i.

1.	~ ((∀x)(∀y)(Fx ⊃ Gy) ≡ (∀x)(Fx ⊃ (∀y)Gy))✓		SM
2.	(∀x)(∀y)(Fx ⊃ Gy)	~ (∀x)(∀y)(Fx ⊃ Gy)✓	1 ~ ≡D
3.	~ (∀x)(Fx ⊃ (∀y)Gy)✓	(∀x)(Fx ⊃ (∀y)Gy)	1 ~ ≡D
4.	(∃x) ~ (Fx ⊃ (∀y)Gy)✓		3 ~ ∀D
5.	~ (Fa ⊃ (∀y)Gy)✓		4 ∃D
6.	Fa		5 ~ ⊃D
7.	~ (∀y)Gy✓		5 ~ ⊃D
8.	(∃y) ~ Gy✓		7 ~ ∀D
9.	~ Gb		8 ∃D
10.	(∀y)(Fa ⊃ Gy)		2 ∀D
11.	Fa ⊃ Gb✓		10 ∀D
12.	~ Fa Gb		11 ⊃D
13.	× ×	(∃x) ~ (∀y)(Fx ⊃ Gy)✓	2 ~ ∀D
14.		~ (∀y)(Fc ⊃ Gy)✓	13 ∃D
15.		(∃y) ~ (Fc ⊃ Gy)✓	14 ~ ∀D
16.		~ (Fc ⊃ Gd)✓	15 ∃D
17.		Fc	16 ~ ⊃D
18.		~ Gd	16 ~ ⊃D
19.		Fc ⊃ (∀y)Gy✓	3 ∀D
20.		~ Fc (∀y)Gy	19 ⊃D
21.		× Gd	20 ∀D
		×	

The tree is closed. Therefore the sentences '(∀x)(∀y)(Fx ⊃ Gy)' and '(∀x)(Fx ⊃ (∀y)Gy)' are quantificationally equivalent.

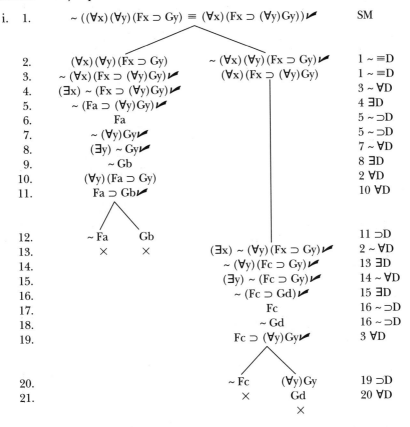

k.	1.	~ ((∀x)(Fa ≡ Gx) ≡ (Fa ≡ (∀x)Gx))✓								SM
	2.	(∀x)(Fa ≡ Gx)				~ (∀x)(Fa ≡ Gx)✓				1 ~ ≡D
	3.	~ (Fa ≡ (∀x)Gx)✓				Fa ≡ (∀x)Gx✓				1 ~ ≡D
	4.	Fa		~ Fa						3 ~ ≡D
	5.	~ (∀x)Gx✓		(∀x)Gx						3 ~ ≡D
	6.	(∃x) ~ Gx✓								5 ~ ∀D
	7.	~ Gb								6 ∃D
	8.	Fa ≡ Gb✓		Fa ≡ Gb✓						2 ∀D
	9.	Fa	~ Fa	Fa	~ Fa					8 ≡D
	10.	Gb	~ Gb	Gb	~ Gb					8 ≡D
	11.	×	×	×	Gb					5 ∀D
	12.				×	(∃x) ~ (Fa ≡ Gx)✓				2 ~ ∀D
	13.					~ (Fa ≡ Gc)✓				12 ∃D
										5 ∀D
	14.					Fa		~ Fa		3 ≡D
	15.					(∀x)Gx		~ (∀x)Gx✓		3 ≡D
	16.					Fa	~ Fa	Fa	~ Fa	13 ~ ≡D
	17.					~ Gc	Gc	~ Gc	Gc	13 ~ ≡D
	18.					Gc	×	×		15 ∀D
	19.					×			(∃x) ~ Gx✓	15 ~ ∀D
	20.								~ Gd	19 ∃D

The tree is open. Therefore the sentences '(∀x)(Fa ≡ Gx)' and '(Fa ≡ (∀x)Gx)' are not quantificationally equivalent.

m.

1.	~ ((∀x)(Fx ⊃ (∀y)Gy) ≡ (∀x)(∀y)(Fx ⊃ Gy))✓		SM
2.	(∀x)(Fx ⊃ (∀y)Gy)	~ (∀x)(Fx ⊃ (∀y)Gy)✓	1 ~ ≡D
3.	~ (∀x)(∀y)(Fx ⊃ Gy)✓	(∀x)(∀y)(Fx ⊃ Gy)	1 ~ ≡D
4.	(∃x) ~ (∀y)(Fx ⊃ Gy)✓		3 ~ ∀D
5.	~ (∀y)(Fa ⊃ Gy)✓		4 ∃D
6.	(∃y) ~ (Fa ⊃ Gy)✓		5 ~ ∀D
7.	~ (Fa ⊃ Gb)✓		6 ∃D
8.	Fa		7 ~ ⊃D
9.	~ Gb		7 ~ ⊃D
10.	Fa ⊃ (∀y)Gy✓		2 ∀D
11.	~ Fa (∀y)Gy		10 ⊃D
12.	× Gb		11 ∀D
13.	×	(∃x) ~ (Fx ⊃ (∀y)Gy)✓	2 ~ ∀D
14.		~ (Fc ⊃ (∀y)Gy)✓	13 ∃D
15.		Fc	14 ~ ⊃D
16.		~ (∀y)Gy✓	14 ~ ⊃D
17.		(∃y) ~ Gy✓	16 ~ ∀D
18.		~ Gd	17 ∃D
19.		(∀y)(Fc ⊃ Gy)	3 ∀D
20.		Fc ⊃ Gd✓	19 ∀D
21.		~ Fc Gd	20 ⊃D
		× ×	

The tree is closed. Therefore the sentences '(∀x)(Fx ⊃ (∀y)Gy)' and '(∀x)(∀y)(Fx ⊃ Gy)' are quantificationally equivalent.

5.a.

1.	(∀x)(Fx ⊃ Gx)	SM
2.	Ga	SM
3.	~ Fa	SM
4.	Fa ⊃ Ga✓	1 ∀D
5.	~ Fa Ga	4 ⊃D

The tree is open. Therefore the argument is quantificationally invalid.

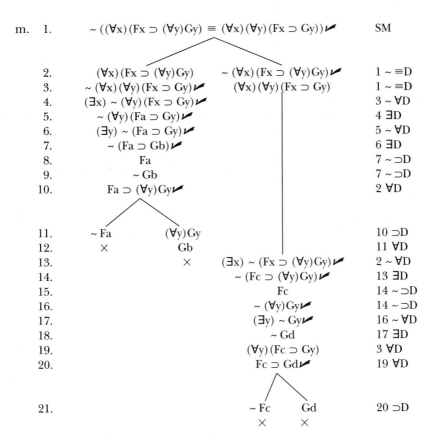

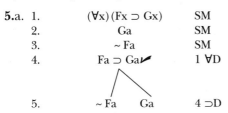

c. 1.	(∀x)(Kx ⊃ Lx)			SM
2.	(∀x)(Lx ⊃ Mx)			SM
3.	~ (∀x)(Kx ⊃ Mx)✔			SM
4.	(∃x) ~ (Kx ⊃ Mx)✔			3 ~ ∀D
5.	~ (Ka ⊃ Ma)✔			4 ∃D
6.	Ka			5 ~ ⊃D
7.	~ Ma			5 ~ ⊃D
8.	Ka ⊃ La✔			1 ∀D
9.	La ⊃ Ma✔			2 ∀D
10.	~ Ka ×	La		8 ⊃D
11.		~ La ×	Ma ×	9 ⊃D

The tree is closed. Therefore the argument is quantificationally valid.

e. 1.	(∀x)(Fx ⊃ Gx) ⊃ (∃x)Nx✔				SM
2.	(∀x)(Nx ⊃ Gx)				SM
3.	~ (∀x)(~ Fx ∨ Gx)✔				SM
4.	(∃x) ~ (~ Fx ∨ Gx)✔				3 ~ ∀D
5.	~ (~ Fa ∨ Ga)✔				4 ∃D
6.	~ ~ Fa✔				5 ~ ∨D
7.	~ Ga				5 ~ ∨D
8.	Fa				6 ~ ~ D
9.	Na ⊃ Ga✔				2 ∀D
10.	~ Na			Ga ×	9 ⊃D
11.	~ (∀x)(Fx ⊃ Gx)✔		(∃x)Nx✔		1 ⊃D
12.			Nb		11 ∃D
13.	(∃x) ~ (Fx ⊃ Gx)✔				11 ~ ∀D
14.	~ (Fb ⊃ Gb)✔				13 ∃D
15.	Fb				14 ~ ⊃D
16.	~ Gb				14 ~ ⊃D
17.	Nb ⊃ Gb✔		Nb ⊃ Gb✔		2 ∀D
18.	~ Nb	Gb ×	~ Nb ×	Gb	17 ⊃D

The tree is open. Therefore the argument is quantificationally invalid.

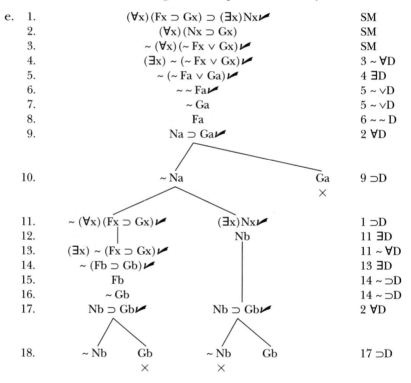

g.	1.	(∀x)(~ Ax ⊃ Kx)		SM
	2.	(∃y) ~ Ky✓		SM
	3.	~ (∃w)(Aw ∨ ~ Lwf)✓		SM
	4.	(∀w) ~ (Aw ∨ ~ Lwf)		3 ~ ∃D
	5.	~ Ka		2 ∃D
	6.	~ Aa ⊃ Ka✓		1 ∀D
	7.	~ (Aa ∨ ~ Laf)✓		4 ∀D
	8.	~ Aa		7 ~ ∨D
	9.	~ ~ Laf✓		7 ~ ∨D
	10.	Laf		9 ~ ~ D
	11.	~ ~ Aa✓	Ka	6 ⊃D
	12.	Aa	×	11 ~ ~ D
		×		

The tree is closed. Therefore the argument is quantificationally valid.

i.	1.	(∀x)(∀y)Cxy				SM
	2.	~ ((Caa & Cab) & (Cba & Cbb))✓				SM
	3.	(∀y)Cay				1 ∀D
	4.	(∀y)Cby				1 ∀D
	5.	Caa				3 ∀D
	6.	Cab				3 ∀D
	7.	Cba				4 ∀D
	8.	Cbb				4 ∀D
	9.	~ (Caa & Cab)✓		~ (Cba & Cbb)✓		2 ~ &D
	10.	~ Caa	~ Cab	~ Cba	~ Cbb	9 ~ &D
		×	×	×	×	

The tree is closed. Therefore the argument is quantificationally valid.

k.	1.	(∀x)(Fx ⊃ Gx)		SM
	2.	~ (∃x)Fx✓		SM
	3.	~ ~ (∃x)Gx✓		SM
	4.	(∃x)Gx✓		3 ~ ~ D
	5.	Ga		4 ∃D
	6.	(∀x) ~ Fx		2 ~ ∃D
	7.	Fa ⊃ Ga✓		1 ∀D
	8.	~ Fa		6 ∀D
	9.	~ Fa	Ga	7 ⊃D

The tree is open. Therefore the argument is quantificationally invalid.

	Line				Justification
m.	1.		(∃x)Cx ⊃ Ch✓		SM
	2.		~ ((∃x)Cx ≡ Ch)✓		SM
	3.	(∃x)Cx✓		~ (∃x)Cx✓	2 ~ ≡D
	4.	~ Ch		Ch	2 ~ ≡D
	5.			(∀x) ~ Cx	3 ~ ∃D
	6.			~ Ch	5 ∀D
	7.	Ca		×	3 ∃D
	8.	~ (∃x)Cx✓	Ch		1 ⊃D
	9.	(∀x) ~ Cx	×		8 ~ ∃D
	10.	~ Ca			9 ∀D
		×			

The tree is closed. Therefore the argument is quantificationally valid.

	Line			Justification
6.a.	1.	(∀x) ~ Jx		SM
	2.	(∃y)(Hby ∨ Ryy) ⊃ (∃x)Jx✓		SM
	3.	~ (∀y) ~ (Hby ∨ Ryy)✓		SM
	4.	(∃y) ~ ~ (Hby ∨ Ryy)✓		3 ~ ∀D
	5.	~ ~ (Hba ∨ Raa)✓		4 ∃D
	6.	Hba ∨ Raa✓		5 ~ ~ D
	7.	~ Ja		1 ∀D
	8.	~ Jb		1 ∀D
	9.	~ (∃y)(Hby ∨ Ryy)✓	(∃x)Jx✓	2 ⊃D
	10.		Jc	9 ∃D
	11.		~ Jc	1 ∀D
	12.	(∀y) ~ (Hby ∨ Ryy)	×	9 ~ ∃D
	13.	~ (Hba ∨ Raa)✓		12 ∀D
	14.	~ Hba		13 ~ ∨D
	15.	~ Raa		13 ~ ∨D
	16.	Hba / Raa		6 ∨D
		× / ×		

The tree is closed. Therefore the entailment does hold.

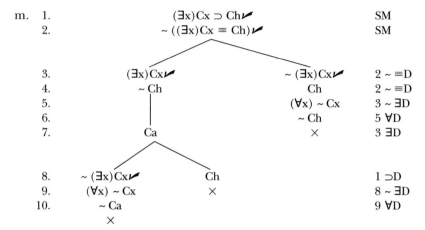

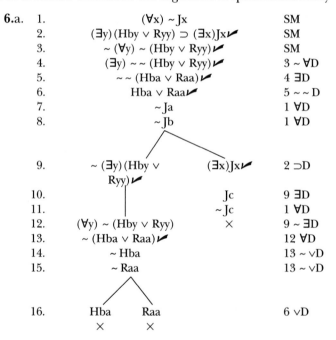

c.	1.	(∀y)((Hy & Fy) ⊃ Gy)		SM
	2.	(∀z)Fz & ~ (∀x)Kxb✓		SM
	3.	~ (∀x)(Hx ⊃ Gx)✓		SM
	4.	(∀z)Fz		2 &D
	5.	~ (∀x)Kxb✓		2 &D
	6.	(∃x) ~ (Hx ⊃ Gx)✓		3 ~ ∀D
	7.	(∃x) ~ Kxb✓		5 ~ ∀D
	8.	~ Kab		7 ∃D
	9.	~ (Hc ⊃ Gc)✓		6 ∃D
	10.	Hc		9 ~ ⊃D
	11.	~ Gc		9 ~ ⊃D
	12.	(Hc & Fc) ⊃ Gc✓		1 ∀D
	13.	~ (Hc & Fc)✓	Gc ×	12 ⊃D
	14.	~ Hc ~ Fc		13 ~ &D
	15.	× Fc ×		4 ∀D

The tree is closed. Therefore the entailment does hold.

e.	1.	(∀z)(Lz ≡ Hz)		SM
	2.	(∀x) ~ (Hx ∨ ~ Bx)		SM
	3.	~ ~ Lb✓		SM
	4.	Lb		3 ~ ~ D
	5.	Lb ≡ Hb✓		1 ∀D
	6.	Lb	~ Lb	5 ≡D
	7.	Hb	~ Hb	5 ≡D
	8.	~ (Hb ∨ ~ Bb)✓	×	2 ∀D
	9.	~ Hb		8 ~ ∨D
	10.	~ ~ Bb ×		8 ~ ∨D

The tree is closed. Therefore the entailment does hold.

Section 9.4E

1.a.	1.	(∀x)Fxx	SM
	2.	(∃x)(∃y) ~ Fxy✓	SM
	3.	(∀x)x = a	SM
	4.	(∃y) ~ Fby✓	2 ∃D
	5.	~ Fbc	4 ∃D
	6.	Faa	1 ∀D
	7.	c = a	3 ∀D
	8.	Fac	6, 7 =D
	9.	b = a	3 ∀D
	10.	Fbc ×	8, 9 =D

The tree is closed. Therefore the set is quantificationally inconsistent.

c.

1.	$(\forall x)(x = a \supset Gxb)$		SM
2.	$\sim (\exists x)Gxx$ ✓		SM
3.	$a = b$		SM
4.	$(\forall x) \sim Gxx$		2 ~ ∃D
5.	$a = a \supset Gab$ ✓		1 ∀D
6.	$\sim a = a$	Gab	5 ⊃D
7.	×	$\sim Gaa$	4 ∀D
8.		Gaa	3, 6 =D
		×	

The tree is closed. Therefore the set is quantificationally inconsistent.

e.

1.	$(\forall x)((Fx \,\&\, \sim Gx) \supset \sim x = a)$			SM
2.	$Fa \,\&\, \sim Ga$ ✓			SM
3.	Fa			2 &D
4.	$\sim Ga$			2 &D
5.	$(Fa \,\&\, \sim Ga) \supset \sim a = a$ ✓			1 ∀D
6.	$\sim (Fa \,\&\, \sim Ga)$ ✓		$\sim a = a$	5 ⊃D
			×	
7.	$\sim Fa$	$\sim\sim Ga$ ✓		6 ~ &D
8.	×	Ga		7 ~ ~ D
		×		

The tree is closed. Therefore the set is quantificationally inconsistent.

2.a.

1.	$\sim (a = b \equiv b = a)$ ✓		SM
2.	$a = b$	$\sim a = b$	1 ~ ≡D
3.	$\sim b = a$	$b = a$	1 ~ ≡D
4.	$\sim a = a$	$\sim b = b$	2, 3 =D
	×	×	

The tree is closed. Therefore 'a = b ≡ b = a' is quantificationally true.

c.

1.	$\sim ((Gab \,\&\, \sim Gba) \supset \sim a = b)$ ✓	SM
2.	$Gab \,\&\, \sim Gba$ ✓	1 ~ ⊃D
3.	$\sim\sim a = b$ ✓	1 ~ ⊃D
4.	Gab	2 &D
5.	$\sim Gba$	2 &D
6.	$a = b$	3 ~ ~ D
7.	Gaa	4, 6 =D
8.	$\sim Gaa$	5, 6 =D
	×	

The tree is closed. Therefore the sentence '(Gab & ~ Gba) ⊃ ~ a = b' is quantificationally true.

e. 1.	~ (Fa ≡ (∃x) (Fx & x = a))✓			SM
2.	Fa		~ Fa	1 ~ ≡D
3.	~ (∃x) (Fx & x = a)✓		(∃x) (Fx & x = a)✓	1 ~ ≡D
4.	(∀x) ~ (Fx & x = a)			3 ~ ∃D
5.	~ (Fa & a = a)✓			4 ∀D
6.	~ Fa	~ a = a		5 ~ &D
7.	×	×	Fb & b = a✓	3 ∃D
8.			Fb	7 &D
9.			b = a	7 &D
10.			~ Fb	2, 9 =D
			×	

The tree is closed. Therefore the sentence 'Fa ≡ (∃x) (Fx & x = a)' is quantificationally true.

g. 1.	~ ((∀x)x = a ⊃ ((∃x)Fx ⊃ (∀x)Fx))✓	SM
2.	(∀x)x = a	1 ~ ⊃D
3.	~ ((∃x)Fx ⊃ (∀x)Fx)✓	1 ~ ⊃D
4.	(∃x)Fx✓	3 ~ ⊃D
5.	~ (∀x)Fx✓	3 ~ ⊃D
6.	(∃x) ~ Fx✓	5 ~ ∀D
7.	Fb	4 ∃D
8.	~ Fc	6 ∃D
9.	c = a	2 ∀D
10.	b = a	2 ∀D
11.	c = b	9, 10 =D
12.	Fc	7, 11 =D
	×	

The tree is closed. Therefore the sentence '(∀x)x = a ⊃ ((∃x)Fx ⊃ (∀x)Fx)' is quantificationally true.

i. 1.	(∀x) (∀y) ~ x = y	SM
2.	(∀y) ~ a = y	1 ∀D
3.	~ a = a	2 ∀D
	×	

The tree is closed. Therefore the sentence '(∀x) (∀y) ~ x = y' is quantificationally false.

k.

1.	$(\exists x)(\exists y) \sim x = y$ ✓	SM
2.	$(\exists y) \sim a = y$ ✓	1 $\exists$D
3.	$\sim a = b$	2 $\exists$D

1.	$\sim (\exists x)(\exists y) \sim x = y$ ✓	SM
2.	$(\forall x) \sim (\exists y) \sim x = y$	1 $\sim \exists$D
3.	$\sim (\exists y) \sim a = y$ ✓	2 $\forall$D
4.	$(\forall y) \sim\sim a = y$	3 $\sim \exists$D
5.	$\sim\sim a = a$ ✓	4 $\forall$D
6.	$a = a$	5 $\sim\sim$D

Both trees are open. Therefore the sentence '$(\exists x)(\exists y) \sim x = y$' is quantificationally indeterminate.

m.

1.	$\sim (\forall x)(\forall y)((Fx \equiv Fy) \supset x = y)$ ✓		SM
2.	$(\exists x) \sim (\forall y)((Fx \equiv Fy) \supset x = y)$ ✓		1 $\sim \forall$D
3.	$\sim (\forall y)((Fa \equiv Fy) \supset a = y)$ ✓		2 $\exists$D
4.	$(\exists y) \sim ((Fa \equiv Fy) \supset a = y)$ ✓		3 $\sim \forall$D
5.	$\sim ((Fa \equiv Fb) \supset a = b)$ ✓		4 $\exists$D
6.	$Fa \equiv Fb$ ✓		5 $\sim \supset$D
7.	$\sim a = b$		5 $\sim \supset$D
8.	Fa	$\sim Fa$	6 $\equiv$D
9.	Fb	$\sim Fb$	6 $\equiv$D

1.	$(\forall x)(\forall y)((Fx \equiv Fy) \supset x = y)$			SM
2.	$(\forall y)((Fa \equiv Fy) \supset a = y)$			1 $\forall$D
3.	$(Fa \equiv Fa) \supset a = a$ ✓			2 $\forall$D
4.	$\sim (Fa \equiv Fa)$ ✓		$a = a$	3 $\supset$D
5.	Fa	$\sim Fa$		4 $\sim \equiv$D
6.	$\sim Fa$	Fa		4 $\sim \equiv$D
	×	×		

Both trees are open. Therefore the sentence '$(\forall x)(\forall y)(Fx \equiv Fy) \supset x = y)$' is quantificationally indeterminate.

o.	1.	~ (((∃x)Gax & ~ (∃x)Gxa) ⊃ (∀x)(Gxa ⊃ ~ x = a)) ✓	SM
	2.	(∃x)Gax & ~ (∃x)Gxa ✓	1 ~ ⊃D
	3.	~ (∀x)(Gxa ⊃ ~ x = a) ✓	1 ~ ⊃D
	4.	(∃x)Gax ✓	2 &D
	5.	~ (∃x)Gxa ✓	2 &D
	6.	(∀x) ~ Gxa	5 ~ ∃D
	7.	(∃x) ~ (Gxa ⊃ ~ x = a) ✓	3 ~ ∀D
	8.	~ (Gba ⊃ ~ b = a) ✓	7 ∃D
	9.	Gac	4 ∃D
	10.	Gba	8 ~ ⊃D
	11.	~ ~ b = a	8 ~ ⊃D
	12.	~ Gba	6 ∀D
		×	

The tree is closed. Therefore the sentence '[(∃x)Gax & ~ (∃x)Gxa] ⊃ (∀x)(Gxa ⊃ ~ x = a)' is quantificationally true.

3.a.	1.	~ (~ a = b ≡ ~ b = a) ✓		SM
	2.	~ a = b	~ ~ a = b ✓	1 ~ ≡D
	3.	~ ~ b = a ✓	~ b = a	1 ~ ≡D
	4.	b = a		3 ~ ~ D
	5.	~ b = b		2, 4 =D
	6.	×	a = b	2 ~ ~ D
	7.		~ a = a	6, 3 =D
			×	

The tree is closed. Therefore the sentences '~ a = b' and '~ b = a' are quantificationally equivalent.

c.	1.	~ ((∀x)x = a ≡ (∀x)x = b) ✓		SM
	2.	(∀x)x = a	~ (∀x)x = a ✓	1 ~ ≡D
	3.	~ (∀x)x = b ✓	(∀x)x = b	1 ~ ≡D
	4.	(∃x) ~ x = b ✓		3 ~ ∀D
	5.	~ c = b		4 ∃D
	6.	b = a		2 ∀D
	7.	c = a		2 ∀D
	8.	c = b		6, 7 =D
	9.	×	(∃x) ~ x = a ✓	2 ~ ∀D
	10.		~ c = a	9 ∃D
	11.		c = b	3 ∀D
	12.		a = b	3 ∀D
	13.		c = a	11, 12 =D
			×	

The tree is closed. Therefore the sentences '(∀x)x = a' and '(∀x)x = b' are quantificationally equivalent.

e.

1.	~((∀x)(∀y)x = y ≡ (∀x)x = a)✓		SM
2.	(∀x)(∀y)x = y	~(∀x)(∀y)x = y✓	1 ~≡D
3.	~(∀x)x = a✓	(∀x)x = a	1 ~≡D
4.	(∃x) ~ x = a✓		3 ~∀D
5.	~b = a		4 ∃D
6.	(∀y)b = y		2 ∀D
7.	b = a		6 ∀D
8.	×	(∃x) ~ (∀y)x = y✓	2 ~∀D
9.		~(∀y)b = y✓	8 ∃D
10.		(∃y) ~ b = y✓	9 ~∀D
11.		~b = c	10 ∃D
12.		b = a	3 ∀D
13.		c = a	3 ∀D
14.		b = c	12, 13 =D
		×	

The tree is closed. Therefore the sentences '(∀x)(∀y)x = y' and '(∀x)x = a' are quantificationally equivalent.

g.

1.	~((∀x)(Fx ⊃ x = a) ≡ (∀x)(Fa ⊃ x = a))✓						SM
2.	(∀x)(Fx ⊃ x = a)		~(∀x)(Fx ⊃ x = a)✓				1 ~≡D
3.	~(∀x)(Fa ⊃ x = a)✓		(∀x)(Fa ⊃ x = a)				1 ~≡D
4.	(∃x) ~ (Fa ⊃ x = a)✓						3 ~∀D
5.	~(Fa ⊃ b = a)✓						4 ∃D
6.	Fa						5 ~⊃D
7.	~b = a						5 ~⊃D
8.	Fb ⊃ b = a✓						2 ∀D
9.	~Fb	b = a					8 ⊃D
10.	Fa ⊃ a = a✓	×					2 ∀D
11.	~Fa	a = a					10 ⊃D
12.	×		(∃x) ~ (Fx ⊃ x = a)✓				2 ~∀D
13.			~(Fb ⊃ b = a)✓				12 ∃D
14.			Fb				13 ~⊃D
15.			~b = a				13 ~⊃D
16.			Fa ⊃ a = a✓				3 ∀D
17.			Fa ⊃ b = a✓				3 ∀D
18.			~Fa		a = a		16 ⊃D
19.			~Fa	b = a	~Fa	b = a	17 ⊃D
				×		×	

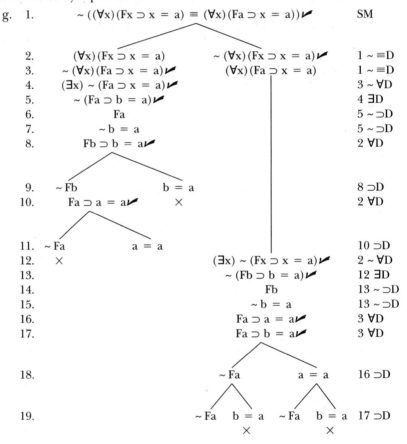

The tree is open. Therefore the sentences '(∀x)(Fx ⊃ x = a)' and '(∀x)(Fa ⊃ x = a)' are not quantificationally equivalent.

i.

1.	~(((∀x)Fx ∨ (∀x) ~Fx) ≡ (∀y)(Fy ⊃ y = b)) ✓						SM
2.	(∀x)Fx ∨ (∀x) ~Fx ✓		~((∀x)Fx ∨ (∀x) ~Fx) ✓				1 ~≡D
3.	~(∀y)(Fy ⊃ y = b) ✓		(∀y)(Fy ⊃ y = b)				1 ~≡D
4.	(∃y) ~(Fy ⊃ y = b) ✓						3 ~∀D
5.	~(Fa ⊃ a = b) ✓						4 ∃D
6.	Fa						5 ~⊃D
7.	~a = b						5 ~⊃D
8.	(∀x)Fx	(∀x) ~Fx					2 ∨D
9.	Fa	~Fa					8 ∀D
10.	Fb	×					8 ∀D
11.			~(∀x)Fx ✓				2 ~∨D
12.			~(∀x) ~Fx ✓				2 ~∨D
13.			(∃x) ~Fx ✓				11 ~∀D
14.			(∃x) ~~Fx ✓				12 ~∀D
15.			~Fa				13 ∃D
16.			~~Fc ✓				14 ∃D
17.			Fc				16 ~~D
18.			Fc ⊃ c = b ✓				3 ∀D
19.			~Fc ×	c = b			18 ⊃D
20.				Fb ⊃ b = b ✓			3 ∀D
21.				~Fb	b = b		20 ⊃D
22.				~Fc ×			19, 21 =D
23.					Fa ⊃ a = b ✓		3 ∀D
24.					~Fa	a = b	23 ⊃D
25.					b = c	b = c	19, 21 =D
26.					c = c	c = c	19, 25 =D
27.						a = c	19, 24 =D
28.						Fa ×	27, 17 =D
29.					Fb		17, 25 =D

The tree is open. Therefore the sentences '(∀x)Fx ∨ (∀x) ~Fx' and '(∀y)(Fy ⊃ y = b)' are not quantificationally equivalent.

k.

1.	$\sim((\exists x)(x = a \,\&\, x = b) \equiv a = b)$ ✓			SM
2.	$(\exists x)(x = a \,\&\, x = b)$ ✓	$\sim(\exists x)(x = a \,\&\, x = b)$ ✓		$1 \sim\equiv D$
3.	$\sim a = b$	$a = b$		$1 \sim\equiv D$
4.		$(\forall x) \sim (x = a \,\&\, x = b)$		$2 \sim\exists D$
5.		$\sim(a = a \,\&\, a = b)$ ✓		$4\ \forall D$
6.		$\sim(b = a \,\&\, b = b)$		$4\ \forall D$
7.		$\sim a = a$	$\sim a = b$	$5 \sim\&D$
8.	$c = a \,\&\, c = b$ ✓	×	×	$2\ \exists D$
9.	$c = a$			$8\ \&D$
10.	$c = b$			$8\ \&D$
11.	$\sim c = b$			$3, 9\ =D$
	×			

The tree is closed. Therefore the sentences '$(\exists x)(x = a \,\&\, x = b)$' and '$a = b$' are quantificationally equivalent.

4.a.

1.	$a = b \,\&\, \sim Bab$ ✓	SM
2.	$\sim\sim(\forall x)Bxx$ ✓	SM
3.	$(\forall x)Bxx$	$2 \sim\sim D$
4.	$a = b$	$1\ \&D$
5.	$\sim Bab$	$1\ \&D$
6.	Bbb	$3\ \forall D$
7.	Bab	$4, 6\ =D$
	×	

The tree is closed. Therefore the argument is quantificationally valid.

c.

1.	$(\forall z)(Gz \supset (\forall y)(Ky \supset Hzy))$			SM
2.	$(Ki \,\&\, Gj) \,\&\, i = j$ ✓			SM
3.	$\sim Hii$			SM
4.	$Ki \,\&\, Gj$ ✓			$2\ \&D$
5.	$i = j$			$2\ \&D$
6.	Ki			$4\ \&D$
7.	Gj			$4\ \&D$
8.	$Gj \supset (\forall y)(Ky \supset Hjy)$ ✓			$1\ \forall D$
9.	$\sim Gj$	$(\forall y)(Ky \supset Hjy)$		$8 \supset D$
10.	×	$Ki \supset Hji$ ✓		$9\ \forall D$
11.		$\sim Ki$	Hji	$10 \supset D$
12.		×	Hii	$5, 11\ =D$
			×	

The tree is closed. Therefore the argument is quantificationally valid.

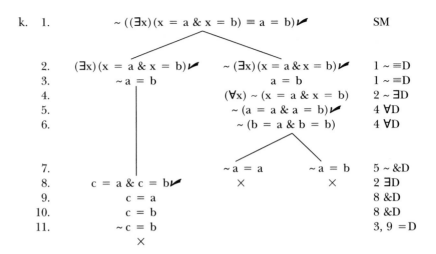

e.	1.	a = b		SM
	2.	~ (Ka ∨ ~ Kb) ✓		SM
	3.	~ Ka		2 ~ ∀D
	4.	~ ~ Kb ✓		2 ~ ∀D
	5.	Kb		4 ~ ~ D
	6.	Ka		1, 5 =D
		×		

The tree is closed. Therefore the argument is quantificationally valid.

g.	1.	(∀x) (x = a ∨ x = b)		SM
	2.	(∃x) (Fxa & Fbx) ✓		SM
	3.	~ (∃x) Fxx		SM
	4.	(∀x) ~ Fxx		3 ~ ∃D
	5.	Fca & Fbc ✓		2 ∃D
	6.	Fca		5 &D
	7.	Fbc		5 &D
	8.	c = a ∨ c = b ✓		1 ∀D
	9.			
	10.	c = a	c = b	8 ∨D
	11.	Fcc		6, 10 =D
	12.		Fcc	7, 10 =D
	13.	~ Fcc	~ Fcc	4 ∀D
		×	×	

The tree is closed. Therefore the argument is quantificationally valid.

i.	1.	(∀x) (∀y) (Fxy ∨ Fyx)		SM
	2.	a = b		SM
	3.	~ (∀x) (Fxa ∨ Fbx) ✓		SM
	4.	(∃x) ~ (Fxa ∨ Fbx) ✓		3 ~ ∀D
	5.	~ (Fca ∨ Fbc) ✓		4 ∃D
	6.	~ Fca		5 ~ ∀D
	7.	~ Fbc		5 ~ ∀D
	8.	(∀y) (Fay ∨ Fya)		1 ∀D
	9.	Fac ∨ Fca ✓		8 ∀D
	10.	Fac	Fca	9 ∀D
	11.	~ Fac	×	2, 7 =D
		×		

The tree is closed. Therefore the argument is quantificationally valid.

k.	1.	$(\forall x)(Fx \equiv \sim Gx)$		SM
	2.	Fa		SM
	3.	Gb		SM
	4.	$\sim\sim a = b$ ✓		SM
	5.	$a = b$		4 ~~D
	6.	$Fa \equiv \sim Ga$ ✓		1 ∀D
	7.	Fa	$\sim Fa$	6 ≡D
	8.	$\sim Ga$	$\sim\sim Ga$	6 ≡D
	9.	Ga	×	3, 5 =D
		×		

The tree is closed. Therefore the argument is quantificationally valid.

m.	1.	$(\forall x)(\forall y)x = y$	SM
	2.	$\sim\sim(\exists x)(\exists y)(Fx \& \sim Fy)$ ✓	SM
	3.	$(\exists x)(\exists y)(Fx \& \sim Fy)$ ✓	2 ~~D
	4.	$(\exists y)(Fa \& \sim Fy)$ ✓	3 ∃D
	5.	$Fa \& \sim Fb$ ✓	4 ∃D
	6.	Fa	5 &D
	7.	$\sim Fb$	5 &D
	8.	$(\forall y)a = y$	1 ∀D
	9.	$a = b$	8 ∀D
	10.	$\sim Fa$	7, 9 =D
		×	

The tree is closed. Therefore the argument is quantificationally valid.

5.a.	1.	$(\forall x)(Fx \supset (\exists y)(Gyx \,\&\, \sim y = x))$		SM
	2.	$(\exists x)Fx$ ✓		SM
	3.	$\sim (\exists x)(\exists y) \sim x = y$ ✓		SM
	4.	$(\forall x) \sim (\exists y) \sim x = y$		$3 \sim \exists D$
	5.	Fa		$2\ \exists D$
	6.	$Fa \supset (\exists y)(Gya \,\&\, \sim y = a)$ ✓		$1\ \forall D$
	7.	$\sim Fa$	$(\exists y)(Gya \,\&\, \sim y = a)$ ✓	$6 \supset D$
	8.	×	$Gba \,\&\, \sim b = a$ ✓	$7\ \exists D$
	9.		Gba	8 &D
	10.		$\sim b = a$	8 &D
	11.		$\sim (\exists y) \sim a = y$ ✓	$4\ \forall D$
	12.		$\sim (uQy) \sim b = y$ ✓	$4\ \forall D$
	13.		$(\forall y) \sim \sim a = y$	$11 \sim \exists D$
	14.		$(\forall y) \sim \sim b = y$	$12 \sim \exists D$
	15.		$\sim \sim a = a$ ✓	$13\ \forall D$
	16.		$\sim \sim a = b$ ✓	$13\ \forall D$
	17.		$\sim \sim b = a$ ✓	$14\ \forall D$
	18.		$\sim \sim b = b$ ✓	$14\ \forall D$
	19.		$a = a$	$15 \sim \sim D$
	20.		$a = b$	$16 \sim \sim D$
	21.		$b = a$	$17 \sim \sim D$
	22.		$b = b$	$18 \sim \sim D$
	23.		$\sim b = b$	10, 21 =D
			×	

The tree is closed. Therefore the alleged entailment does hold.

c.	1.	$(\forall x)(Fx \supset \sim x = a)$		SM
	2.	$(\exists x)Fx$ ✓		SM
	3.	$\sim (\exists x)(\exists y) \sim x = y$ ✓		SM
	4.	Fb		$2\ \exists D$
	5.	$(\forall x) \sim (\exists y) \sim x = y$		$3 \sim \exists D$
	6.	$Fb \supset \sim b = a$ ✓		$1\ \forall D$
	7.	$\sim Fb$	$\sim b = a$	$6 \supset D$
	8.	×	$\sim (\exists y) \sim a = y$ ✓	$5\ \forall D$
	9.		$(\forall y) \sim \sim a = y$	$8 \sim \exists D$
	10.		$\sim \sim a = b$ ✓	$9\ \forall D$
	11.		$a = b$	$10 \sim \sim D$
	12.		$\sim a = a$	7, 11 =D
			×	

The tree is closed. Therefore the alleged entailment does hold.

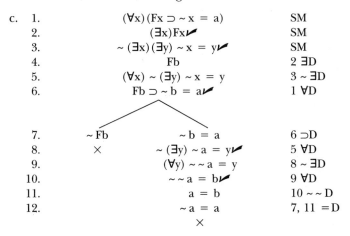

e.

1.	(∃w)(∃z) ~ w = z✓	SM
2.	(∃w)Hw✓	SM
3.	~ (∃w) ~ Hw✓	SM
4.	(∀w) ~ ~ Hw	3 ~ ∃D
5.	(∃z) ~ a = z✓	1 ∃D
6.	Hb	2 ∃D
7.	~ a = c	5 ∃D
8.	~ ~ Ha✓	4 ∀D
9.	~ ~ Hb✓	4 ∀D
10.	~ ~ Hc✓	4 ∀D
11.	Ha	8 ~ ~ D
12.	Hb	9 ~ ~ D
13.	Hc	10 ~ ~ D

The tree is open. Therefore the alleged entailment does not hold.

g.

1.	(∀x)(∀y)((Fx ≡ Fy) ≡ x = y)	SM
2.	(∃z)Fz✓	SM
3.	~ (∃x)(∃y)(~ x = y & (Fx & ~ Fy))✓	SM
4.	(∀x) ~ (∃y)(~ x = y & (Fx & ~ Fy))	3 ~ ∃D
5.	Fa	2 ∃D
6.	~ (∃y)(~ a = y & (Fa & ~ Fy))✓	4 ∀D
7.	(∀y) ~ (~ a = y & (Fa & ~ Fy))	6 ~ ∃D
8.	~ (~ a = a & (Fa & ~ Fa))✓	7 ∀D
9.	(∀y)((Fa ≡ Fy) ≡ a = y)	1 ∀D
10.	(Fa ≡ Fa) ≡ a = a✓	9 ∀D

11.	~ ~ a = a✓				~ (Fa &~ Fa)✓			8 ~ &D
12.	a = a							11 ~ ~ D
13.				~ Fa	~ ~ Fa✓			11 ~ &D
14.				×	Fa			13 ~ ~ D
15.	Fa ≡ Fa✓		~ (Fa ≡ Fa)✓		Fa ≡ Fa✓		~ (Fa ≡ Fa)✓	10 ≡D
16.	a = a		~ a = a		a = a		~ a = a	10 ≡D
17.			×				×	
18.	Fa	~ Fa			Fa	~ Fa		15 ≡D
19.	Fa	~ Fa			Fa	~ Fa		15 ≡D
20.		×				×		

The tree is open. Therefore the alleged entailment does not hold.

Section 9.5E

Note: Branches that are open but not completed are so indicated by a series of dots below the branch.

1.a.

1.	(∀x)Jx				SM
2.	(∀x)(Jx ≡ (∃y)(Gyx ∨ Ky))				SM
3.	Ja				1 ∀D
4.	Ja ≡ (∃y)(Gya ∨ Ky) ✓				2 ∀D
5.	Ja		~Ja		4 ≡D
6.	(∃y)(Gya ∨ Ky) ✓		~ ∃y)(Gya ∨ Ky)		4 ≡D
			×		
7.	Gaa ∨ Ka ✓		Gba ∨ Kb ✓		6 ∃D2
8.	Gaa	Ka	Gba	Kb	7 ∨D
			⋮	⋮	

The tree has at least one completed open branch. Therefore the set is quantificationally consistent.

c.

1.	(∃x)Fx ✓		SM
2.	(∃x) ~ Fx ✓		SM
3.	Fa		1 ∃D2
4.	~ Fa	~ Fb	2 ∃D2
	×		

The tree has a completed open branch. Therefore the set is quantificationally consistent.

e.

1.	(∃x)Fx & (∃x) ~ Fx ✓			SM
2.	(∃x)Fx ⊃ (∀x) ~ Fx ✓			SM
3.	(∃x)Fx ✓			1 &D
4.	(∃x) ~ Fx ✓			1 &D
5.	Fa			3 ∃D2
6.	~ Fa	~ Fb		4 ∃D2
	×			
7.		~ (∃x)Fx ✓	(∀x) ~ Fx	2 ⊃D
8.		(∀x) ~ Fx		7 ~ ∃D
9.		~ Fa		8 ∀D
		×	~ Fa	7 ∀D
			×	

The tree is closed. Therefore the set is quantificationally inconsistent.

g.			
1.	(∀x)(∃y)Fxy		SM
2.	(∃y)(∀x) ~ Fyx✓		SM
3.	(∀x) ~ Fax		2 ∃D2
4.	(∃y)Fay✓		1 ∀D
5.	~ Faa		3 ∀D
6.	Faa	Fab	4 ∃D2
7.	×	(∃y)Fby	1 ∀D
8.		~ Fab	3 ∀D
		×	

The tree is closed. Therefore the set is quantificationally inconsistent.

i.									
1.				(∃x)Hx✓					SM
2.				~ (∀x)Hx✓					SM
3.				(∀x)(Hx ⊃ Kx)					SM
4.				(∃x)(Kx & Hx)✓					SM
5.				(∃x) ~ Hx✓					2 ~ ∀D
6.				Ka & Ha✓					4 ∃D2
7.				Ka					6 &D
8.				Ha					6 &D
9.		Ha					Hb		1 ∃D2
10.	~ Ha		~ Hb		~ Ha	~ Hb	~ Hc		5 ∃D2
11.	×		Ha ⊃ Ka✓		×	×	Ha ⊃ Ka✓		3 ∀D
12.			Hb ⊃ Kb✓				Hb ⊃ Kb✓		3 ∀D
13.							Hc ⊃ Kc		3 ∀D
14.		~ Ha	Ka				~ Ha	Ka	11 ⊃D
		×					×		
15.			~ Hb	Kb			~ Hb	Kb	12 ⊃D
							×	⋮	

The tree has at least one completed open branch. The set is quantificationally consistent.

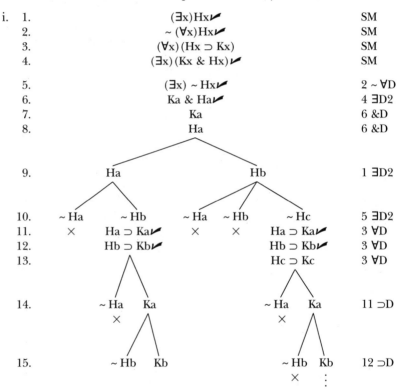

k.

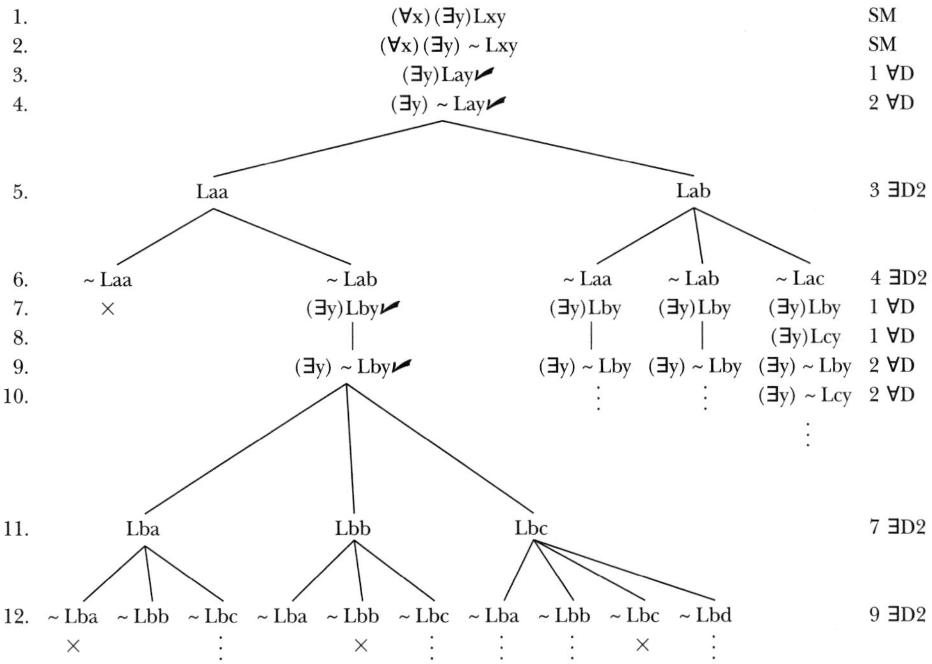

The tree has at least one completed open branch. Therefore the set is quantificationally consistent.

m.

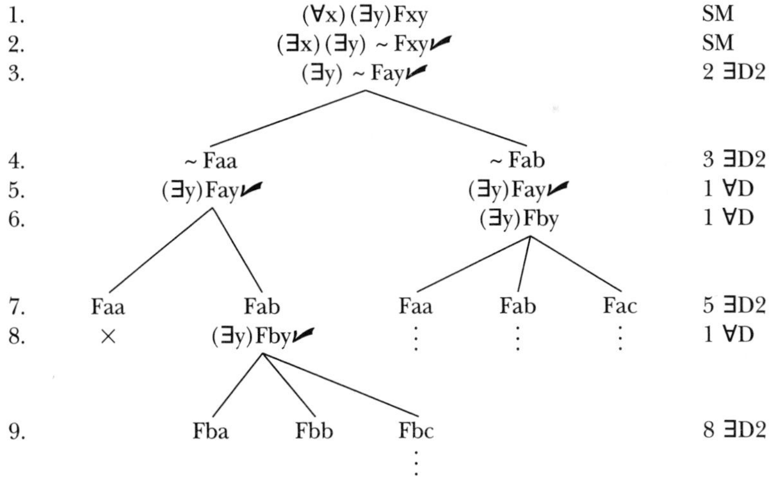

The tree has at least one completed open branch. Therefore the set is quantificationally consistent.

o.

1.	~ (∀x)(Kx ⊃ (∀y)(Ky ∨ Lxy))✓					SM
2.	(∀y)(Ky ⊃ (∀x)(Rx ⊃ Lyx))					SM
3.	(∀x)Rx					SM
4.	(∃x) ~ (Kx ⊃ (∀y)(Ky ∨ Lxy))✓					1 ~ ∀D
5.	~ (Ka ⊃ (∀y)(Ky ∨ Lay))✓					4 ∃D2
6.	Ka					5 ~ ⊃D
7.	~ (∀y)(Ky ∨ Lay)✓					5 ~ ⊃D
8.	(∃y) ~ (Ky ∨ Lay)✓					7 ~ ∀D
9.	~ (Ka ∨ Laa)✓	~ (Kb ∨ Lab)✓				8 ∃D2
10.	~ Ka	~ Kb				9 ~ ∨D
11.	~ Laa	~ Lab				9 ~ ∨D
12.	×	Ka ⊃ (∀x)(Rx ⊃ Lax)✓				2 ∀D
13.		Kb ⊃ (∀x)(Rx ⊃ Lbx)✓				2 ∀D
14.		Ra				3 ∀D
15.		Rb				3 ∀D
16.		~ Ka	(∀x)(Rx ⊃ Lax)			12 ⊃D
		×				
17.			~ Kb	(∀x)(Rx ⊃ Lbx)		13 ⊃D
18.			Ra ⊃ Laa	Ra ⊃ Laa		16 ∀D
19.			Rb ⊃ Lab✓	Rb ⊃ Lab✓		16 ∀D
20.				Ra ⊃ Lba		17 ∀D
21.				Rb ⊃ Lbb		17 ∀D
22.			~ Rb Lab	~ Rb Lab		19 ⊃D
			× ×	× ×		

The tree is closed. Therefore the set is quantificationally inconsistent.

2.a.

1.	(∀x)(Fax ⊃ (∃y)Fya)		SM
2.	Faa ⊃ (∃y)Fya✓		1 ∀D
3.	~ Faa	(∃y)Fya	2 ⊃D
		⋮	

1.	~ (∀x)(Fax ⊃ (∃y)Fya)✓		SM
2.	(∃x) ~ (Fax ⊃ (∃y)Fya)✓		1 ~ ∀D
3.	~ (Faa ⊃ (∃y)Fya)✓	~ (Fab ⊃ (∃y)Fya)✓	2 ∃D2
4.	Faa	Fab	3 ~ ⊃D
5.	~ (∃y)Fya✓	~ (∃y)Fya✓	3 ~ ⊃D
6.	(∀y) ~ Fya	(∀y) ~ Fya	5 ~ ∃D
7.	~ Faa	~ Faa	6 ∀D
8.	×	~ Fba	6 ∀D

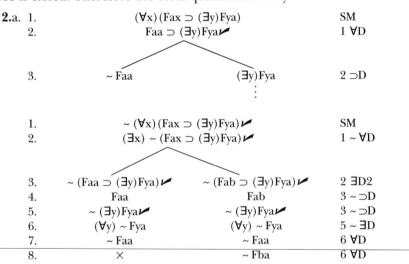

Both the tree for the sentence and the tree for its negation have at least one completed open branch. Therefore the sentence is quantificationally indeterminate.

c.

1.	$\sim (\forall x)(Fx \supset (\forall y)(Hy \supset Fy))$ ✓		SM
2.	$(\exists x) \sim (Fx \supset (\forall y)(Hy \supset Fy))$ ✓		$1 \sim \forall D$
3.	$\sim (Fa \supset (\forall y)(Hy \supset Fy))$ ✓		$2\ \exists D2$
4.	Fa		$3 \sim \supset D$
5.	$\sim (\forall y)(Hy \supset Fy)$ ✓		$3 \sim \supset D$
6.	$(\exists y) \sim (Hy \supset Fy)$ ✓		$5 \sim \forall D$
7.	$\sim (Ha \supset Fa)$ ✓	$\sim (Hb \supset Fb)$ ✓	$6\ \exists D2$
8.	Ha	Hb	$7 \sim \supset D$
9.	$\sim Fa$	$\sim Fb$	$7 \sim \supset D$
	×		

1.	$(\forall x)(Fx \supset (\forall y)(Hy \supset Fy))$		SM
2.	$Fa \supset (\forall y)(Hy \supset Fy)$ ✓		$1\ \forall D$
3.	$\sim Fa$	$(\forall y)(Hy \supset Fy)$	$2 \supset D$
		⋮	

Both the tree for the sentence and the tree for its negation have at least one completed open branch. Therefore the sentence is quantificationally indeterminate.

e.

1.	$\sim ((\exists x)(Fx \vee \sim Fx) \equiv ((\exists x)Fx \vee (\exists x) \sim Fx))$ ✓				SM
2.	$(\exists x)(Fx \vee \sim Fx)$ ✓		$\sim (\exists x)(Fx \vee \sim Fx)$ ✓		$1 \sim \equiv D$
3.	$\sim ((\exists x)Fx \vee (\exists x) \sim Fx)$ ✓		$(\exists x)Fx \vee (\exists x) \sim Fx$ ✓		$1 \sim \equiv D$
4.	$\sim (\exists x)Fx$ ✓				$3 \sim \vee D$
5.	$\sim (\exists x) \sim Fx$ ✓				$3 \sim \vee D$
6.	$(\forall x) \sim Fx$				$4 \sim \exists D$
7.	$(\forall x) \sim\sim Fx$				$5 \sim \exists D$
8.	$Fa \vee \sim Fa$ ✓				$2\ \exists D2$
9.	Fa	$\sim Fa$			
10.			$(\forall x) \sim (Fx \vee \sim Fx)$		$2 \sim \exists D$
11.			$(\exists x)Fx$ ✓	$(\exists x) \sim Fx$ ✓	$3\ \vee D$
			Fa	$\sim Fa$	$11\ \exists D2$
12.	$\sim Fa$	$\sim Fa$			$6\ \forall D$
13.	×	$\sim\sim Fa$ ✓			$7\ \forall D$
14.		Fa			$13 \sim\sim D$
15.		×	$\sim (Fa \vee \sim Fa)$ ✓	$\sim (Fa \vee \sim Fa)$ ✓	$10\ \forall D$
16.			$\sim Fa$	$\sim Fa$	$15 \sim \vee D$
17.			$\sim\sim Fa$	$\sim\sim Fa$ ✓	$15 \sim \vee D$
18.			×	Fa	$17 \sim\sim D$
				×	

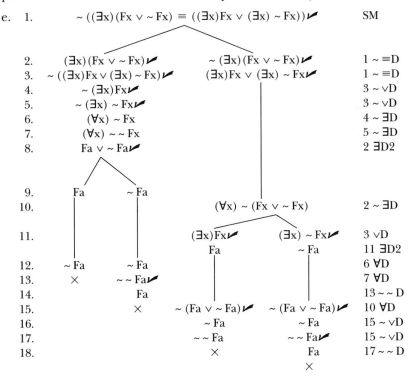

The tree for the negation of the sentence is closed. Therefore the sentence is quantificationally true.

g.

1.	~ ((∀x)(Fx ⊃ ((∃y)Gyx ⊃ H)) ⊃ (∀x)(Fx ⊃ (∃y)(Gyx ⊃ H))) ✓			SM
2.	(∀x)(Fx ⊃ ((∃y)Gyx ⊃ H))			1 ~ ⊃D
3.	~ (∀x)(Fx ⊃ (∃y)(Gyx ⊃ H)) ✓			1 ~ ⊃D
4.	(∃x) ~ (Fx ⊃ (∃y)(Gyx ⊃ H)) ✓			3 ~ ∀D
5.	~ (Fa ⊃ (∃y)(Gya ⊃ H)) ✓			4 ∃D2
6.	Fa			5 ~ ⊃D
7.	~ (∃y)(Gya ⊃ H) ✓			5 ~ ⊃D
8.	(∀y) ~ (Gya ⊃ H)			7 ~ ∃D
9.	~ (Gaa ⊃ H) ✓			8 ∀D
10.	Fa ⊃ ((∃y)Gya ⊃ H) ✓			2 ∀D
11.	Gaa			9 ~ ⊃D
12.	~ H			9 ~ ⊃D
13.	~ Fa	(∃y)Gya ⊃ H ✓		10 ⊃D
	×			
14.		~ (∃y)Gya ✓	H	13 ⊃D
15.		(∀y) ~ Gya	×	14 ~ ∃D
16.		~ Gaa		15 ∀D
		×		

The tree for the negation of the sentence is closed. Therefore the sentence is quantificationally true.

3.a.

1.	Fa									SM
2.	(∀x)(Fx ⊃ Cx)									SM
3.	~ (∀x)(Fx & Cx) ✓									SM
4.	(∃x) ~ (Fx & Cx) ✓									2 ~ ∀D
5.	~ (Fa & Ca) ✓			~ (Fb & Cb) ✓						4 ∃D2
6.	~ Fa	~ Ca		~ Fb			~ Cb			5 ~ &D
7.	×	Fa ⊃ Ca ✓		Fa ⊃ Ca ✓			Fa ⊃ Ca ✓			2 ∀D
8.				Fb ⊃ Cb ✓			Fb ⊃ Cb ✓			2 ∀D
9.		~ Fa	Ca	~ Fa	Ca		~ Fa	Ca		7 ⊃D
		×	×	×			×			
10.					~ Fb	Cb		~ Fb	Cb	8 ⊃D
									×	

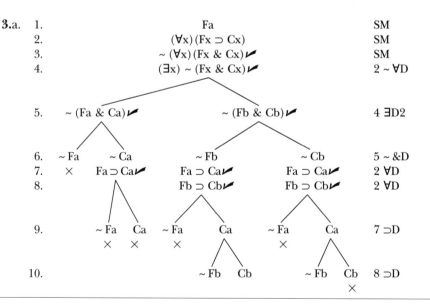

The tree for the premises and the negation of the conclusion has at least one completed open branch. Therefore the argument is quantificationally invalid.

c.

1.	Fa	SM
2.	$(\forall x)(Fx \supset Cx)$	SM
3.	$\sim (\exists x)(Fx \;\&\; Cx)$ ✓	SM
4.	$(\forall x) \sim (Fx \;\&\; Cx)$	$3 \sim \exists D$
5.	$Fa \supset Ca$ ✓	$2\ \forall D$
6.	$\sim (Fa \;\&\; Ca)$ ✓	$4\ \forall D$
7.	$\sim Fa$ × | Ca	$5 \supset D$
8.	(under Ca:) $\sim Fa$ × | $\sim Ca$ ×	$6 \sim \&D$

The tree for the premises and the negation of the conclusion is closed. Therefore the argument is quantificationally valid.

e.

1.	$(\forall x)(\forall y)(\forall z)((Lxy \;\&\; Lyz) \supset Lxz)$	SM
2.	$(\forall x)(\forall y)(Lxy \supset Lyx)$	SM
3.	$\sim (\forall x)Lxx$ ✓	SM
4.	$(\exists x) \sim Lxx$ ✓	$3 \sim \forall D$
5.	$\sim Laa$	$4\ \exists D2$
6.	$(\forall y)(\forall z)((Lay \;\&\; Lyz) \supset Laz)$	$1\ \forall D$
7.	$(\forall y)(Lay \supset Lya)$	$2\ \forall D$
8.	$(\forall z)((Laa \;\&\; Laz) \supset Laz)$	$6\ \forall D$
9.	$Laa \supset Laa$ ✓	$7\ \forall D$
10.	$(Laa \;\&\; Laa) \supset Laa$ ✓	$8\ \forall D$
11.	$\sim (Laa \;\&\; Laa)$ ✓ | Laa ×	$10 \supset D$
12.	(under $\sim (Laa \;\&\; Laa)$:) $\sim Laa$ | Laa ×	$9 \supset D$
13.	(under $\sim Laa$:) $\sim Laa$ | $\sim Laa$	$11 \sim \&D$

The tree for the premises and the negation of the conclusion has at least one completed open branch. Therefore the argument is quantificationally invalid.

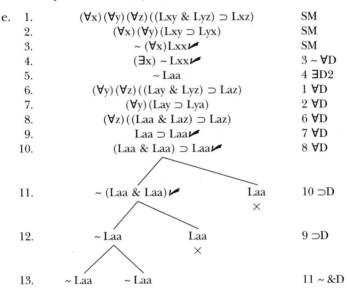

g.

1.		(∃x)((Lx ∨ Sx) ∨ Kx)✓		SM
2.		(∀y) ~ (Ly ∨ Ky)		SM
3.		~ (∃x)Sx✓		SM
4.		(La ∨ Sa) ∨ Ka✓		1 ∃D2
5.		(∀x) ~ Sx		3 ~ ∃D
6.	La ∨ Sa✓		Ka	4 ∨D
7.	La	Sa		6 ∨D
8.	~ (La ∨ Ka)✓	~ (La ∨ Ka)	~ (La ∨ Ka)✓	2 ∀D
9.	~ Sa	~ Sa	~ Sa	5 ∀D
10.	~ La	×	~ La	8 ~ ∨D
11.	~ Ka		~ Ka	8 ~ ∨D
	×		×	

The tree for the premises and the negation of the conclusion is closed. Therefore the argument is quantificationally valid.

i.

1.			(∀x)(Hx ⊃ Kcx)			SM
2.			(∀x)(Lx ⊃ ~ Kcx)			SM
3.			Ld			SM
4.			~ (∃y) ~ Hy✓			SM
5.			(∀y) ~ ~ Hy			4 ~ ∃D
6.			Hc ⊃ Kcc✓			1 ∀D
7.			Hd ⊃ Kcd✓			1 ∀D
8.			Lc ⊃ ~ Kcc✓			2 ∀D
9.			Ld ⊃ ~ Kcd✓			2 ∀D
10.			~ ~ Hc✓			5 ∀D
11.			~ ~ Hd✓			5 ∀D
12.			Hc			10 ~ ~ D
13.			Hd			11 ~ ~ D
14.	~ Hc		Kcc			6 ⊃D
	×					
15.		~ Hd	Kcd			7 ⊃D
		×				
16.			~ Lc		~ Kcc	8 ⊃D
					×	
17.			~ Ld	~ Kcd		9 ⊃D
			×	×		

The tree for the premises and the negation of the conclusion is closed. Therefore the argument is quantificationally valid.

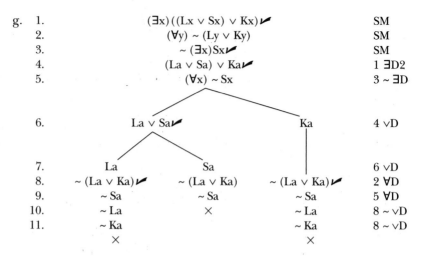

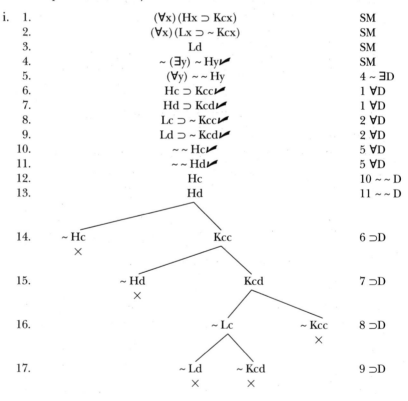

4.a.

1.	~ ((∀x) (∀y) ~ Sxy ≡ ~ (∃x) (∃y) Sxy) ✓				SM
2.	(∀x) (∀y) ~ Sxy		~ (∀x) (∀y) ~ Sxy ✓		1 ~ ≡D
3.	~ ~ (∃x) (∃y) Sxy ✓		~ (∃x) (∃y) Sxy ✓		1 ~ ≡D
4.	(∃x) (∃y) Sxy ✓				3 ~ ~ D
5.	(∃y) Say ✓				4 ∃D2
6.	Saa	Sab			5 ∃D2
7.			(∃x) ~ (∀y) ~ Sxy ✓		2 ~ ∀D
8.			(∀x) ~ (∃y) Sxy		3 ~ ∃D
9.			~ (∀y) ~ Say ✓		7 ∃D2
10.			(∃y) ~ ~ Say ✓		9 ~ ∀D
11.			~ ~ Saa ✓	~ ~ Sab ✓	10 ∃D2
12.			Saa	Sab	11 ~ ~ D
13.			~ (∃y) Say ✓	~ (∃y) Say ✓	8 ∀D
14.				~ (∃y) Sby ✓	8 ∀D
15.	(∀y) ~ Say	(∀y) ~ Say			2 ∀D
16.		(∀y) ~ Sby			2 ∀D
17.	~ Saa	~ Sab			15 ∀D
18.	×	×	(∀y) ~ Say	(∀y) ~ Say	13 ~ ∃D
19.				(∀y) ~ Sby	14 ~ ∃D
20.			~ Saa	~ Sab	18 ∀D
			×	×	

The tree for the negation of the corresponding biconditional is closed. Therefore the sentences are equivalent.

c.

1.	~ ((∃x) (∀x ⊃ B) ≡ ((∀x) Ax ⊃ B)) ✓				SM
2.	(∃x) (Ax ⊃ B) ✓		~ (∃x) (Ax ⊃ B) ✓		1 ~ ≡D
3.	~ ((∀x) Ax ⊃ B) ✓		(∀x) Ax ⊃ B ✓		1 ~ ≡D
4.	(∀x) Ax				3 ~ ⊃D
5.	~ B				3 ~ ⊃D
6.	Aa ⊃ B ✓				2 ∃D2
7.	~ Aa	B			6 ⊃D
8.		×	(∀x) ~ (Ax ⊃ B)		2 ~ ∃D
9.			~ (∀x) Ax ✓	B	3 ⊃D
10.			(∃x) ~ Ax ✓		9 ~ ∀D
11.			~ Aa		10 ∃D2
12.	Aa				4 ∀D
13.	×		~ (Aa ⊃ B) ✓	~ (Aa ⊃ B) ✓	8 ∀D
14.			Aa	Aa	13 ~ ⊃D
15.			~ B	~ B	13 ~ ⊃D
			×	×	

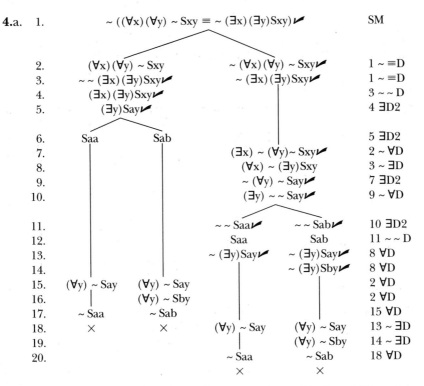

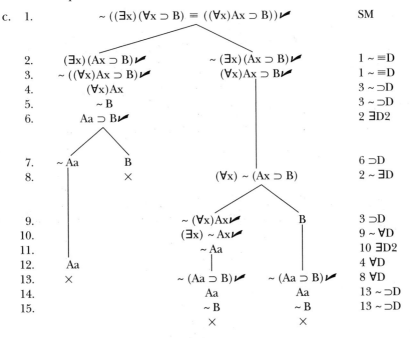

The tree for the negation of the corresponding biconditional is closed. Therefore the sentences are equivalent.

e.

Line	Left branch		Right branch		Justification
1.	~ ((∀x)(Ax ⊃ B) ≡ ((∃x)Ax ⊃ B)) ✓				SM
2.	(∀x)(Ax ⊃ B)		~ (∀x)(Ax ⊃ B) ✓		1 ~ ≡D
3.	~ ((∃x)Ax ⊃ B) ✓		(∃x)Ax ⊃ B ✓		1 ~ ≡D
4.	(∃x)Ax ✓				3 ~ ⊃D
5.	~ B				3 ~ ⊃D
6.	Aa				4 ∃D2
7.			(∃x) ~ (Ax ⊃ B) ✓		2 ~ ∀D
8.			~ (Aa ⊃ B) ✓		7 ∃D2
9.			Aa		8 ~ ⊃D
10.			~ B		8 ~ ⊃D
11.			~ (∃x)Ax ✓	B	3 ⊃D
12.			(∀x) ~ Ax	×	11 ~ ∃D
13.			~ Aa		12 ∀D
14.	Aa ⊃ B ✓		×		2 ∀D
15.	~ Aa	B			14 ⊃D
	×	×			

The tree for the negation of the corresponding biconditional is closed. Therefore the sentences are equivalent.

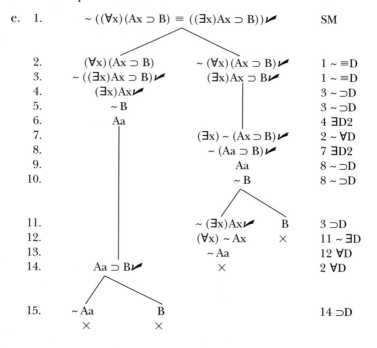

g.

1.	~((∃x)(∃y)Hxy ≡ (∃y)(∃x)Hxy) ✓				SM
2.	(∃x)(∃y)Hxy ✓		~(∃x)(∃y)Hxy ✓		1 ~≡D
3.	~(∃y)(∃x)Hxy ✓		(∃y)(∃x)Hxy ✓		1 ~≡D
4.	(∃y)Hay ✓				2 ∃D2
5.	(∀y) ~(∃x)Hxy				3 ~∃D
6.			(∃x)Hxa ✓		3 ∃D2
7.	Haa	Hab			4 ∃D2
8.			(∀x) ~(∃y)Hxy		2 ~∃D
9.			Haa	Hba	6 ∃D2
10.	~(∃x)Hxa ✓	~(∃x)Hxa ✓			5 ∀D
11.		~(∃x)Hxb ✓			5 ∀D
12.			~(∃y)Hay ✓	~(∃y)Hay ✓	8 ∀D
13.				~(∃y)Hby ✓	8 ∀D
14.	(∀x) ~Hxa	(∀x) ~Hxa			10 ~∃D
15.		(∀x) ~Hxb			11 ~∃D
16.			(∀y) ~Hay	(∀y) ~Hay	12 ~∃D
17.				(∀y) ~Hby	13 ~∃D
18.	~Haa	~Haa			14 ∀D
19.	×	~Hab			15 ∀D
20.		×	~Haa		16 ∀D
21.			×	~Hba	17 ∀D
				×	

The tree for the negation of the corresponding biconditional is closed. Therefore the sentences are equivalent.

5.a.

1.	(∀x)(Fax ⊃ Fxa)			SM
2.	~(Fab ∨ Fba) ✓			SM
3.	~Fab			2 ~∨D
4.	~Fba			2 ~∨D
5.	Faa ⊃ Faa ✓			1 ∀D
6.	Fab ⊃ Fba ✓			1 ∀D
7.	~Fab		Fba	6 ⊃D
			×	
8.	~Faa	Faa		5 ⊃D

The tree has at least one completed open branch. Therefore the given set does not quantificationally entail the given sentence.

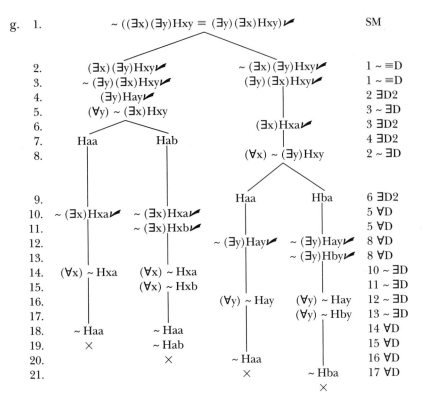

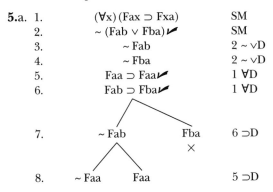

c. 1.		~ Fa			SM
2.		(∀x) (Fa ⊃ (∃y) Gxy)			SM
3.		~ ~ (∃y) Gay✓			SM
4.		(∃y) Gay✓			3 ~ ~ D
5.	Gaa		Gab		4 ∃D2
6.	Fa ⊃ (∃y) Gay✓		Fa ⊃ (∃y) Gay✓		2 ∀D
7.			Fa ⊃ (∃y) Gby✓		2 ∀D
			⋮		
8.	~ Fa	(∃y) Gay			6 ⊃D
		⋮			

The tree has at least one completed open branch. Therefore the given set does not quantificationally entail the given sentence.

e. 1.			(∃x) Gx✓			SM
2.			(∀x) (Gx ⊃ Dxx)			SM
3.			~ (∃x) (Gx & (∀y) Dxy)✓			SM
4.			(∀x) ~ (Gx & (∀y) Dxy)			3 ~ ∃D
5.			Ga			1 ∃D2
6.			Ga ⊃ Daa✓			2 ∀D
7.			~ (Ga & (∀y) Day)✓			4 ∀D
8.	~ Ga ×|		~ (∀y) Day✓			7 ~ &D
9.		~ Ga ×		Daa		6 ⊃D
10.				(∃y) ~ Day✓		8 ~ ∀D
11.	~ Daa ×			~ Dab		10 ∃D2
12.				Gb ⊃ Dbb✓		2 ∀D
13.				~ (Gb & (∀y) Dby)✓		4 ∀D
14.		~ Gb		~ (∀y) Dby		13 ~ &D
15.		~ Gb	Dbb	~ Gb	Dbb	12 ⊃D
				⋮	⋮	

The tree has at least one completed open branch. Therefore the given set does not quantificationally entail the given sentence.

7. If a tree is closed, then on each branch of that tree there is some atomic sentence 𝒫 and its negation, ~ 𝒫. One of these sentences occurs subsequent to

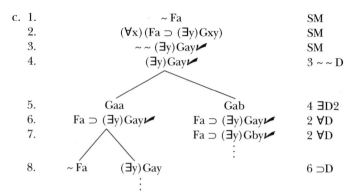

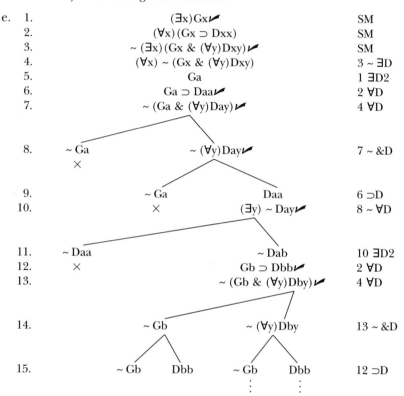

the other on the branch in question. Let $\mathcal{Q}$ be the latter of the two sentences and let n be the number of the line on which $\mathcal{Q}$ occurs. Then n is either the last line of the branch or the second to the last line of the branch. The reason is that once both an atomic sentence and its negation have been added to a branch, that branch is closed and no further sentences can be added to the branch after the current decomposition has been completed. (Some decomposition rules do add two sentences to each branch passing through the sentence being decomposed.) Hence such a branch is finite—for no infinite branch can have a last member.

9. No. For example, consider the sentence '(∃x) (Fx & ~ Fb)' and its substitution instance 'Fb & ~ Fb'. Clearly, every tree for the unit set of the latter sentence closes, but the systematic tree for the unit set of '(∃x) (Fx & ~ Fb)' does not close. Rather it has at least one completed open branch:

1.	(∃x) (Fx & ~ Fb) ✓		SM
2.	Fb & ~ Fb ✓	Fa & ~ Fb ✓	1 ∃D2
3.	Fb	Fa	2 &D
4.	~ Fb	~ Fb	2 &D
	×		

11. Since it has already been specified that stage 1 is done before stage 2 and stage 2 before stage 3, we would have to specify the order in which work within each stage is to be done, and what constants are to be used in what order.

CHAPTER TEN

Section 10.1.1E

a. Derive: Fa & Fb

1	(∀x)Fx	Assumption
2	Fa	1 ∀E
3	Fb	1 ∀E
4	Fa & Fb	2, 3 &I

c. Derive: ~ Qe

1	(∀z)Mz	Assumption
2	(∀z) ~ Mz	Assumption
3	Qe	Assumption
4	Ma	1 ∀E
5	~ Ma	2 ∀E
6	~ Qe	3–5 ~ I

Section 10.1.2E

a. Derive: (∃x) (Ax & Jx)

1	Jc	Assumption
2	Ac	Assumption
3	Ac & Jc	1, 2 &I
4	(∃x) (Ax & Jx)	3 ∃I

c. Derive: (∃y) (∃z) Cyz

1	(∀w) (∀z) Cwz	Assumption
2	(∀z) Ckz	1 ∀E
3	Ckr	2 ∀E
4	(∃z) Ckz	3 ∃I
5	(∃y) (∃z) Cyz	4 ∃I

Section 10.1.3E

a. Derive: (∀y) Hy

1	(∀x) Hx	Assumption
2	Ha	1 ∀E
3	(∀y) Hy	2 ∀I

c. Derive: (∀x) (Ex ⊃ Kx)

1	(∀x) (Ex ⊃ Sx)	Assumption
2	(∀x) (Sx ⊃ Kx)	Assumption
3	Es	Assumption
4	Es ⊃ Ss	1 ∀E
5	Ss	3, 4 ⊃E
6	Ss ⊃ Ks	2 ∀E
7	Ks	5, 6 ⊃E
8	Es ⊃ Ks	3–7 ⊃I
9	(∀x) (Ex ⊃ Kx)	8 ∀I

Section 10.1.4E

1.a. Derive: (∃y)(Zy ∨ Hy)

1	(∃x)Zx	Assumption
2	Za	Assumption
3	Za ∨ Ha	2 ∨I
4	(∃y)(Zy ∨ Hy)	3 ∃I
5	(∃y)(Zy ∨ Hy)	1, 2–4 ∃E

c. Derive: (∀x)(∃y)Bxy

1	(∃y)(∀y)Bxy	Assumption
2	(∀x)Bxf	Assumption
3	Bhf	2 ∀E
4	(∃y)Bhy	3 ∃I
5	(∀x)(∃y)Bxy	4 ∀I
6	(∀x)(∃y)Bxy	1, 2–5 ∃E

2.a. This sentence can be derived by ∀E applied to the sentence on line 1.

c. This sentence cannot be derived. Note that 'Saaab' is not a substitution instance of '(∀x)Saaxx'. Either 'a' can replace the free variable in the open sentence 'Saaxx', or 'b' can replace it, but they cannot both replace it in forming a substitution instance.

e. This sentence can be derived by ∃I applied to the sentence on line 2.

g. This sentence can be derived by ∃I applied to the sentence on line 2. Note that 'Saabb' is a substitution instance of '(∃w)Swwbb'.

i. This sentence cannot be derived. Note that ∀I cannot be used to derive this sentence, for 'a' occurs in an undischarged assumption on line 1, which violates the first restriction on using ∀I.

k. This sentence cannot be derived. Note that 'Saabb' is *not* a substitution instance of '(∀x)Saxxb'.

Section 10.2E

1.a. Derive: (Mk & Gh) & Md

1	(∀x)(Mx & Gx)	Assumption
2	Mk & Gk	1 ∀E
3	Mk	2 &E
4	Mh & Gh	1 ∀E
5	Gh	4 &E
6	Mk & Gh	3, 5 &I
7	Md & Gd	1 ∀E
8	Md	7 &E
9	(Mk & Gh) & Md	6, 8 &I

c. Derive: (∃x)(~ Bxx ⊃ (∀z)Msz)

1	Bnn ∨ (Kn & Lj)	Assumption
2	~ (∀z)Msz ⊃ ~ Kn	Assumption
3	~ Bnn	Assumption
4	Bnn	Assumption
5	~ Kn	Assumption
6	Bnn	4 R
7	~ Bnn	3 R
8	Kn	5–7 ~ E
9	Kn & Lj	Assumption
10	Kn	9 &E
11	Kn	1, 4–8, 9–10 ∨E
12	~ (∀z)Msz	Assumption
13	~ Kn	2, 12 ⊃E
14	Kn	11 R
15	(∀z)Msz	12–14 ~ E
16	~ Bnn ⊃ (∀z)Msz	3–15 ⊃I
17	(∃x)(~ Bxx ⊃ (∀z)Msz)	16 ∃I

e. Derive: ((∀x)Hxg ∨ Rg) ∨ Lg

1	(∀z)[(Rz ∨ (∀x)Hxz) ≡ Kzzz]	Assumption
2	Kggg	Assumption
3	(Rg ∨ (∀x)Hxg) ≡ Kggg	1 ∀E
4	Rg ∨ (∀x)Hxg	2, 3 ≡E
5	Rg	Assumption
6	(∀x)Hxg ∨ Rg	5 ∨I
7	(∀x)Hxg	Assumption
8	(∀x)Hxg ∨ Rg	7 ∨I
9	(∀x)Hxg ∨ Rg	4, 5–6, 7–8 ∨E
10	((∀x)Hxg Rg) ∨ Lg	9 ∨I

g. Derive: (∀w)(∃z) ~ (Hz & Rzw)

1	(∀z)[Hz ⊃ (Rzz ⊃ Gz)]	Assumption
2	(∀z)(Gz ⊃ Bz) & (∀z) ~ Bz	Assumption
3	Ha ⊃ (Raa ⊃ Ga)	1 ∀E
4	(∀z)(Gz ⊃ Bz)	2 &E
5	Ga ⊃ Ba	4 ∀E
6	(∀z) ~ Bz	2 &E
7	Ha & Raa	Assumption
8	Ha	7 &E
9	Raa ⊃ Ga	8, 3 ⊃E
10	Raa	7 &E
11	Ga	9, 10 ⊃E
12	Ba	5, 11 ⊃E
13	~ Ba	6 ∀E
14	~ (Ha & Raa)	7–13 ~ I
15	(∃z) ~ (Hz & Rza)	14 ∃I
16	(∀w)(∃z) ~ (Hz & Rzw)	15 ∀I

i. Derive: Sc

1	(∃x)Px ⊃ Sc	Assumption
2	(∃x)[Txx & (∃y)(Py & ~ Jy)]	Assumption
3	Taa & (∃y)(Py & ~ Jy)	Assumption
4	(∃y)(Py & ~ Jy)	3 &E
5	Pb & ~ Jb	Assumption
6	Pb	5 &E
7	(∃x)Px	6 ∃I
8	Sc	1, 7 ⊃E
9	Sc	4, 5–8 ∃E
10	Sc	2, 3–9 ∃E

2.a. Derive ~ Na

1	(∀x)Hx ⊃ ~ (∃y)Ky	Assumption
2	Ha ⊃ Na	Assumption
3	Ha	1 ∀E ⟵ ERROR!
4	Na	2, 3 ⊃E

'Ha' cannot be derived from the sentence on line 1 which is a conditional sentence. The rule Universal Elimination can be used only on universally quantified sentences.

c. Derive (∃x)Zx

1	(∃x)Qx	Assumption
2	(∀x)(Zx ≡ Qx)	Assumption
3	Zd ≡ Qd	2 ∀E
4	Qd	1 ∃E ⟵ ERROR!
5	Zd	3, 4 ≡E
6	(∃x)Zx	5 ∃I

This is a tempting move but not a use of the rule Existential Elimination which requires the use of a subderivation. Here is a oorrect derivation:

1	(∃x)Qx	Assumption
2	(∀x)(Zx ≡ Qx)	Assumption
3	Zd ≡ Qd	2 ∀E
4	Qd	Assumption
5		
6	Zd	3, 4 ≡E
7	(∃x)Zx	5 ∃I
8	(∃x)Zx	1, 4–6 ∃E

e. Derive: (∀x)(Jx & Gc) ∨ Lc

1	(∀x)(∀y)(Jx & Gy)	Assumption
2	(∀x)(Jx & Gc)	1 ∀E ⟵ ERROR!
3	(∀x)(Jx & Gc) ∨ Lc	2 ∨I

This is not a substitution instance of the sentence on line 1. To generate a proper substitution instance the leading quantifier must be dropped (not a quantifier located internally) and the free variable(s) replaced with the same constant. Here is a correct derivation:

1	(∀x)(∀y)(Jx & Gy)	Assumption
2	(∀y)(Jb & Gy)	1 ∀E
3	Jb & Gc	2 ∀E
4	(∀x)(Jx & Gc)	3 ∀I
5	(∀x)(Jx & Gc) ∨ Lc	4 ∨I

Notice that the leading quantifier in line 1, '(∀x)', has been dropped in forming the substitution instance on line 2.

g. Derive: (∃x)(∃z)Azx

1	(∃w)(∃y)Awy	Assumption
2	(∃y)Aky	Assumption
3	Aka	Assumption
4	(∃z)Aza	3 ∃I
5	(∃z)Aza	2, 3–4 ∃E ⟵ ERROR!
6	(∃x)(∃z)Azx	5 ∃I
7	(∃x)(∃z)Azx	1, 2–6 ∃E

The application of Existential Elimination on line 5 is a mistake because the instantiating constant 'a' occurring on line 3 occurs in the last sentence in the subderivation on line 4. This violates the third condition on the rule Existential Elimination.

Here is a correct version of the derivation:

1	(∃w)(∃y)Awy	Assumption
2	(∃y)Aky	Assumption
3	Aka	Assumption
4	(∃z)Aza	3 ∃I
5	(∃x)(∃z)Azx	4 ∃I
6	(∃x)(∃z)Azx	2, 3–5 ∃E
7	(∃x)(∃z)Azx	1, 2–6 ∃E

Section 10.4E

1. Goal analysis

Part (i)

a. Derive: (∀x)Ax ≡ (∀x)(Ax & Ax)

	1	(∀x)Ax	Assumption
Subgoal ⟶		(∀x)(Ax & Ax)	
		(∀x)(Ax & Ax)	Assumption
Subgoal ⟶		(∀x)Ax	
Goal ⟶		(∀x)Ax ≡ (∀x)(Ax & Ax)	1–_, _–_ ≡I

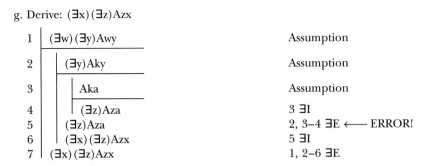

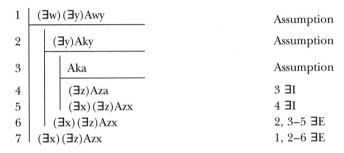

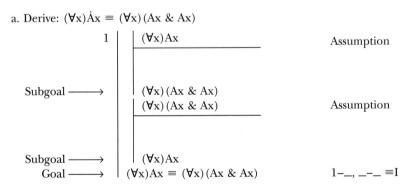

c. Derive: (∀x)(Fx ⊃ Hx)

	1	(∀x)(Fx ⊃ Gx)	Assumption
	2	(∀x)(Gx ⊃ Hx)	Assumption
Subgoal ⟶		Fa ⊃ Ha	
Goal ⟶		(∀x)(Fx ⊃ Hx)	_ ∀I

Notice that unlike exercise (b) the goal sentence is a quantified conditional sentence not a conditional sentence. Thus the appropriate subgoal is a substitution instance of the goal sentence to be derived on the last line.

e. Derive: (∀x)(Hx ∨ ~ Sx)

	1	(∀x) ~ Kx	Assumption
	2	(∀x)(~ Kx ⊃ ~ Sx)	Assumption
Subgoal ⟶		~ Ka ⊃ ~ Sa	
Goal ⟶		~ Sa	
		Ha ∨ ~ Sa	_ ∨I
		(∀x)(Hx ∨ ~ Sx)	_ ∀I

'~ Sa' is the current goal sentence. At this point a glance at the assumptions shows that '~ Sx' is a subformula of the second assumption which suggests that a substitution instance of the second assumption might be a good subgoal.

g. Derive: (∃x) ~ Cx

	1	(∃x) ~ (Cx ∨ ~ Rx)	Assumption
	2	~ (Ca ∨ ~ Ra)	Assumption
Subgoal ⟶		(∃x) ~ Cx	
Goal ⟶		(∃x) ~ Cx	1, 2–_ ∃E

Given that the goal sentence must come from an existentially quantified primary assumption, it is advisable to set up a subderivation for the application of the rule Existential Elimination and then take the goal sentence as the new subgoal within the scope of the subderivation.

i. Derive: (∃x)(∃y)(~ Kx & ~ Oy)

```
                 1 | (∃x)(Mx & ~ Kx)                    Assumption
                 2 | (∃y)(~ Oy & Wy)                    Assumption
                   |--------------------------
                 3 |  | Mj & ~ Kj                       Assumption
                   |  |-----------------------
                 4 |  |  | ~ Oc & Wc                    Assumption
                   |  |  |--------------------
                   |  |  |
                   |  |  |
Subgoal ———→       |  |  | (∃x)(∃y)(~ Kx & ~Oy)
Goal ———→          |  | (∃x)(∃y)(~ Kx & ~ Oy)           2, 4–_ ∃E
                   | (∃x)(∃y)(~ Kx & ~ Oy)              1, 3–_ ∃E
```

The goal sentence contains the subformula '~ Oy' which very likely can be derived using the assumption on line 2 which also contains the same subformula. Therefore, setting up another subderivation within the first allows for the use of the rule Existential Elimination. Notice that the assumption on line 4 is a substitution instance of the sentence on line 2 and that the instantiating constant is different from the one used on line 3.

k. Derive: (∀x)(Fx ⊃ (∃y)(Gxy ∨ ~ Hxy))

```
                 1 | (∀x)(Fx ⊃ (∃y)Gxy)                 Assumption
                   |--------------------------
                 2 |  | Fa                              Assumption
                   |  |-----------------------
                   |  |
                   |  |  | Gab                          Assumption
                   |  |  |--------------------
                   |  |  |
Subgoal ———→       |  |  | (∃y)(Gay ∨ ~ Hay)
Goal ———→          |  | (∃y)(Gay ∨ ~ Hay)               _, _–_ ∃E
                   | Fa ⊃ (∃y)(Gay ∨ ~ Hay)             2–_ ⊃I
                   | (∀x)(Fx ⊃ (∃y)(Gxy ∨ ~ Hxy))       _ ∀I
```

This may be difficult to see at first because the key subformula is '(∃y)Gxy' and is buried within the assumption on line 1. Eventually this subformula must be derived to support the use of Existential Elimination. We know this subformula is crucial because it contains the predicate 'G' which is found in the goal sentence. Another way to approach the problem is to derive 'Fa ⊃ (∃y)Gay' and then derive '(∃y)Gay' which suggests the use of Existential Elimination and the next subgoal.

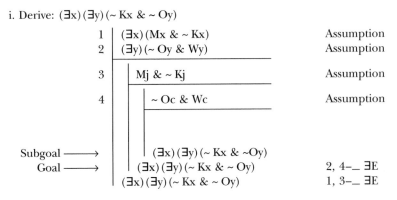

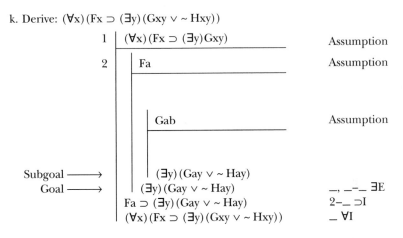

	1	(∀x)(Fx ⊃ (∃y)Gxy)	Assumption
	2	│ Fa	Assumption
	3	│ Fa ⊃ (∃y)Gay	1 ∀E
	4	│ (∃y)Gay	2, 3 ⊃E
	5	│ │ Gab	Assumption
Subgoal ⟶		│ │ (∃y)(Gay ∨ ~ Hay)	
Goal ⟶		│ (∃y)(Gay ∨ ~ Hay)	4, 5–_ ∃E
		Fa ⊃ (∃y)(Gay ∨ ~ Hay)	2–_ ⊃I
		(∀x)(Fx ⊃ (∃y)(Gxy ∨ ~ Hxy))	_ ∀I

Part (ii)

a. Derive: (∀x) Ax ≡ (∀x)(Ax & Ax)

1	│ (∀x)Ax	Assumption
2	│ Ab	1 ∀E
3	│ Ab & Ab	2, 2 &I
4	│ (∀x)(Ax & Ax)	3 ∀I
5	│ (∀x)(Ax & Ax)	Assumption
6	│ Ab & Ab	5 ∀E
7	│ Ab	6 &E
8	│ (∀x)Ax	7 ∀I
9	(∀x)Ax ≡ (∀x)(Ax & Ax)	1–4, 5–8 ≡I

c. Derive: (∀x)(Fx ⊃ Hx)

1	(∀x)(Fx ⊃ Gx)	Assumption
2	(∀x)(Gx ⊃ Hx)	Assumption
3	│ Fa	Assumption
4	│ Fa ⊃ Ga	1 ∀E
5	│ Ga	3, 4 ⊃E
6	│ Ga ⊃ Ha	2 ∀E
7	│ Ha	5, 6 ⊃E
8	Fa ⊃ Ha	3–7 ⊃I
9	(∀x)(Fx ⊃ Hx)	8 ∀I

e. Derive: (∀x)(Hx ∨ ~ Sx)

1	(∀x) ~ Kx	Assumption
2	(∀x)(~ Kx ⊃ ~ Sx)	Assumption
3	~ Ka	1 ∀E
4	~ Ka ⊃ ~ Sa	2 ∀E
5	~ Sa	3, 4 ⊃E
6	Ha ∨ ~ Sa	5 ∨I
7	(∀x)(Hx ∨ ~ Sx)	6 ∀I

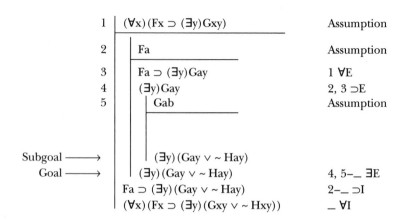

g. Derive: (∃x) ~ Cx

1	(∃x) ~ (Cx ∨ ~ Rx)	Assumption
2	~ (Ca ∨ ~ Ra)	Assumption
3	Ca	Assumption
4	Ca ∨ ~ Ra	3 ∨I
5	~ (Ca ∨ ~ Ra)	2 R
6	~ Ca	3–5 ~ I
7	(∃x) ~ Cx	6 ∃I
8	(∃x) ~ Cx	1, 2–7 ∃E

i. Derive: (∃x) (∃y) (~ Kx & ~ Oy)

1	(∃x) (Mx & ~ Kx)	Assumption
2	(∃y) (~ Oy & Wy)	Assumption
3	Mj & ~ Kj	Assumption
4	~ Oc & Wc	Assumption
5	~ Kj	3 &E
6	~ Oc	4 &E
7	~ Kj & ~ Oc	5, 6 &I
8	(∃y) (~ Kj & ~ Oy)	7 ∃I
9	(∃x) (∃y) (~ Kx & ~ Oy)	8 ∃I
10	(∃x) (∃y) (~ Kx & ~ Oy)	2, 4–9 ∃E
11	(∃x) (∃y) (~ Kx & ~ Oy)	1, 3–10 ∃E

k. Derive: (∀x) (Fx ⊃ (∃y) (Gxy ∨ ~ Hxy))

1	(∀x) (Fx ⊃ (∃y) Gxy)	Assumption
2	Fa	Assumption
3	Fa ⊃ (∃y) Gay	1 ∀E
4	(∃y) Gay	2, 3 ⊃E
5	Gab	Assumption
6	Gab ∨ ~ Hab	5 ∨I
7	(∃y) (Gay ∨ ~ Hay)	6 ∃I
8	(∃y) (Gay ∨ ~ Hay)	4, 5–7 ∃E
9	Fa ⊃ (∃y) (Gay ∨ ~ Hay)	2–8 ⊃I
10	(∀x) (Fx ⊃ (∃y) (Gxy ∨ ~ Hxy))	9 ∀I

2. Derivability

a. Derive: (∀z) Kzz

1	(∀x) Kxx	Assumption
2	Kcc	1 ∀E
3	(∀z) Kzz	2 ∀I

c. Derive: (∃y)Hy

1	(∀z)(Gz ⊃ Hz)	Assumption
2	Gi	Assumption
3	Gi ⊃ Hi	1 ∀E
4	Hi	2, 3 ⊃E
5	(∃y)Hy	4 ∃I

e. Derive: (∃x)(∃y)(∃z)Bxyz

1	(∃y)Byyy	Assumption
2	Bjjj	Assumption
3	(∃z)Bjjz	2 ∃I
4	(∃y)(∃z)Bjyz	3 ∃I
5	(∃x)(∃y)(∃z)Bxyz	4 ∃I
6	(∃x)(∃y)(∃z)Bxyz	1, 2–5 ∃E

3. Validity

a. Derive: (Caa & Cab) & (Cba & Cbb)

1	(∀x)(∀y)Cxy	Assumption
2	(∀y)Cay	1 ∀E
3	Caa	2 ∀E
4	Cab	2 ∀E
5	Caa & Cab	3, 4 &I
6	(∀y)Cby	1 ∀E
7	Cba	6 ∀E
8	Cbb	6 ∀E
9	Cba & Cbb	7, 8 &I
10	(Caa & Cab) & (Cba & Cbb)	5, 9 &I

c. Derive: (∀x)(Hx ⊃ Gx)

1	(∀y)[(Hy & Fy) ⊃ Gy]	Assumption
2	(∀z)Fz & ~ (∀x)Kxb	Assumption
3	Hm	Assumption
4	(Hm & Fm) ⊃ Gm	1 ∀E
5	(∀z)Fz	2 &E
6	Fm	5 ∀E
7	Hm & Fm	3, 6 &I
8	Gm	4, 7 ⊃E
9	Hm ⊃ Gm	3–8 ⊃I
10	(∀x)(Hx ⊃ Gx)	9 ∀I

e. Derive: (∃w) (Aw ∨ ~ Lwf)

```
 1 | (∀x) (~ Ax ⊃ Kx)                 Assumption
 2 | (∃y) ~ Ky                        Assumption
   |---------------------
 3 | | ~ Ka                           Assumption
   | |----------
 4 | | ~ Aa ⊃ Ka                      1 ∀E
 5 | | | ~ Aa                         Assumption
   | | |--------
 6 | | | Ka                           4, 5 ⊃E
 7 | | | ~ Ka                         3 R
 8 | | Aa                             5–7 ~ E
 9 | | Aa ∨ ~ Laf                     8 ∨I
10 | | (∃w) (Aw ∨ ~ Lwf)              9 ∃I
11 | (∃w) (Aw ∨ ~ Lwf)                2, 3–10 ∃E
```

4. Theorems

a. Derive: (∀x) (∃y) (Ay ⊃ Ax)

```
1 | | Ac                              Assumption
  | |--------
2 | | Ac                              1 R
3 | Ac ⊃ Ac                           1–2 ⊃I
4 | (∃y) (Ay ⊃ Ac)                    3 ∃I
5 | (∀x) (∃y) (Ay ⊃ Ax)               4 ∀I
```

c. Derive: (∀x) (Ax ⊃ Bx) ⊃ ((∀x)Ax ⊃ (∀x)Bx)

```
1 | | (∀x) (Ax ⊃ Bx)                          Assumption
  | |------------------
2 | | | (∀x)Ax                                Assumption
  | | |----------------
3 | | | Ac ⊃ Bc                               1 ∀E
4 | | | Ac                                    2 ∀E
5 | | | Bc                                    3, 4 ⊃E
6 | | | (∀x)Bx                                5 ∀I
7 | | (∀x)Ax ⊃ (∀x)Bx                         2–6 ⊃I
8 | (∀x) (Ax ⊃ Bx) ⊃ ((∀x)Ax ⊃ (∀x)Bx)        1–7 ⊃I
```

e. Derive: (∀x)(Bi ⊃ Ax) ≡ (Bi ⊃ (∀x)Ax)

1	(∀x)(Bi ⊃ Ax)	Assumption
2	Bi	Assumption
3	Bi ⊃ Ac	1 ∀E
4	Ac	2, 3 ⊃E
5	(∀x)Ax	4 ∀I
6	Bi ⊃ (∀x)Ax	2–5 ⊃I
7	Bi ⊃ (∀x)Ax	Assumption
8	Bi	Assumption
9	(∀x)Ax	7, 8 ⊃E
10	Ac	9 ∀E
11	Bi ⊃ Ac	8–10 ⊃I
12	(∀x)(Bi ⊃ Ax)	11 ∀I
13	(∀x)(Bi ⊃ Ax) ≡ (Bi ⊃ (∀x)Ax)	1–6, 7–12 ≡I

5. Equivalence

a. Derive: (∀x)(Ax & Ax)

1	(∀x)Ax	Assumption
2	Ak	1 ∀E
3	Ak & Ak	2, 2 &I
4	(∀x)(Ax & Ax)	3 ∀I

Derive: (∀x)Ax

1	(∀x)(Ax & Ax)	Assumption
2	Ai & Ai	1 ∀E
3	Ai	2 &E
4	(∀x)Ax	3 ∀I

c. Derive: (∃x)Ax ∨ (∃x)Bx

1	(∃x)(Ax ∨ Bx)	Assumption
2	Aa ∨ Ba	Assumption
3	Aa	Assumption
4	(∃x)Ax	3 ∃I
5	(∃x)Ax ∨ (∃x)Bx	4 ∨I
6	Ba	Assumption
7	(∃x)Bx	6 ∃I
8	(∃x)Ax ∨ (∃x)Bx	7 ∨I
9	(∃x)Ax ∨ (∃x)Bx	2, 3–5, 6–8 ∨E
10	(∃x)Ax ∨ (∃x)Bx	1, 2–9 ∃E

Derive: $(\exists x)(Ax \vee Bx)$

1	$(\exists x)Ax \vee (\exists x)Bx$	Assumption
2	$\quad (\exists x)Ax$	Assumption
3	$\quad\quad Aa$	Assumption
4	$\quad\quad Aa \vee Ba$	3 $\vee$I
5	$\quad\quad (\exists x)(Ax \vee Bx)$	4 $\exists$I
6	$\quad (\exists x)(Ax \vee Bx)$	2, 3–5 $\exists$E
7	$\quad (\exists x)Bx$	Assumption
8	$\quad\quad Ba$	Assumption
9	$\quad\quad Aa \vee Ba$	8 $\vee$I
10	$\quad\quad (\exists x)(Ax \vee Bx)$	9 $\exists$I
11	$\quad (\exists x)(Ax \vee Bx)$	7, 8–10 $\exists$E
12	$(\exists x)(Ax \vee Bx)$	1, 2–6, 7–11 $\vee$E

e. Derive: $(\exists x) \sim Ax$

1	$\sim (\forall x)Ax$	Assumption
2	$\quad \sim (\exists x) \sim Ax$	Assumption
3	$\quad\quad \sim Ac$	Assumption
4	$\quad\quad (\exists x) \sim Ax$	3 $\exists$I
5	$\quad\quad \sim (\exists x) \sim Ax$	2 R
6	$\quad Ac$	3–5 $\sim$E
7	$\quad (\forall x)Ax$	6 $\forall$I
8	$\quad \sim (\forall x)Ax$	1 R
9	$(\exists x) \sim Ax$	2–8 $\sim$E

Derive: $\sim (\forall x)Ax$

1	$(\exists x) \sim Ax$	Assumption
2	$\quad \sim Ac$	Assumption
3	$\quad\quad (\forall x)Ax$	Assumption
4	$\quad\quad Ac$	3 $\forall$E
5	$\quad\quad \sim Ac$	2 R
6	$\quad \sim (\forall x)Ax$	3–5 $\sim$I
7	$\sim (\forall x)Ax$	1, 2–6 $\exists$E

6. Inconsistency

a.

1	(∀x)Hx	Assumption
2	(∀y) ~ (Hy ∨ Byy)	Assumption
3	Hc	1 ∀E
4	Hc ∨ Bcc	3 ∨I
5	~ (Hc ∨ Bcc)	2 ∀E

c.

1	(∀x)Rx	Assumption
2	(∃x) ~ Rx	Assumption
3	~ Ri	Assumption
4	(∀x)Rx	Assumption
5	~ Ri	3 R
6	Ri	1 ∀E
7	~ (∀x)Rx	4–6 ~ I
8	~ (∀x)Rx	2, 3–7 ∃E
9	(∀x)Rx	1 R

e.

1	(∀w)(∀z)(Jwz ≡ ~Jwz)	Assumption
2	(∀z)(Jaz ≡ ~Jaz)	1 ∀E
3	Jab ≡ ~Jab	2 ∀E
4	Jab	Assumption
5	~Jab	3, 4 ≡E
6	Jab	4 R
7	~Jab	4–6 ~ I
8	Jab	3, 7 ≡E

7. Derivability

a. Derive: (∃x)Bx

1	(∀x)(~ Bx ⊃ ~ Wx)	Assumption
2	(∃x)Wx	Assumption
3	Wa	Assumption
4	~ Ba ⊃ ~ Wa	1 ∀E
5	~ Ba	Assumption
6	~ Wa	4, 5 ⊃E
7	Wa	3 R
8	Ba	5–7 ~ E
9	(∃x)Bx	8 ∃I
10	(∃x)Bx	2, 3–9 ∃E

c. Derive: Ha ⊃ (∃x)Sxcc

1	(∀x)(Hx ⊃ (∀y)Rxyb)	Assumption
2	(∀x)(∀z)(Razx ⊃ Sxzz)	Assumption
3	Ha	Assumption
4	Ha ⊃ (∀y)Rayb	1 ∀E
5	(∀y)Rayb	3, 4 ⊃E
6	Racb	5 ∀E
7	(∀z)(Razb ⊃ Sbzz)	2 ∀E
8	Racb ⊃ Sbcc	7 ∀E
9	Sbcc	6, 8 ⊃E
10	(∃x)Sxcc	9 ∃I
11	Ha ⊃ (∃x)Sxcc	3–10 ⊃I

e. Derive: (∃z)Lz ⊃ (∃y)Ky

1	(∀z)(~ Lz ∨ (∃y)Ky)	Assumption
2	(∃z)Lz	Assumption
3	La	Assumption
4	~ La ∨ (∃y)Ky	1 ∀E
5	~ La	Assumption
6	~ (∃y)Ky	Assumption
7	La	3 R
8	~ La	5 R
9	(∃y)Ky	6–8 ~ E
10	(∃y)Ky	Assumption
11	(∃y)Ky	10 R
12	(∃y)Ky	4, 5–9, 10–11 ∨E
13	(∃y)Ky	2, 3–12 ∃E
14	(∃z)Lz ⊃ (∃y)Ky	2–13 ⊃I

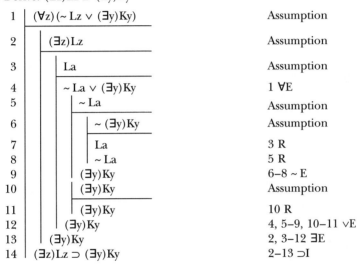

g. Derive: (∃x)Cx

Line	Formula	Justification
1	(∃x)(Cx ∨ (∀y)(Wxy ⊃ Cy))	Assumption
2	(∀x)(Wxa & ~ Ca)	Assumption
3	│ Cb ∨ (∀y)(Wby ⊃ Cy)	Assumption
4	│ │ Cb	Assumption
5	│ │ (∃x)Cx	4 ∃I
6	│ │ (∀y)(Wby ⊃ Cy)	Assumption
7	│ │ │ ~ (∃x)Cx	Assumption
8	│ │ │ Wba ⊃ Ca	6 ∀E
9	│ │ │ Wba & ~ Ca	2 ∀E
10	│ │ │ Wba	9 &E
11	│ │ │ Ca	8, 10 ⊃E
12	│ │ │ ~ Ca	9 &E
13	│ │ (∃x)Cx	7–12 ~ E
14	│ (∃x)Cx	3, 4–5, 6–13 ∨E
15	(∃x)Cx	1, 3–14 ∃E

8. Validity

a. Derive: (∀x)(Zx ⊃ (∃y)(Ky ∨ Sy))

Line	Formula	Justification
1	(∀x)(Zx ⊃ (∃y)Ky)	Assumption
2	Za ⊃ (∃y)Ky	1 ∀E
3	│ Za	Assumption
4	│ (∃y)Ky	2, 3 ⊃E
5	│ │ Kb	Assumption
6	│ │ Kb ∨ Sb	5 ∨I
7	│ │ (∃y)(Ky ∨ Sy)	6 ∃I
8	│ (∃y)(Ky ∨ Sy)	4, 5–7 ∃E
9	Za ⊃ (∃y)(Ky ∨ Sy)	3–8 ⊃I
10	(∀x)(Zx ⊃ (∃y)(Ky ∨ Sy))	9 ∀I

c. Derive: (∀x)(Hx ⊃ Wxx)

Line	Formula	Justification
1	(∀x)(Hx ⊃ Fx)	Assumption
2	(∀x)((Fx & Uxx) ⊃ Wxx)	Assumption
3	(∀z)Uzz	Assumption
4	│ Ha	Assumption
5	│ Ha ⊃ Fa	1 ∀E
6	│ Fa	4, 5 ⊃E
7	│ Uaa	3 ∀E
8	│ Fa & Uaa	6, 7 &I
9	│ (Fa & Uaa) ⊃ Waa	2 ∀E
10	│ Waa	8, 9 ⊃E
11	Ha ⊃ Waa	4–10 ⊃I
12	(∀x)(Hx ⊃ Wxx)	11 ∀I

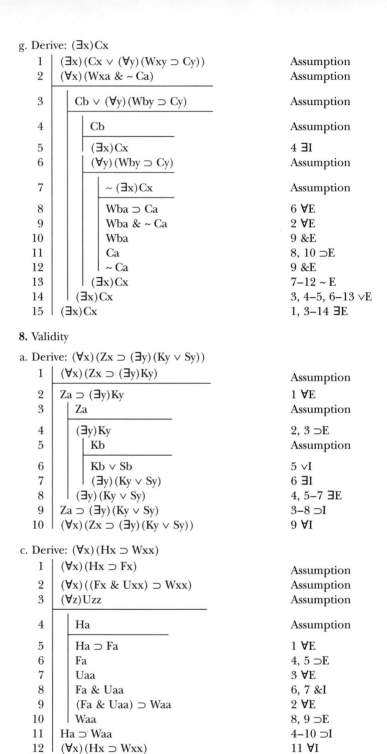

e. Derive: ~ (∀x) (Cx ⊃ Lx)

```
 1  │ (∀x) (Lx ⊃ Yx)                          Assumption
 2  │ (∃x) (Cx & Yx) & (∃x) (Cx & ~ Yx)       Assumption
    ├──────────────────────────────────
 3  │ (∃x) (Cx & ~ Yx)                        2 &E
 4  │ │ Cb & ~ Yb                              Assumption
    │ ├────────────────────────────
 5  │ │ │ (∀x) (Cx ⊃ Lx)                      Assumption
    │ │ ├──────────────────────
 6  │ │ │ Cb ⊃ Lb                             5 ∀E
 7  │ │ │ Cb                                  4 &E
 8  │ │ │ Lb ⊃ Yb                             1 ∀E
 9  │ │ │ Lb                                  6, 7 ⊃E
10  │ │ │ Yb                                  8, 9 ⊃E
11  │ │ │ ~ Yb                                4 &E
12  │ │ ~ (∀x) (Cx ⊃ Lx)                      5–11 ~ I
13  │ ~ (∀x) (Cx ⊃ Lx)                        3, 4–12 ∃E
```

g. Derive: (∃x) ~ Kx

```
 1  │ (∀x) (∀y) ((Ry ∨ Dx) ⊃ ~ Ky)            Assumption
 2  │ (∀x) (∃y) (Ax ⊃ ~ Ky)                   Assumption
 3  │ (∃x) (Ax ∨ Rx)                          Assumption
    ├──────────────────────────────────
 4  │ │ Aa ∨ Ra                                Assumption
    │ ├────────────────────────────
 5  │ │ │ Aa                                  Assumption
    │ │ ├──────────────────────
 6  │ │ │ (∃y) (Aa ⊃ ~ Ky)                    2 ∀E
 7  │ │ │ │ Aa ⊃ ~ Kb                         Assumption
    │ │ │ ├────────────────
 8  │ │ │ │ ~ Kb                              5, 7 ⊃E
 9  │ │ │ │ (∃x) ~ Kx                         8 ∃I
10  │ │ │ (∃x) ~ Kx                           6, 7–9 ∃E
11  │ │ │ Ra                                  Assumption
    │ │ ├──────────────────────
12  │ │ │ (∀y) ((Ry ∨ Dc) ⊃ ~ Ky)             1 ∀E
13  │ │ │ (Ra ∨ Dc) ⊃ ~ Ka                    12 ∀E
14  │ │ │ Ra ∨ Dc                             11 ∨I
15  │ │ │ ~ Ka                                13, 14 ⊃E
16  │ │ │ (∃x) ~ Kx                           15 ∃I
17  │ │ (∃x) ~ Kx                             4, 5–10, 11–16 ∨E
18  │ (∃x) ~ Kx                               3, 4–17 ∃E
```

i. Derive: $(\exists z)[Bz \,\&\, (\forall y)(By \supset Hzy)]$

1	$(\forall x)(\forall y)[(Hky \,\&\, Hxk) \supset Hxy]$	Assumption
2	$(\forall z)(Bz \supset Hkz)$	Assumption
3	$(\exists x)(Bx \,\&\, Hxk)$	Assumption
4	$Bi \,\&\, Hik$	Assumption
5	Ba	Assumption
6	$Ba \supset Hka$	2 $\forall$E
7	Hka	5, 6 $\supset$E
8	Hik	4 &E
9	$Hka \,\&\, Hik$	7, 8 &I
10	$(\forall y)[(Hky \,\&\, Hik) \supset Hiy]$	1 $\forall$E
11	$(Hka \,\&\, Hik) \supset Hia$	10 $\forall$E
12	Hia	9, 11 $\supset$E
13	$Ba \supset Hia$	5–12 $\supset$I
14	$(\forall y)(By \supset Hiy)$	13 $\forall$I
15	Bi	4 &E
16	$Bi \,\&\, (\forall y)(By \supset Hiy)$	15, 14 &I
17	$(\exists z)[Bz \,\&\, (\forall y)(By \supset Hzy)]$	16 $\exists$I
18	$(\exists z)[Bz \,\&\, (\forall y)(By \supset Hzy)]$	3, 4–17 $\exists$E

k. Derive: (∀w)([Gw & (∃z)(Gz & Hwz)] ⊃ Hww)

1	(∀x)(∀y)[(Gx & Gy) ⊃ (Hxy ⊃ Hyx)]	Assumption
2	(∀x)(∀y)(∀z)([(Gx & Gy) & Gz] ⊃ [(Hxy & Hyz) ⊃ Hxz])	Assumption
3	Ga & (∃z)(Gz & Haz)	Assumption
4	(∃z)(Gz & Haz)	3 &E
5	Gb & Hab	Assumption
6	(∀y)[(Ga & Gy) ⊃ (Hay ⊃ Hya)]	1 ∀E
7	(Ga & Gb) ⊃ (Hab ⊃ Hba)	6 ∀E
8	Gb	5 &E
9	Ga	3 &E
10	Ga & Gb	9, 8 &I
11	Hab ⊃ Hba	10, 7 ⊃E
12	Hab	5 &E
13	Hba	11, 12 ⊃E
14	Hab & Hba	12, 13 &I
15	(∀y)(∀z)([(Ga & Gy) & Gz] ⊃ [(Hay & Hyz) ⊃ Haz])	2 ∀E
16	(∀z)([(Ga & Gb) & Gz] ⊃ [(Hab & Hbz) ⊃ Haz])	15 ∀E
17	[(Ga & Gb) & Ga] ⊃ [(Hab & Hba) ⊃ Haa]	16 ∀E
18	(Ga & Gb) & Ga	10, 9 &I
19	(Hab & Hba) ⊃ Haa	17, 18 ⊃E
20	Haa	14, 19 ⊃E
21	Haa	4, 5–20 ∃E
22	[Ga & (∃z)(Gz & Haz)] ⊃ Haa	3–21 ⊃I
23	(∀w)([Gw & (∃z)(Gz & Hwz)] ⊃ Hww)	22 ∀I

9. Theorems

a. Derive: [(∀x)(∀y)Axy & (∀x)(Axx ⊃ Bi)] ⊃ Bi

1	(∀x)(∀y)Axy & (∀x)(Axx ⊃ Bi)	Assumption
2	(∀x)(Axx ⊃ Bi)	1 &E
3	Akk ⊃ Bi	2 ∀E
4	(∀x)(∀y)Axy	1 &E
5	(∀y)Aky	4 ∀E
6	Akk	5 ∀E
7	Bi	3, 6 ⊃E
8	[(∀x)(∀y)Axy & (∀x)(Axx ⊃ Bi)] ⊃ Bi	1–7 ⊃I

c. Derive: $(\forall x)Ax \equiv \sim(\exists x) \sim Ax$

1	$(\forall x)Ax$	Assumption
2	$(\exists x) \sim Ax$	Assumption
3	$\sim Ac$	Assumption
4	$(\exists x) \sim Ax$	Assumption
5	Ac	1 ∀E
6	$\sim Ac$	3 R
7	$\sim(\exists x) \sim Ax$	4–6 ~ I
8	$\sim(\exists x) \sim Ax$	2, 3–7 ∃E
9	$(\exists x) \sim Ax$	2 R
10	$\sim(\exists x) \sim Ax$	2–9 ~ I
11	$\sim(\exists x) \sim Ax$	Assumption
12	$\sim Ac$	Assumption
13	$(\exists x) \sim Ax$	12 ∃I
14	$\sim(\exists x) \sim Ax$	11 R
15	Ac	12–14 ~ E
16	$(\forall x)Ax$	15 ∀I
17	$(\forall x)Ax \equiv \sim(\exists x) \sim Ax$	1–10, 11–16 ≡I

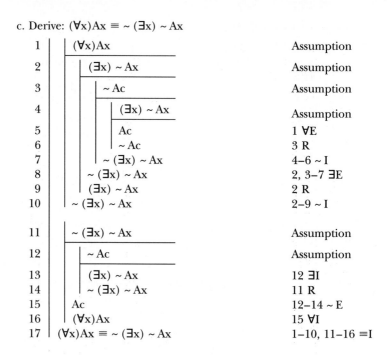

e. Derive: (∃x)(Bi ⊃ Ax) ≡ (Bi ⊃ (∃x)Ax)

1	│ │ (∃x)(Bi ⊃ Ax)	Assumption
2	│ │ │ Bi	Assumption
3	│ │ │ │ Bi ⊃ Ac	Assumption
4	│ │ │ │ Ac	2, 3 ⊃E
5	│ │ │ │ (∃x)Ax	4 ∃I
6	│ │ │ (∃x)Ax	1, 3–5 ∃E
7	│ │ Bi ⊃ (∃x)Ax	2–6 ⊃I
8	│ │ Bi ⊃ (∃x)Ax	Assumption
9	│ │ │ ~ (∃x)(Bi ⊃ Ax)	Assumption
10	│ │ │ │ Bi	Assumption
11	│ │ │ │ (∃x)Ax	8, 10 ⊃E
12	│ │ │ │ │ Ac	Assumption
13	│ │ │ │ │ │ ~ Ad	Assumption
14	│ │ │ │ │ │ │ Bi	Assumption
15	│ │ │ │ │ │ │ Ac	12 R
16	│ │ │ │ │ │ Bi ⊃ Ac	14–15 ⊃I
17	│ │ │ │ │ │ (∃x)(Bi ⊃ Ax)	16 ∃I
18	│ │ │ │ │ │ ~ (∃x)(Bi ⊃ Ax)	9 R
19	│ │ │ │ │ Ad	13–18 ~ E
20	│ │ │ │ Ad	11, 12–19 ∃E
21	│ │ │ Bi ⊃ Ad	10–20 ⊃I
22	│ │ │ (∃x)(Bi ⊃ Ax)	21 ∃I
23	│ │ │ ~ (∃x)(Bi ⊃ Ax)	9 R
24	│ │ (∃x)(Bi ⊃ Ax)	9–23 ~ E
25	│ (∃x)(Bi ⊃ Ax) ≡ (Bi ⊃ (∃x)Ax)	1–7, 8–24 ≡I

10. Equivalence

a. Derive: (∀x)(Bx ⊃ Bx)

1	│ (∀x)(Ax ⊃ Ax)	Assumption
2	│ │ Ba	Assumption
3	│ │ Ba	2 R
4	│ Ba ⊃ Ba	2–3 ⊃I
5	│ (∀x)(Bx ⊃ Bx)	4 ∀I

Derive: (∀x)(Ax ⊃ Ax)

1	│ (∀x)(Bx ⊃ Bx)	Assumption
2	│ │ Aa	Assumption
3	│ │ Aa	2 R
4	│ Aa ⊃ Aa	2–3 ⊃I
5	│ (∀x)(Ax ⊃ Ax)	4 ∀I

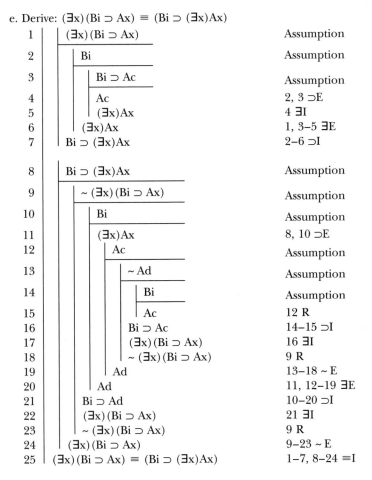

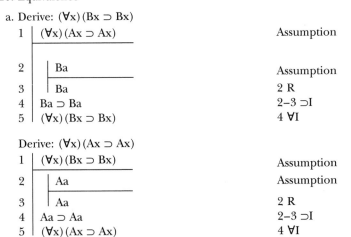

c. Derive: (∃y) ~ By ⊃ (∀x) ~ Ax

1	(∀x) (∀y) (Ax ⊃ By)	Assumption
2	│ (∃y) ~ By	Assumption
3	│ │ ~ Ba	Assumption
4	│ │ (∀y) (Ab ⊃ By)	1 ∀E
5	│ │ Ab ⊃ Ba	4 ∀E
6	│ │ │ Ab	Assumption
7	│ │ │ Ba	5, 6 ⊃E
8	│ │ │ ~ Ba	3 R
9	│ │ ~ Ab	6–8 ~ I
10	│ │ (∀x) ~ Ax	9 ∀I
11	│ (∀x) ~ Ax	2, 3–10 ∃E
12	(∃y) ~ By ⊃ (∀x) ~ Ax	2–11 ⊃I

Derive: (∀x) (∀y) (Ax ⊃ By)

1	(∃y) ~ By ⊃ (∀x) ~ Ax	Assumption
2	│ Aa	Assumption
3	│ │ ~ Bb	Assumption
4	│ │ (∃y) ~ By	3 ∃I
5	│ │ (∀x) ~ Ax	1, 4 ⊃E
6	│ │ ~ Aa	5 ∀E
7	│ │ Aa	2 R
8	│ Bb	3–7 ~ E
9	Aa ⊃ Bb	2–8 ⊃I
10	(∀y) (Aa ⊃ By)	9 ∀I
11	(∀x) (∀y) (Ax ⊃ By)	10 ∀I

e. Derive: ~ (∀x)Ax ∨ (∀y)By

1	(∃x) (∀y) (Ax ⊃ By)	Assumption
2	│ (∀y) (Aa ⊃ By)	Assumption
3	│ Aa ⊃ Bb	2 ∀E
4	│ │ ~ (~ (∀x)Ax ∨ (∀y)By)	Assumption
5	│ │ │ (∀x)Ax	Assumption
6	│ │ │ Aa	5 ∀E
7	│ │ │ Bb	3, 6 ⊃E
8	│ │ │ (∀y)By	7 ∀I
9	│ │ │ ~ (∀x)Ax ∨ (∀y)By	8 ∨I
10	│ │ │ ~ (~ (∀x)Ax ∨ (∀y)By)	4 R
11	│ │ ~ (∀x)Ax	5–10 ~ I
12	│ │ ~ (∀x)Ax ∨ (∀y)By	11 ∨I
13	│ │ ~ (~ (∀x)Ax ∨ (∀y)By)	4 R
14	│ ~ (∀x)Ax ∨ (∀y)By	4–13 ~ E
15	~ (∀x)Ax ∨ (∀y)By	1, 2–14 ∃E

Derive: $(\exists x)(\forall y)(Ax \supset By)$

1	$\sim (\forall x)Ax \vee (\forall y)By$	Assumption
2	$\sim (\forall x)Ax$	Assumption
3	$\sim (\exists x)(\forall y)(Ax \supset By)$	Assumption
4	$\sim Aa$	Assumption
5	Aa	Assumption
6	$\sim Bb$	Assumption
7	$\sim Aa$	4 R
8	Aa	5 R
9	Bb	6–8 $\sim$ E
10	$Aa \supset Bb$	5–9 $\supset$I
11	$(\forall y)(Aa \supset By)$	10 $\forall$I
12	$(\exists x)(\forall y)(Ax \supset By)$	11 $\exists$I
13	$\sim (\exists x)(\forall y)(Ax \supset By)$	3 R
14	Aa	4–13 $\sim$ E
15	$(\forall x)Ax$	14 $\forall$I
16	$\sim (\forall x)Ax$	2 R
17	$(\exists x)(\forall y)(Ax \supset By)$	3–16 $\sim$ E
18	$(\forall y)By$	Assumption
19	Aa	Assumption
20	Bb	18 $\forall$E
21	$Aa \supset Bb$	19–20 $\supset$I
22	$(\forall y)(Aa \supset By)$	21 $\forall$I
23	$(\exists x)(Ay)(Ax \supset By)$	22 $\exists$I
24	$(\exists x)(\forall y)(Ax \supset By)$	1, 2–17, 18–23 $\vee$E

11. Inconsistency

a.

1	$(\forall y)(\exists z)Byz$	Assumption
2	$(\forall w) \sim Baw$	Assumption
3	$(\exists z)Baz$	1 $\forall$E
4	Bab	Assumption
5	$(\forall w) \sim Baw$	Assumption
6	$\sim Bab$	5 $\forall$E
7	Bab	4 R
8	$\sim (\forall w) \sim Baw$	5–7 $\sim$ I
9	$\sim (\forall w) \sim Baw$	3, 4–8 $\exists$E
10	$(\forall w) \sim Baw$	2 R

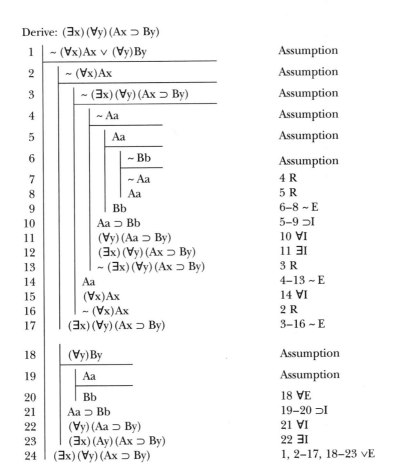

c.

1	(∃x)(~ Bx & Lxx)	Assumption
2	(∀z)(Cz & Bz)	Assumption
3	(∀y)[(By & ~ Cy) ≡ Lyy]	Assumption
4	~ Bi & Lii	Assumption
5	(Bi & ~ Ci) ≡ Lii	3 ∀E
6	Lii	4 &E
7	Bi & ~ Ci	5, 6 ≡E
8	(∀z)(Cz & Bz)	Assumption
9	Bi	7 &E
10	~ Bi	4 &E
11	~ (∀z)(Cz & Bz)	8–10 ~ I
12	~ (∀z)(Cz & Bz)	1, 4–11 ∃E
13	(∀z)(Cz & Bz)	2 R

e.

1	(∃x)(∃y)Fxy ∨ (∀x)(∀y)(∀z)Hxxyz	Assumption
2	(∃x)(∃y)Fxy ⊃ ~ Haaab	Assumption
3	(Hbbba ∨ ~ Haaab) ≡ (∀x) ~ (∀x ∨ ~ Ax)	Assumption
4	(∃x)(∃y)Fxy	Assumption
5	~ Haaab	2, 4 ⊃E
6	Hbbba ∨ ~ Haaab	5 ∨I
7	(∀x)(∀y)(∀z)Hxxyz	Assumption
8	(∀y)(∀z)Hbbyz	7 ∀E
9	(∀z)Hbbbz	8 ∀E
10	Hbbba	9 ∀E
11	Hbbba ∨ ~ Haaab	10 ∨I
12	Hbbba ∨ ~ Haaab	1, 4–6, 7–11 ∨E
13	(∀x) ~ (Ax ∨ ~ Ax)	3, 12 ≡E
14	Ac	Assumption
15	Ac ∨ ~ Ac	14 ∨I
16	~ (Ac ∨ ~ Ac)	13 ∀E
17	~ Ac	14–16 ~ I
18	Ac ∨ ~ Ac	17 ∨I
19	~ (Ac ∨ ~ Ac)	13 ∀E

12. Validity

a. Derive: (∃x)(Fxg & Cx)

1	(∀x)[Sx ⊃ (Cx ∨ Bx)]	Assumption
2	(∃x)[Fxg & (Sx & ~ Bx)]	Assumption
3	Fkg & (Sk & ~ Bk)	Assumption
4	Sk ⊃ (Ck ∨ Bk)	1 ∀E
5	Sk & ~ Bk	3 &E
6	Sk	5 &E
7	Ck ∨ Bk	4, 6 ⊃E
8	Ck	Assumption
9	Ck	8 R
10	Bk	Assumption
11	~ Ck	Assumption
12	Bk	10 R
13	~ Bk	5 &E
14	Ck	11–13 ~ E
15	Ck	7, 8–9, 10–14 ∨E
16	Fkg	3 &E
17	Fkg & Ck	16, 15 &I
18	(∃x)(Fxg & Cx)	17 ∃I
19	(∃x)(Fxg & Cx)	2, 3–18 ∃E

c. Derive: Fnm

1	(∀x)[(∃y)(∃z)[~ Iyz & (Lyx & Lzx)] ⊃ (∀z)((∃y)[Lyz & (∀w)(Lwz ⊃ Iwy)] ⊃ Fxz)]	Assumption
2	~ Ihg & (Lhn & Lgn)	Assumption
3	Ldm & (∀w)(Lwm ⊃ Iwd)	Assumption
4	(∃y)(∃z)[~ Iyz & (Lyn & Lzn)] ⊃ (∀z)((∃y)[Lyz & (∀w)(Lwz ⊃ Iwy)] ⊃ Fnz)	1 ∀E
5	(∃z)[~ Ihz & (Lhn & Lzn)]	2 ∃I
6	(∃y)(∃z)[~ Iyz & (Lyn & Lzn)]	5 ∃I
7	(∀z)((∃y)[Lyz & (∀w)(Lwz ⊃ Iwy)] ⊃ Fnz)	4, 6 ⊃E
8	(∃y)[Lym & (∀w)(Lwm ⊃ Iwy)] ⊃ Fnm	7 ∀E
9	(∃y)[Lym & (∀w)(Lwm ⊃ Iwy)]	3 ∃I
10	Fnm	8, 9 ⊃E

e. Derive: (∀x) [Hx ⊃ ~ (∃y) (Hy & Sxy)] ⊃ (∃z) (Lz & Szz)

1	(∃x) [Hx & (∃y) (Dy & Sxy)]	Assumption
2	(∃x) [Hx & (∀y) (Dy ⊃ ~ Sxy)]	Assumption
3	(∀x) (∀y) ([(Px & Sxy) & (Dy ∨ Hy)] ⊃ Lx)	Assumption
4	(∀x) [Hx ⊃ (Px & (∀y) [Sxy ⊃ (Dy ∨ Hy)])]	Assumption
5	(∀x) (Hx ⊃ (∃y) Sxy)	Assumption
6	(∀x) [Hx ⊃ ~ (∃y) (Hy & Sxy)]	Assumption
7	Ha & (∀y) (Dy ⊃ ~ Say)	Assumption
8	Ha ⊃ (Pa & (∀y) [Say ⊃ (Dy ∨ Hy)])	4 ∀E
9	Ha	7 &E
10	Pa & (∀y) [Say ⊃ (Dy ∨ Hy)]	8, 9 ⊃E
11	(∀y) [Say ⊃ (Dy ∨ Hy)]	10 &E
12	Ha ⊃ (∃y) Say	5 ∀E
13	(∃y) Say	9, 12 ⊃E
14	Sab	Assumption
15	Sab ⊃ (Db ∨ Hb)	11 ∀E
16	Db ∨ Hb	14, 15 ⊃E
17	Db	Assumption
18	(∀y) (Dy ⊃ ~ Say)	7 &E
19	Db ⊃ ~ Sab	18 ∀E
20	~ Hb	Assumption
21	~ Sab	17, 19 ⊃E
22	Sab	14 R
23	Hb	20–22 ~ E
24	Hb	Assumption
25	Hb	24 R
26	Hb	16, 17–23, 24–25 ∨E
27	Hb & Sab	26, 14 &I
28	(∃y) (Hy & Say)	27 ∃I
29	(∃y) (Hy & Say)	13, 14–28 ∃E
30	~ (∃z) (Lz & Szz)	Assumption
31	(∃y) (Hy & Say)	29 R
32	Ha ⊃ ~ (∃y) (Hy & Say)	6 ∀E
33	~ (∃y) (Hy & Say)	9, 32 ⊃E
34	(∃z) (Lz & Szz)	30–33 ~ E
35	(∃z) (Lz & Szz)	2, 7–34 ∃E
36	(∀x) [Hx ⊃ ~ (∃y) (Hy & Sxy)] ⊃ (∃z) (Lz & Szz)	6–35 ⊃I

13. Inconsistency

a.

1	(∃x) [Px & (∀y) (Uxy ≡ ~ Uyy)]	Assumption
2	Pa & (∀y) (Uay ≡ ~ Uyy)	Assumption
3	(∀y) (Uay ≡ ~ Uyy)	2 &E
4	Uaa ≡ ~ Uaa	3 ∀E
5	~ (Hi & ~ Hi)	Assumption
6	Uaa	Assumption
7	~ Uaa	4, 6 ≡E
8	Uaa	6 R
9	~ Uaa	6–8 ~ I
10	Uaa	4, 9 ≡E
11	Hi & ~ Hi	5–10 ~ E
12	Hi & ~ Hi	1, 2–11 ∃E
13	Hi	12 &E
14	~ Hi	12 &E

c.

1	(∀x) [(Px & Bx) ⊃ ~ Mx]	Assumption
2	(∀x) [(Px & Rx) ⊃ Bx]	Assumption
3	(∀x) [(Px & Rx) ⊃ Mx]	Assumption
4	(∃x) (Px & Rx)	Assumption
5	Pm & Rm	Assumption
6	(Pm & Rm) ⊃ Mm	3 ∀E
7	(Pm & Rm) ⊃ Bm	2 ∀E
8	Bm	5, 7 ⊃E
9	(Pm & Bm) ⊃ ~ Mm	1 ∀E
10	Pm	5 &E
11	Pm & Bm	10, 8 &I
12	(∃x) (Px & Rx)	Assumption
13	Mm	5, 6 ⊃E
14	~ Mm	9, 11 ⊃E
15	~ (∃x) (Px & Rx)	12–14 ~ I
16	~ (∃x) (Px & Rx)	4, 5–15 ∃E
17	(∃x) (Px & Rx)	4 R

Section 10.5E

1. Derivability

a. Derive: (∃y) (~ Fy ∨ ~ Gy)

1	~ (∀y) (Fy & Gy)	Assumption
2	(∃y) ~ (Fy & Gy)	1 QN
3	(∃y) (~ Fy ∨ ~ Gy)	2 DeM

c. Derive: (∃z)(Az & ~ Cz)

1	(∃z)(Gz & Az)	Assumption
2	(∀y)(Cy ⊃ ~ Gy)	Assumption
3	Gh & Ah	Assumption
4	Ch ⊃ ~ Gh	2 ∀E
5	Gh	3 &E
6	~ ~ Gh	5 DN
7	~ Ch	4, 6 MT
8	Ah	3 &E
9	Ah & ~ Ch	8, 7 &I
10	(∃z)(Az & ~ Cz)	9 ∃I
11	(∃z)(Az & ~ Cz)	1, 3–10 ∃E

e. Derive: (∃x)Cxb

1	(∀x)[(~ Cxb ∨ Hx) ⊃ Lxx]	Assumption
2	(∃y) ~ Lyy	Assumption
3	~ Lmm	Assumption
4	(~ Cmb ∨ Hm) ⊃ Lmm	1 ∀E
5	~ (~ Cmb ∨ Hm)	3, 4 MT
6	~ ~ Cmb & ~ Hm	5 DeM
7	~ ~ Cmb	6 &E
8	Cmb	7 DN
9	(∃x)Cxb	8 ∃I
10	(∃x)Cxb	2, 3–9 ∃E

2. Validity

a. Derive: (∀y) ~ (Hby ∨ Ryy)

1	(∀y) ~Jx	Assumption
2	(∃y)(Hby ∨ Ryy) ⊃ (∃x)Jx	Assumption
3	~ (∃x)Jx	1 QN
4	~ (∃y)(Hby ∨ Ryy)	2, 3 MT
5	(∀y) ~ (Hby ∨ Ryy)	4 QN

c. Derive: (∀x)(∀y)Hxy & (∀x) ~ Tx

1	(∀x) ~ ((∀y)Hyx ∨ Tx)	Assumption
2	~ (∃y)(Ty ∨ (∃x) ~ Hxy)	Assumption
3	(∀y) ~ (Ty ∨ (∃x) ~ Hxy)	2 QN
4	~ (Ta ∨ (∃x) ~ Hxa)	3 ∀E
5	~ Ta & ~ (∃x) ~ Hxa	4 DeM
6	~ (∃x) ~ Hxa	5 &E
7	(∀x) ~ ~ Hxa	6 QN
8	~ ~ Hba	7 ∀E
9	Hba	8 DN
10	(∀y)Hby	9 ∀I
11	(∀x)(∀y)Hxy	10 ∀I
12	~ Ta	5 &E
13	(∀x) ~ Tx	12 ∀I
14	(∀x)(∀y)Hxy & (∀x) ~ Tx	11, 13 &I

e. Derive: (∃x) ~ Kxx

1	(∀z)[Kzz ⊃ (Mz & Nz)]	Assumption
2	(∃z) ~ Nz	Assumption
3	~ Ng	Assumption
4	Kgg ⊃ (Mg & Ng)	1 ∀E
5	~ Mg ∨ ~ Ng	3 ∨I
6	~ (Mg & Ng)	5 DeM
7	~ Kgg	4, 6 MT
8	(∃x) ~ Kxx	7 ∃I
9	(∃x) ~ Kxx	2, 3–8 ∃E

g. Derive: (∃w)(Qw & Bw) ⊃ (∀y)(Lyy ⊃ ~ Ay)

1	(∃z)Qz ⊃ (∀w)(Lww ⊃ ~ Hw)	Assumption
2	(∃x)Bx ⊃ (∀y)(Ay ⊃ Hy)	Assumption
3	(∃w)(Qw & Bw)	Assumption
4	Qm & Bm	Assumption
5	Qm	4 &E
6	(∃z)Qz	5 ∃I
7	(∀w)(Lww ⊃ ~ Hw)	1, 6 ⊃E
8	Lcc ⊃ ~ Hc	7 ∀E
9	Bm	4 &E
10	(∃x)Bx	9 ∃I
11	(∀y)(Ay ⊃ Hy)	2, 10 ⊃E
12	Ac ⊃ Hc	11 ∀E
13	~ Hc ⊃ ~ Ac	12 Trans
14	Lcc ⊃ ~ Ac	8, 13 HS
15	(∀y)(Lyy ⊃ ~ Ay)	14 ∀I
16	(∀y)(Lyy ⊃ ~ Ay)	3, 4–15 ∃E
17	(∃w)(Qw & Bw) ⊃ (∀y)(Lyy ⊃ ~ Ay)	3–16 ⊃I

i. Derive: ~ (∀x) (∀y)Bxy ⊃ (∀x) (~ Px ∨ ~ Hx)

1	~ (∀x) (~ Px ∨ ~ Hx) ⊃ (∀x) [Cx & (∀y) (Ly ⊃ Axy)]	Assumption
2	(∃x) [Hx & (∀y) (Ly ⊃ Axy)] ⊃ (∀x) (Rx & (∀y)Bxy)	Assumption
3	~ (∀x) (~ Px ∨ ~ Hx)	Assumption
4	(∃x) ~ (~ Px ∨ ~ Hx)	3 QN
5	~ (~ Pi ∨ ~ Hi)	Assumption
6	~ ~ Pi & ~ ~ Hi	5 DeM
7	~ ~ Hi	6 &E
8	Hi	7 DN
9	(∀x) [Cx & (∀y) (Ly ⊃ Axy)]	1, 3 ⊃E
10	Ci & (∀y) (Ly ⊃ Aiy)	9 ∀E
11	(∀y) (Ly ⊃ Aiy)	10 &E
12	Hi & (∀y) (Ly ⊃ Aiy)	8, 11 &I
13	(∃x) [Hx & (∀y) (Ly ⊃ Axy)]	12 ∃I
14	(∀x) (Rx & (∀y) Bxy)	2, 13 ⊃E
15	Rj & (∀y)Bjy	14 ∀E
16	(∀y) Bjy	15 &E
17	(∀x) (∀y) Bxy	16 ∀I
18	(∀x) (∀y) Bxy	4, 5–17 ∃E
19	~ (∀x) (~ Px ∨ ~ Hx) ⊃ (∀x) (∀y) Bxy	3–18 ⊃I
20	~ (∀x) (∀y) Bxy ⊃ ~ ~ (∀x) (~ Px ∨ ~ Hx)	19 Trans
21	~ (∀x) (∀y) Bxy ⊃ (∀x) (~ Px ∨ ~ Hx)	20 DN

3. Theorems

a. Derive: (∀x) (Ax ⊃ Bx) ⊃ (∀x) (Bx ∨ ~ Ax)

1	(∀x) (Ax ⊃ Bx)	Assumption
2	(∀x) (~ Ax ∨ Bx)	1 Impl
3	(∀x) (Bx ∨ ~ Ax)	2 Com
4	(∀x) (Ax ⊃ Bx) ⊃ (∀x) (Bx ∨ ~ Ax)	1–3 ⊃I

c. Derive: ~ (∃x) (Ax ∨ Bx) ⊃ (∀x) ~ Ax

1	~ (∃x) (Ax ∨ Bx)	Assumption
2	(∀x) ~ (Ax ∨ Bx)	1 QN
3	~ (Ac ∨ Bc)	2 ∀E
4	~ Ac & ~ Bc	3 DeM
5	~ Ac	4 &E
6	(∀x) ~ Ax	5 ∀I
7	~ (∃x) (Ax ∨ Bx) ⊃ (∀x) ~ Ax	1–6 ⊃I

e. Derive: $((\exists x)Ax \supset (\exists x)Bx) \supset (\exists x)(Ax \supset Bx)$

1	$\sim(\exists x)(Ax \supset Bx)$	Assumption
2	$(\forall x) \sim (Ax \supset Bx)$	1 QN
3	$\sim(Ac \supset Bc)$	2 ∀E
4	$\sim(\sim Ac \lor Bc)$	3 Impl
5	$\sim\sim Ac \;\&\; \sim Bc$	4 DeM
6	$\sim\sim Ac$	5 &E
7	$(\exists x) \sim\sim Ax$	6 ∃I
8	$\sim(\forall x) \sim Ax$	7 QN
9	$\sim\sim(\exists x)Ax$	8 QN
10	$\sim Bc$	5 &E
11	$(\forall x) \sim Bx$	10 ∀I
12	$\sim(\exists x)Bx$	11 QN
13	$\sim\sim(\exists x)Ax \;\&\; \sim(\exists x)Bx$	9, 12 &I
14	$\sim(\sim(\exists x)Ax \lor (\exists x)Bx)$	13 DeM
15	$\sim((\exists x)Ax \supset (\exists x)Bx)$	14 Impl
16	$\sim(\exists x)(Ax \supset Bx) \supset \sim((\exists x)Ax \supset (\exists x)Bx)$	1–15 ⊃I
17	$((\exists x)Ax \supset (\exists x)Bx) \supset (\exists x)(Ax \supset Bx)$	16 Trans

4. Equivalence

a. Derive: $(\exists x)(Ax \;\&\; \sim Bx)$

1	$\sim(\forall x)(Ax \supset Bx)$	Assumption
2	$(\exists x) \sim (Ax \supset Bx)$	1 QN
3	$(\exists x) \sim (\sim Ax \lor Bx)$	2 Impl
4	$(\exists x)(\sim\sim Ax \;\&\; \sim Bx)$	3 DeM
5	$(\exists x)(Ax \;\&\; \sim Bx)$	4 DN

Derive: $\sim(\forall x)(Ax \supset Bx)$

1	$(\exists x)(Ax \;\&\; \sim Bx)$	Assumption
2	$(\exists x)(\sim\sim Ax \;\&\; \sim Bx)$	1 DN
3	$(\exists x) \sim (\sim Ax \lor Bx)$	2 DeM
4	$(\exists x) \sim (Ax \supset Bx)$	3 Impl
5	$\sim(\forall x)(Ax \supset Bx)$	4 QN

c. Derive: $(\exists x)[\sim Ax \lor (\sim Cx \supset \sim Bx)]$

1	$\sim(\forall x) \sim [(Ax \;\&\; Bx) \supset Cx]$	Assumption
2	$(\exists x) \sim\sim [(Ax \;\&\; Bx) \supset Cx]$	1 QN
3	$(\exists x)[(Ax \;\&\; Bx) \supset Cx]$	2 DN
4	$(\exists x)[Ax \supset (Bx \supset Cx)]$	3 Exp
5	$(\exists x)[\sim Ax \lor (Bx \supset Cx)]$	4 Impl
6	$(\exists x)[\sim Ax \lor (\sim Cx \supset \sim Bx)]$	5 Trans

Derive: $\sim (\forall x) \sim [(Ax \mathbin{\&} Bx) \supset Cx]$

1	$(\exists x)[\sim Ax \lor (\sim Cx \supset \sim Bx)]$	Assumption
2	$(\exists x)[\sim Ax \lor (Bx \supset Cx)]$	1 Trans
3	$(\exists x)[Ax \supset (Bx \supset Cx)]$	2 Impl
4	$(\exists x)[(Ax \mathbin{\&} Bx) \supset Cx]$	3 Exp
5	$\sim\sim (\exists x)[(Ax \mathbin{\&} Bx) \supset Cx]$	4 DN
6	$\sim (\forall x) \sim [(Ax \mathbin{\&} Bx) \supset Cx]$	5 QN

e. Derive: $\sim (\exists x)[(\sim Ax \lor \sim Bx) \mathbin{\&} (Ax \lor Bx)]$

1	$(\forall x)(Ax \equiv Bx)$	Assumption
2	$\sim\sim (\forall x)(Ax \equiv Bx)$	1 DN
3	$\sim (\exists x) \sim (Ax \equiv Bx)$	2 QN
4	$\sim (\exists x) \sim [(Ax \mathbin{\&} Bx) \lor (\sim Ax \mathbin{\&} \sim Bx)]$	3 Equiv
5	$\sim (\exists x)[\sim (Ax \mathbin{\&} Bx) \mathbin{\&} \sim (\sim Ax \mathbin{\&} \sim Bx)]$	4 DeM
6	$\sim (\exists x)[(\sim Ax \lor \sim Bx) \mathbin{\&} \sim (\sim Ax \mathbin{\&} \sim Bx)]$	5 DeM
7	$\sim (\exists x)[(\sim Ax \lor \sim Bx) \mathbin{\&} (\sim\sim Ax \lor \sim\sim Bx)]$	6 DeM
8	$\sim (\exists x)[(\sim Ax \lor \sim Bx) \mathbin{\&} (Ax \lor \sim\sim Bx)]$	7 DN
9	$\sim (\exists x)[(\sim Ax \lor \sim Bx) \mathbin{\&} (Ax \lor Bx)]$	8 DN

Derive: $(\forall x)(Ax \equiv Bx)$

1	$\sim (\exists x)[(\sim Ax \lor \sim Bx) \mathbin{\&} (Ax \lor Bx)]$	Assumption
2	$\sim (\exists x)[(\sim Ax \lor \sim Bx) \mathbin{\&} (Ax \lor \sim\sim Bx)]$	1 DN
3	$\sim (\exists x)[(\sim Ax \lor \sim Bx) \mathbin{\&} (\sim\sim Ax \lor \sim\sim Bx)]$	2 DN
4	$\sim (\exists x)[(\sim Ax \lor \sim Bx) \mathbin{\&} \sim (\sim Ax \mathbin{\&} \sim Bx)]$	3 DeM
5	$\sim (\exists x)[\sim (Ax \mathbin{\&} Bx) \mathbin{\&} \sim (\sim Ax \mathbin{\&} \sim Bx)]$	4 DeM
6	$\sim (\exists x) \sim [(Ax \mathbin{\&} Bx) \lor (\sim Ax \mathbin{\&} \sim Bx)]$	5 DeM
7	$\sim (\exists x) \sim (Ax \equiv Bx)$	6 Equiv
8	$\sim\sim (\forall x)(Ax \equiv Bx)$	7 QN
9	$(\forall x)(Ax \equiv Bx)$	8 DN

5. Inconsistency

a.

1	$[(\forall x)(Mx \equiv Jx) \mathbin{\&} \sim Mc] \mathbin{\&} (\forall x)Jx$	Assumption
2	$(\forall x)(Mx \equiv Jx) \mathbin{\&} \sim Mc$	1 &E
3	$(\forall x)(Mx \equiv Jx)$	2 &E
4	$Mc \equiv Jc$	3 ∀E
5	$(Mc \supset Jc) \mathbin{\&} (Jc \supset Mc)$	4 Equiv
6	$Jc \supset Mc$	5 &E
7	$\sim Mc$	2 &E
8	$\sim Jc$	6, 7 MT
9	$(\forall x)Jx$	1 &E
10	Jc	9 ∀E

c.

1	(∀x)(∀y)Lxy ⊃ ~ (∃z)Tz	Assumption
2	(∀x)(∀y)Lxy ⊃ ((∃w)Cww ∨ (∃z)Tz)	Assumption
3	(~ (∀x)(∀y)Lxy ∨ (∀z)Bzzk) & (~ (∀z)Bzzk ∨ ~ (∃w)Cww)	Assumption
4	(∀x)(∀y)Lxy	Assumption
5	~ (∃z)Tz	1, 4 ⊃E
6	(∃w)Cww ∨ (∃z)Tz	2, 4 ⊃E
7	(∃w)Cww	5, 6 DS
8	~ (∀x)(∀y)Lxy ∨ (∀z)Bzzk	3 &E
9	(∀x)(∀y)Lxy ⊃ (∀z)Bzzk	8 Impl
10	(∀z)Bzzk	4, 9 ⊃E
11	~ (∀z)Bzzk ∨ ~ (∃w)Cww	3 &E
12	(∀z)Bzzk ⊃ ~ (∃w)Cww	11 Impl
13	~ (∃w)Cww	10, 12 ⊃E

e.

1	(∀x)(∀y)(Gxy ⊃ Hc)	Assumption
2	(∃x)Gix & (∀x)(∀y)(∀z)Lxyz	Assumption
3	~ Lcib ∨ ~ (Hc ∨ Hc)	Assumption
4	(∃x)Gix	2 &E
5	Gik	Assumption
6	(∀y)(Giy ⊃ Hc)	1 ∀E
7	Gik ⊃ Hc	6 ∀E
8	Hc	5, 7 ⊃E
9	Hc	4, 5–8 ∃E
10	(∀x)(∀y)(∀z)Lxyz	2 &E
11	(∀y)(∀z)Lcyz	10 ∀E
12	(∀z)Lciz	11 ∀E
13	Lcib	12 ∀E
14	~ ~ Lcib	13 DN
15	~ (Hc ∨ Hc)	3, 14 DS
16	~ Hc	15 Idem

6.a. Suppose there is a sentence on an accessible line i of a derivation to which Universal Elimination can be properly applied at line n. The sentence that would be derived by Universal Elimination can also be derived by using the routine beginning at line n:

i	$(\forall x)\mathscr{P}$	
n	$\sim \mathscr{P}(a/x)$	Assumption
$n + 1$	$(\exists x) \sim \mathscr{P}$	n ∃I
$n + 2$	$\sim (\forall x)\mathscr{P}$	$n + 1$ QN
$n + 3$	$(\forall x)\mathscr{P}$	i R
$n + 4$	$\mathscr{P}(a/x)$	n – $n+3$ ~ E

Suppose there is a sentence on an accessible line i of a derivation to which Universal Intorduction can be properly applied at line n. The sentence that would be derived by Universal Introduction can also be derived by using the routine beginning at line n:

i	$\mathscr{P}(a/x)$	
n	| $\sim (\forall x)\mathscr{P}$	Assumption
$n + 1$	| $(\exists x) \sim \mathscr{P}$	n QN
$n + 2$	| | $\sim \mathscr{P}(a/x)$	Assumption
$n + 3$	| | | $\sim (\forall x)\mathscr{P}$	Assumption
$n + 4$	| | | $\mathscr{P}(a/x)$	i R
$n + 5$	| | | $\sim \mathscr{P}(a/x)$	$n + 2$ R
$n + 6$	| | $(\forall x)\mathscr{P}$	$n+3 - n+5 \sim$ E
$n + 7$	| $(\forall x)\mathscr{P}$	$n+1, n+2 - n+6$ $\exists$ E
$n + 8$	| $\sim (\forall x)\mathscr{P}$	n R
$n + 9$	$(\forall x)\mathscr{P}$	$n - n+8 \sim$ E

No restriction on the use of Existential Elimination was violated at line $n + 7$. We assumed that we could have applied Universal Introduction at line n to $\mathscr{P}(a/x)$ on line i. So a does not occur in any undischarged assumption prior to line n, and a does not occur in $(\forall x)\mathscr{P}$. So a does not occur in $\mathscr{P}$. Hence

(i) a does not occur in any undischarged assumption prior to $n + 7$. Note that the assumptions on lines n PL 2 and $n + 3$ have been discharged and that a cannot occur in the assumption on line n, for a does not occur in $\mathscr{P}$.

(ii) a does not occur in $(\exists x) \sim \mathscr{P}$, for a does not occur in $\mathscr{P}$.

(iii) a does not occur in $(\forall x)\mathscr{P}$, for a does not occur in $\mathscr{P}$.

Section 10.6E

1.a. Derive: a= b ⊃ b = a

1	| a = b	Assumption
2	| a = a	1, 1 =E
3	| b = a	1, 2 =E
4	a = b ⊃ b = a	1-3 ⊃I

c. Derive: (~ a= b & b = c) ⊃ ~ a = c

1	| ~ a = b & b = c	Assumption
2	| ~ a = b	1 &E
3	| b = c	1 &E
4	| ~ a = c	2, 3 =E
5	(~ a = b & B = c) ⊃ ~ a c)	1-4 ⊃I

e. Derive: ~ a = c ⊃ (~ a = b ∨ ~ b = c)

```
 1 | | ~ a = c                          Assumption
   | |---------
 2 | | | ~ (~ a = b ∨ ~ b = c)          Assumption
   | | |----------------------
 3 | | | | ~ a = b                    Assumption
   | | | |--------
 4 | | | | ~ a = b ∨ ~ b = c          3 ∨I
 5 | | | | ~ (~ a = b ∨ ~ b = c)      3 R
 6 | | | a = b                        3-5 ~ E
 7 | | | ~ b = c                      1, 6 =E
 8 | | | ~ a = b ∨ ~ b = c            7 ∨I
 9 | | | ~ (~ a = b ∨ ~ b = c)        2 R
10 | | ~ a = b ∨ ~ b = c              2-9 ~E
11 | ~ a = c ⊃ (~ a = b ∨ ~ b = c)    1-10 ⊃I
```

2.a. Derive: ~ (∀x)Bxx

```
1 | a = b & ~ Bab                     Assumption
  |--------------
2 | ~ Bab                             1 &E
3 | a = b                             1 &E
4 | | (∀x)Bxx                         Assumption
  | |--------
5 | | Baa                             4 ∀E
6 | | ~ Baa                           2, 3 =E
7 | ~ (∀x)Bxx                         4-6 ~I
```

c. Derive: Hii

```
 1 | (∀z)[Gz ⊃ (∀y)(Ky ⊃ Hzy)]        Assumption
 2 | (Ki & Gj) & i = j                Assumption
   |--------------------------
 3 | Gj ⊃ (∀y)(Ky ⊃ Hjy)              1 ∀E
 4 | Ki & Gj                          2 & E
 5 | Gj                               4 & E
 6 | (∀y)(Ky ⊃ Hjy)                   3, 5 ⊃E
 7 | Ki ⊃ Hji                         7 ∀E
 8 | Ki                               4 & E
 9 | Hji                              7, 8 ⊃E
10 | i = j                            2 &E
11 | Hii                              9, 10 =E
```

e. Derive: Ka ∨ ~ Kb

1	a = b	Assumption
2	| ~ (Ka ∨ ~ Ka)	Assumption
3	| | Ka	Assumption
4	| | Ka ∨ ~ Ka	3 ∨I
5	| | ~ (Ka ∨ ~ Ka)	2 R
6	| ~ Ka	3–5 ~ I
7	| Ka ∨ ~ Ka	6 ∨I
8	| ~ (Ka ∨ ~ Ka)	2 R
9	Ka ∨ ~ Ka	2–8 ~ E
10	Ka ∨ ~ Kb	1, 9 =E

3. a. Derive: (∀x) (x = x ∨ ~ x = x)

1	(∀x)x = x	=I
2	a = a	1 ∀E
3	a = a ∨ ~ a = a	2 ∨I
4	(∀x) (x = x ∨ ~ x = x)	3 ∀I

c. Derive: (∀x) (∀y) (x = y ≡ y = x)

1	| a = b	Assumption
2	| a = a	1, 1 =E
3	| b = a	1, 2 =E
4	| b = a	Assumption
5	| b = b	4, 4 =E
6	| a = b	4, 5 =E
7	a = b ≡ b = a	1–3, 4–6 ≡I
8	(∀y) (a = y ≡ y = a)	7 ∀I
9	(∀x) (∀y) (x = y ≡ y = x)	8 ∀I

e. Derive: ~ (∃x) ~ x = x

1	| (∃x) ~ x = x	Assumption
2	| | ~ a = a	Assumption
3	| | | (∃x) ~ x = x	Assumption
4	| | | (∀x)x = x	=I
5	| | | a = a	4 ∀E
6	| | | ~ a = a	2 R
7	| | ~ (∃x) ~ x = x	3–6, ~ I
8	| ~ (∃x) ~ x = x	1, 2–7 ∃E
9	| (∃x) ~ x = x	1 R
10	~ (∃x) ~ x = x	1–9 ~ I

4.a. Derive: (∃x)(∃y)[(Ex & Ey) & ~ x = y]

1	~ t = f	Assumption
2	Et & Ef	Assumption
3	(Et & Ef) & ~ t = f	1, 2 &I
4	(∃y)[(Et & Ey) & ~ t = y]	3 ∃I
5	(∃x)(∃y)[(Ex & Ey) & ~ x = y]	4 ∃I

c. Derive: ~ s = b

1	~ Ass & Aqb	Assumption
2	(∀x)[(∃y)Ayx ⊃ Abx]	Assumption
3	s = b	Assumption
4	(∃y)Ayb ⊃ Abb	2 ∀E
5	Aqb	1 &E
6	(∃y)Ayb	5 ∃I
7	Abb	4, 6 ⊃E
8	~ Ass	1 &E
9	~ Abb	3, 8 =E
10	~ s = b	3–9 ~ I

e. Derive: (∃x)[(Rxe & Pxa) & (~ x = e & ~ x = a)]

1	(∃x)(Rxe & Pxa)	Assumption
2	~ Ree	Assumption
3	~ Paa	Assumption
4	Rie & Pia	Assumption
5	i = e	Assumption
6	Rie	4 &E
7	Ree	5, 6 =E
8	~ Ree	2 R
9	~ i = e	5–8 ~ I
10	i = a	Assumption
11	Pia	4 &E
12	Paa	10, 11 =E
13	~ Paa	3 R
14	~ i = a	10–13 ~ I
15	~ i = e & ~ i = a	9, 14 &I
16	(Rie & Pia) & (~ i = e & ~ i = a)	4, 15 &I
17	(∃x)[(Rxe & Pxa) & (~ x = e & ~ x = a)]	16 ∃I
18	(∃x)[(Rxe & Pxa) & (~ x = e & ~ x = a)]	1, 4–17 ∃E

Section 11.1E

5. Let $\Gamma \cup \{(\exists x)\mathscr{P}\}$ be a quantificationally consistent set of sentences, none of which contains the constant a. Then there is some interpretation **I** on which every member of $\Gamma \cup \{(\exists x)\mathscr{P}\}$ is true. Because $(\exists x)\mathscr{P}$ is true on **I**, we know that for any variable assignment **d**, there is a member **u** of the UD such that $\mathbf{d}[\mathbf{u}/x]$ satisfies $\mathscr{P}$ on **I**. Let **I**′ be the interpretation that is just like **I** except that $\mathbf{I}'(a) = \mathbf{u}$. Because a does not occur in $\Gamma \cup \{(\exists x)\mathscr{P}\}$, it follows from 11.1.7 that every member of $\Gamma \cup \{(\exists x)\mathscr{P}\}$ is true on **I**′.

On our assumption that $\mathbf{d}[\mathbf{u}/x]$ satisfies $\mathscr{P}$ on **I**, it follows from 11.1.6 that $\mathbf{d}[\mathbf{u}/x]$ satisfies $\mathscr{P}$ on **I**′. By the way that we have constructed **I**′, **u** is $\mathbf{I}'(a)$, and so $\mathbf{d}[\mathbf{u}/x]$ is $\mathbf{d}[\mathbf{I}'(a)/x]$. From result 11.1.1, we therefore know that **d** satisfies $\mathscr{P}(a/x)$ on **I**′. By 11.1.3, then, every variable assignment on **I**′ satisfies $\mathscr{P}(a/x)$, and so it is true on **I**′.

Every member of $\Gamma \cup \{(\exists x)\mathscr{P}, \mathscr{P}(a/x)\}$ being true on **I**′, we conclude that the extended set is quantificationally consistent.

6. Assume that **I** is an interpretation on which each member of the UD is assigned to at least one individual constant and that every substitution instance of $(\forall x)\mathscr{P}$ is true on **I**. Now $(\forall x)\mathscr{P}$ is true on **I** if every variable assignment satisfies $(\forall x)\mathscr{P}$ and, by 11.1.3, if some variable assignment **d** satisfies $(\forall x)\mathscr{P}$. The latter is the case if for every member **u** of the UD, $\mathbf{d}[\mathbf{u}/x]$ satisfies $\mathscr{P}$. Consider an arbitrary member **u** of the UD. By our assumption, $\mathbf{u} = \mathbf{I}(a)$ for some individual constant a. Also by assumption, $\mathscr{P}(a/x)$ is true on **I**—so **d** satisfies $\mathscr{P}(a/x)$. By 11.1.1, then, $\mathbf{d}[\mathbf{I}(a)/x]$, which is $\mathbf{d}[\mathbf{u}/x]$, satisfies $\mathscr{P}$. We conclude that for every member **u** of the UD, $\mathbf{d}[\mathbf{u}/x]$ satisfies $\mathscr{P}$, that **d** therefore satisfies $(\forall x)\mathscr{P}$, and that $(\forall x)\mathscr{P}$ is true on **I**.

Section 11.2E

1.a. Assume that an argument of *PL* is valid in *PD*. Then the conclusion is derivable in *PD* from the set consisting of the premises. By Metatheorem 11.1, it follows that the conclusion is quantificationally entailed by the set consisting of the premises. Therefore the argument is quantificationally valid.

b. Assume that a sentence $\mathscr{P}$ is a theorem in *PD*. Then $\varnothing \vdash \mathscr{P}$. So $\varnothing \vDash \mathscr{P}$, by Metatheorem 11.1, and $\mathscr{P}$ is quantificationally true.

2. Our induction will be on the number of occurrences of *logical operators* in $\mathscr{P}$, for we must now take into account the quantifiers as well as the truth-functional connectives.

Basis clause: Thesis 11.2.3 holds for every atomic formula of *PL*.

> **Proof:** Assume that $\mathscr{P}$ is an atomic formula and that $\mathscr{Q}$ is a subformula of $\mathscr{P}$. Then $\mathscr{P}$ and $\mathscr{Q}$ are identical. For any formula $\mathscr{Q}_1$, then, $[\mathscr{P}](\mathscr{Q}_1//\mathscr{Q})$ is simply $\mathscr{Q}_1$. It is trivial that the thesis holds in this case.

Inductive step: Let $\mathscr{P}$ be a formula with $k + 1$ occurrences of logical operators, let $\mathscr{Q}$ be a subformula of $\mathscr{P}$, and let $\mathscr{Q}_1$ be a formula related to $\mathscr{Q}$ as stipulated. Assume (the inductive hypothesis) that 11.2.3 holds for every formula with k or fewer occurrences of logical operators. We now establish that 11.2.3 holds for $\mathscr{P}$ as well. Suppose first that $\mathscr{Q}$ and $\mathscr{P}$ are identical. In this case, that 11.2.3 holds for $\mathscr{P}$ and $[\mathscr{P}](\mathscr{Q}_1//\mathscr{Q})$ is established as in the proof of the basis clause. So assume that $\mathscr{Q}$ is a subformula of $\mathscr{P}$ that is not identical with $\mathscr{P}$ (in which case we say that $\mathscr{Q}$ is a *proper subformula* of $\mathscr{P}$). We consider each form that $\mathscr{P}$ may have.

(i) $\mathscr{P}$ is of the form $\sim \mathscr{R}$. Since $\mathscr{Q}$ is a proper subformula of $\mathscr{P}$, $\mathscr{Q}$ is a subformula of $\mathscr{R}$. Therefore $[\mathscr{P}](\mathscr{Q}_1//\mathscr{Q})$ is $\sim [\mathscr{R}](\mathscr{Q}_1//\mathscr{Q})$. Since $\mathscr{R}$ has fewer than $k + 1$ occurrences of logical operators, it follows from the inductive hypothesis that, on any interpretation, a variable assignment satisfies $\mathscr{R}$ if and only if it satisfies $[\mathscr{R}](\mathscr{Q}_1//\mathscr{Q})$. Since an assignment satisfies a formula if and only if it fails to satisfy the negation of the formula, it follows that on any interpretation a variable assignment satisfies $\sim \mathscr{R}$ if and only if it satisfies $\sim [\mathscr{R}](\mathscr{Q}_1//\mathscr{Q})$.

(ii)–(v) $\mathscr{P}$ is of the form $\mathscr{R}\ \&\ \mathscr{S}$, $\mathscr{R} \vee \mathscr{S}$, $\mathscr{R} \supset \mathscr{S}$, or $\mathscr{R} \equiv \mathscr{S}$. These cases are handled similarly to case (ii) in the inductive proof of Lemma 6.1 (in Chapter 6), with obvious adjustments as in case (i).

(vi) $\mathscr{P}$ is of the form $(\forall x)\mathscr{R}$. Since $\mathscr{Q}$ is a proper subformula of $\mathscr{P}$, $\mathscr{Q}$ is a subformula of $\mathscr{R}$. Therefore $[\mathscr{P}](\mathscr{Q}_1//\mathscr{Q})$ is $(\forall x)[\mathscr{R}](\mathscr{Q}_1//\mathscr{Q})$. Since $\mathscr{R}$ has fewer than $k + 1$ occurrences of logical operators, it follows, by the inductive hypothesis, that on any interpretation a variable assignment satisfies $\mathscr{R}$ if and only if that assignment satisfies $[\mathscr{R}](\mathscr{Q}_1//\mathscr{Q})$. Now $(\forall x)\mathscr{R}$ is satisfied by a variable assignment **d** if and only if for each member **u** of the UD, $\mathbf{d}[\mathbf{u}/x]$ satisfies $\mathscr{R}$. The latter is the case just in case $[\mathscr{R}](\mathscr{Q}_1//\mathscr{Q})$ is satisfied by every variant $\mathbf{d}[\mathbf{u}/x]$. And this is the case if and only if $(\forall x)[\mathscr{R}](\mathscr{Q}_1//\mathscr{Q})$ is satisfied by **d**. Therefore on any interpretation $(\forall x)\mathscr{R}$ is satisfied by a variable assignment if and only if $(\forall x)[\mathscr{R}](\mathscr{Q}_1//\mathscr{Q})$ is satisfied by that assignment.

(vii) $\mathscr{P}$ is of the form $(\exists x)\mathscr{R}$. This case is similar to case (vi).

3. $\mathscr{Q}_{k+1}$ is justified at position $k + 1$ by Quantifier Negation. Then $\mathscr{Q}_{k+1}$ is derived as follows:

h	$\mathscr{S}$	
$k + 1$	$\mathscr{Q}_{k+1}$	h QN

where some component $\mathscr{R}$ of $\mathscr{S}$ has been replaced by a component $\mathscr{R}_1$ to obtain $\mathscr{Q}_{k+1}$ and the four forms that $\mathscr{R}$ and $\mathscr{R}_1$ may have are

$\mathscr{R}$ is	$\mathscr{R}_1$ is
$\sim (\forall x)\mathscr{P}$	$(\exists x) \sim \mathscr{P}$
$(\exists x) \sim \mathscr{P}$	$\sim (\forall x)\mathscr{P}$
$\sim (\exists x)\mathscr{P}$	$(\forall x) \sim \mathscr{P}$
$(\forall x) \sim \mathscr{P}$	$\sim (\exists x)\mathscr{P}$

Whichever pair $\mathscr{R}$ and $\mathscr{R}_1$ constitute, the two sentences contain exactly the same nonlogical constants. We first establish that on any interpretation variable assignment **d** satisfies $\mathscr{R}$ if and only if **d** satisfies $\mathscr{R}_1$.

(i) Either $\mathcal{R}$ is $\sim (\forall x)\mathcal{P}$ and $\mathcal{R}_1$ is $(\exists x) \sim \mathcal{P}$, or $\mathcal{R}$ is $(\exists x) \sim \mathcal{P}$ and $\mathcal{R}_1$ is $\sim (\forall x)\mathcal{P}$. Assume that a variable assignment **d** satisfies $\sim (\forall x)\mathcal{P}$. Then **d** does not satisfy $(\forall x)\mathcal{P}$. There is then at least one variant **d**[**u**/x] that does not satisfy $\mathcal{P}$. Hence **d**[**u**/x] satisfies $\sim \mathcal{P}$. It follows that **d**[**u**/x] satisfies $(\exists x) \sim \mathcal{P}$. Now assume that a variable assignment **d** satisfies $(\exists x) \sim \mathcal{P}$. Then some variant **d**[**u**/x] satisfies $\sim \mathcal{P}$. This variant does not satisfy $\mathcal{P}$. Therefore **d** does not satisfy $(\forall x)\mathcal{P}$ and does satisfy $\sim (\forall x)\mathcal{P}$.

(ii) Either $\mathcal{R}$ is $\sim (\exists x)\mathcal{P}$ and $\mathcal{R}_1$ is $(\forall x) \sim \mathcal{P}$, or $\mathcal{R}$ is $(\forall x) \sim \mathcal{P}$ and $\mathcal{R}_1$ is $\sim (\exists x)\mathcal{P}$. This case is similar to case (i).

$\mathcal{R}$ and $\mathcal{R}_1$ contain the same nonlogical symbols and variables, so it follows, by 11.2.3 (Exercise 2), that $\mathcal{S}$ is satisfied by a variable assignment if and only if $\mathcal{Q}_{k+1}$ is satisfied by that assignment. So on any interpretation $\mathcal{S}$ and $\mathcal{Q}_{k+1}$ have the same truth-value.

By the inductive hypothesis, $\Gamma_k \vDash \mathcal{S}$. But Γ_k is a subset of Γ_{k+1}, and so $\Gamma_{k+1} \vDash \mathcal{S}$, by 11.2.1. Since $\mathcal{S}$ and $\mathcal{Q}_{k+1}$ have the same truth-value on any interpretation, it follows that $\Gamma_{k+1} \vDash \mathcal{Q}_{k+1}$.

Section 11.3E

2. Assume that $\Gamma \cup \{\sim \mathcal{P}\}$ is inconsistent in *PD*. Then there is a derivation of the following sort, where $\mathcal{Q}_1, \ldots, \mathcal{Q}_n$ are members of Γ:

1	$\mathcal{Q}_1$	Assumption
.	.	
n	$\mathcal{Q}_n$	Assumption
$n + 1$	$\sim \mathcal{P}$	Assumption
.	.	
m	$\mathcal{S}$	
.	.	
p	$\sim \mathcal{S}$	

We construct a new derivation as follows:

1	$\mathcal{Q}_1$	Assumption
.	.	
n	$\mathcal{Q}_n$	Assumption
$n + 1$	$\sim \mathcal{P}$	Assumption
.	.	
m	$\mathcal{S}$	
.	.	
p	$\sim \mathcal{S}$	
$p + 1$	$\mathcal{P}$	$n+1 - p$ $\sim$E

where lines 1 to p are as in the original derivation, except that $\sim \mathcal{P}$ is now an auxiliary assumption. This shows that $\Gamma \vDash \mathcal{P}$.

3.a. Assume that an argument of *PL* is quantificationally valid. Then the set consisting of the premises quantificationally entails the conclusion. By Metatheorem 11.2, the conclusion is derivable from that set in *PD*. Therefore the argument is valid in *PD*.

b. Assume that a sentence $\mathscr{P}$ is quantificationally true. Then $\varnothing \vDash \mathscr{P}$. By Metatheorem 11.2, $\varnothing \vdash \mathscr{P}$. So $\mathscr{P}$ is a theorem in *PD*.

4. We shall associate with each symbol of *PL* a numeral as follows. With each symbol of *PL* that is a symbol of *SL*, associate the two-digit numeral that is associated with that symbol in the enumeration of Section 6.4. With the symbol ′ (the prime) associate the numeral '66'. With the nonsubscripted lowercase letters 'a', 'b', . . . , 'z', associate the numerals '67', '68', . . . , '92', respectively. With the symbols '∀' and '∃' associate the numerals '93' and '94', respectively. (Note that the numerals '66' to '94' are not associated with any symbol of *SL*.) We then associate with each sentence of *PL* the numeral that consists of the associated numerals of each of the symbols that occur in the sentence, in the order in which the symbols occur. We now enumerate the sentences of *PL* by letting the first sentence be the sentence whose numeral designates a number that is smaller than the number designated by any other sentence's associated numeral; the second sentence is the sentence whose numeral designates the next largest number designated by the associated numeral of any sentence; and so on.

5. Assume that $\Gamma \vdash \mathscr{P}$. Then there is a derivation

$$
\begin{array}{r|l}
1 & \mathscr{Q}_1 \\
\cdot & \cdot \\
n & \mathscr{Q}_n \\
\cdot & \cdot \\ \hline
m & \mathscr{P}
\end{array}
$$

where $\mathscr{Q}_1, \ldots, \mathscr{Q}_m$ are all members of Γ. The primary assumptions are all members of any superset Γ' of Γ, and so $\Gamma' \vdash \mathscr{P}$ as well.

6.a. Assume that a does not occur in any member of the set $\Gamma \cup \{(\exists x)\mathscr{P}\}$ and that the set is consistent in *PD*. Assume, contrary to what we want to prove, that $\Gamma \cup \{(\exists x)\mathscr{P}, \mathscr{P}(a/x)\}$ is *in*consistent in *PD*. Then there is a derivation of the sort

$$
\begin{array}{r|l}
1 & \mathscr{Q}_1 \\
\cdot & \cdot \\
n & \mathscr{Q}_n \\
n+1 & (\exists x)\mathscr{P} \\
n+2 & \mathscr{P}(a/x) \\ \hline
m & \mathscr{R} \\
\cdot & \cdot \\
p & \sim \mathscr{R}
\end{array}
$$

where $\mathscr{Q}_1, \ldots, \mathscr{Q}_n$ are all members of Γ. We may convert this into a derivation showing that $\Gamma \cup \{(\exists x)\mathscr{P}\}$ is inconsistent in *PD*, contradicting our initial assumption:

1	$\mathscr{Q}_1$	
.	.	
n	$\mathscr{Q}_n$	
$n + 1$	$(\exists x)\mathscr{P}$	
$n + 2$	$\mathscr{P}(a/x)$	
$n + 3$	$(\exists x)\mathscr{P}$	
.	.	
$m + 1$	$\mathscr{R}$	
.	.	
$p + 1$	$\sim \mathscr{R}$	
$p + 2$	$\sim (\exists x)\mathscr{P}$	$n+3 - p+1$ ~I
$p + 3$	$\sim (\exists x)\mathscr{P}$	$n+2 - p+2$ ∃E
$p + 4$	$(\exists x)\mathscr{P}$	$n+1$ R

(Note that use of ∃E is legitimate at line $p + 3$ because a, by our initial hypothesis, does not occur in $(\exists x)\mathscr{P}$ or in any member of Γ.)

We conclude that if the set $\Gamma \cup \{(\exists x)\mathscr{P}\}$ is consistent in *PD* and a does not occur in any member of that set, then $\Gamma \cup \{(\exists x)\mathscr{P}(a/x)\}$ is also consistent in *PD*.

b. Let Γ^* be constructed as in our proof of Lemma 11.2. Assume that $(\exists x)\mathscr{P}$ is a member of Γ^* and that $(\exists x)\mathscr{P}$ is the ith sentence in our enumeration of the sentences of *PL*. Then, by the way each member of the infinite sequence $\Gamma_1, \Gamma_2, \Gamma_3, \ldots$ is constructed, Γ_{i+1} contains $(\exists x)\mathscr{P}$ and a substitution instance of $(\exists x)\mathscr{P}$ if $\Gamma_i \cup \{(\exists x)\mathscr{P}\}$ is consistent in *PD*. Since each member of the infinite sequence is consistent in *PD*, Γ_i is consistent to *PD*. So assume that $\Gamma_i \cup \{(\exists x)\mathscr{P}\}$ is inconsistent in *PD*. Then, since we assumed that $\mathscr{P}_i$, that is, $(\exists x)\mathscr{P}$, is a member of Γ^* and since every member of Γ_i is a member of Γ^*, it follows that Γ^* is inconsistent in *PD*. But this contradicts our original assumption, and so $\Gamma_i \cup \{(\exists x)\mathscr{P}\}$ is consistent in *PD*. Hence Γ_{i+1} is $\Gamma_i \cup \{(\exists x)\mathscr{P}, \mathscr{P}(a/x)\}$ for some constant a, and so some substitution instance of $(\exists x)\mathscr{P}$ is a member of Γ_{i+1} and thus of Γ^*.

7. We shall prove that the sentence at each position i in the new derivation can be justified by the same rule that was used at position i in the original derivation.

Basis clause: Let $i = 1$. The sentence at position 1 of the original derivation is an assumption, and so the sentence at position 1 of the new sequence can be justified similarly.

Inductive step: Assume (the inductive hypothesis) that at every position i prior to position $k + 1$, the new sequence contains a sentence that may be justified by the rule justifying the sentence at position i of the original derivation. We now prove that the sentence at position $k + 1$ of the new sequence can be justified by the rule justifying the sentence at position $k + 1$ of the original derivation. We shall consider the rules by which the sentence at position $k + 1$ of the original derivation could have been justified:

1. $\mathscr{P}$ is justified at position $k + 1$ by Assumption. Obviously, $\mathscr{P}^*$ can be justified by Assumption at position $k + 1$ of the new sequence.

2. $\mathscr{P}$ is justified at position $k + 1$ by Reiteration. Then $\mathscr{P}$ occurs at an accessible earlier position in the original derivation. Therefore $\mathscr{P}^*$ occurs at an accessible earlier position in the new sequence, so $\mathscr{P}^*$ can be justified at position $k + 1$ by Reiteration.

3. $\mathscr{P}$ is a conjunction $\mathscr{Q}$ & $\mathscr{R}$ justified at position $k + 1$ by Conjunction Introduction. Then the conjuncts $\mathscr{Q}$ and $\mathscr{R}$ of $\mathscr{P}$ occur at accessible earlier positions in the original derivation. Therefore $\mathscr{Q}^*$ and $\mathscr{R}^*$ occur at accessible earlier positions in the new sequence. So $\mathscr{P}^*$, which is just $\mathscr{Q}^*$ & $\mathscr{R}^*$, can be justified at position $k + 1$ by Conjunction Introduction.

4–12. $\mathscr{P}$ is justified by one of the other truth-functional connective introduction or elimination rules. These cases are as straightforward as case 3, so we move on to the quantifier rules.

13. $\mathscr{P}$ is a sentence $\mathscr{Q}(a/x)$ justified at position $k + 1$ by ∀E, appealing to an accessible earlier position with $(\forall x)\mathscr{Q}$. Then $(\forall x)\mathscr{Q}^*$ occurs at the accessible earlier position of the new sequence, and $\mathscr{Q}(a/x)^*$ occurs at position $k + 1$. But $\mathscr{Q}(a/x)^*$ is just a substitution instance of $(\forall x)\mathscr{Q}^*$. So $\mathscr{Q}(a/x)^*$ can be justified at position $k + 1$ by ∀E.

14. $\mathscr{P}$ is a sentence $(\exists x)\mathscr{Q}$ and is justified at position $k + 1$ by ∃I. This case is similar to case 13.

15. $\mathscr{P}$ is a sentence $(\forall x)\mathscr{Q}$ and is justified at position $k + 1$ by ∀I. Then some substitution instance occurs at an accessible earlier position j, where a is a constant that does not occur in any undischarged assumption prior to position $k + 1$ or in $(\forall x)\mathscr{Q}$. $\mathscr{Q}(a/x)^*$ and $(\forall x)\mathscr{Q}^*$ occur at positions j and $k + 1$ of the new sequence. $\mathscr{Q}(a/x)^*$ is a substitution instance of $(\forall x)\mathscr{Q}^*$. The instantiating constant a in $\mathscr{Q}(a/x)$ is some a_i, and so the instantiating constant in $\mathscr{Q}(a/x)^*$ is b_i. Since a_i did not occur in any undischarged assumption before position $k + 1$ or in $(\forall x)\mathscr{Q}$ in the original derivation and b_i does not occur in the original derivation, b_i does not occur in any undischarged assumption prior to position $k + 1$ of the new sequence or in $(\forall x)\mathscr{Q}^*$. So $(\forall x)\mathscr{Q}^*$ can be justified by ∀I at position $k + 1$ in the new sequence.

16. $\mathscr{P}$ is justified at position $k + 1$ by ∃E. This case is similar to case 15.

Since every sentence in the new sequence can be justified by a rule of *PD*, it follows that the new sequence is indeed a derivation of *PD*.

10. We required that Γ^* be ∃-complete so that we could construct an interpretation I* for which we could *prove* that every member of Γ^* is true on I*. In requiring that Γ be ∃-complete in addition to being maximally consistent in *PD*, we were guaranteed that Γ^* had property g of sets that are both maximally consistent in *PD* and ∃-complete; and we used this fact in case 7 of the proof that every member of Γ* is true on I*.

11. To prove that *PD** is complete for predicate logic, it will suffice to show that with ∀E* instead of ∀E, every set Γ* of *PD** that is both maximally consistent in *PD** and ∃-complete has property f (i.e., $(\forall x)\mathscr{P} \in \Gamma^*$ if and only if for every constant a, $\mathscr{P}(a/x) \in \Gamma^*$). For the properties a to e and g can be shown to characterize such sets by appealing to the rules of *PD** that are rules of *PD*. Here is our proof:

> **Proof:** Assume that $(\forall x)\mathscr{P} \in \Gamma^*$. Then, since $\{(\forall x)\mathscr{P}\} \vdash \sim (\exists x) \sim \mathscr{P}$ by ∀E*, it follows from 11.3.3 that $\sim (\exists x) \sim \mathscr{P} \in \Gamma^*$. Then $(\exists x) \sim \mathscr{P} \notin \Gamma^*$, by a. Assume that for some substitution instance $\mathscr{P}(a/x)$ of $(\forall x)\mathscr{P}$, $\mathscr{P}(a/x) \notin \Gamma^*$. Then, by a, $\sim \mathscr{P}(a/x) \in \Gamma^*$. Since $\{\sim \mathscr{P}(a/x)\} \vdash (\exists x) \sim \mathscr{P}$ (without use of ∀E), it follows that $(\exists x) \sim \mathscr{P} \in \Gamma^*$. But we have just shown that $(\exists x) \sim \mathscr{P} \notin \Gamma^*$. Hence, if $(\forall x)\mathscr{P} \in \Gamma^*$, then every substitution instance $\mathscr{P}(a/x)$ of $(\forall x)\mathscr{P}$ is a member of Γ*.
>
> Now assume that $(\forall x)\mathscr{P} \notin \Gamma^*$. Then, by a, $\sim (\forall x)\mathscr{P} \in \Gamma^*$. But then, since $\{\sim (\forall x)\mathscr{P}\} \vdash (\exists x) \sim \mathscr{P}$ (without use of ∀E), it follows that $(\exists x) \sim \mathscr{P} \in \Gamma^*$. Since Γ* is ∃-complete, some substitution instance $\sim \mathscr{P}(a/x)$ of $(\exists x) \sim \mathscr{P}$ is a member of Γ*. By a, $\mathscr{P}(a/x) \notin \Gamma^*$.

13. Assume that some sentence $\mathscr{P}$ is not quantificationally false. Then $\mathscr{P}$ is true on at least one interpretation, so $\{\mathscr{P}\}$ is quantificationally consistent. Now suppose that $\{\mathscr{P}\}$ is inconsistent in *PD*. Then some sentences $\mathscr{Q}$ and $\sim \mathscr{Q}$ are derivable from $\{\mathscr{P}\}$ in *PD*. By Metatheorem 11.1, it follows that $\{\mathscr{P}\} \vDash \mathscr{Q}$ and $\{\mathscr{P}\} \vDash \sim \mathscr{Q}$. But then $\mathscr{P}$ cannot be true on any interpretation, contrary to our assumption. So $\{\mathscr{P}\}$ is consistent in *PD*. By Lemma 11.2, $\{\mathscr{P}_e\}$—the set resulting from doubling the subscript of every individual constant in $\mathscr{P}$—is a subset of a set Γ* that is both maximally consistent in *PD* and ∃-complete. It follows from Lemma 11.3 that Γ* is quantificationally consistent. But, in proving 11.3, we actually showed more—for the characteristic interpretation I* that we constructed for Γ* has the set of positive integers as UD. Hence every member of Γ* is true on some interpretation with the set of positive integers as UD, and thus $\mathscr{P}_e$ is true on some interpretation with the set of positive integers as UD. $\mathscr{P}$ can also be shown true on some interpretation with that UD, using 11.1.13.

16. Consider the sentence '(∀x)(∀y)x = y'. This sentence is not quantificationally false; it is true on every interpretation with a one-member UD. In addition, however, it is true on *only* those interpretations that have one-member UDs. (This is because for any variable assignment and any members $\mathbf{u}_1$ and $\mathbf{u}_2$ of a UD, $\mathbf{d}[\mathbf{u}_1/x, \mathbf{u}_2/y]$ satisfies 'x = y' as required for the truth of '(∀x)(∀y)x = y' if and only if $\mathbf{u}_1$ and $\mathbf{u}_2$ are the same object.) So there can be no interpretation with the set of positive integers as UD on which the sentence is true.

Section 11.4E

2.a. Assume that for some sentence $\mathscr{P}$, $\{\mathscr{P}\}$ has a closed truth-tree. Then, by Exercise 1, $\{\mathscr{P}\}$ is quantificationally inconsistent. Hence there is no interpretation on which $\mathscr{P}$, the sole member of $\{\mathscr{P}\}$, is true. Therefore $\mathscr{P}$ is quantificationally false.

b. Assume that for some sentence $\mathscr{P}$, $\{\sim \mathscr{P}\}$ has a closed truth-tree. Then, by Exercise 1, $\{\sim \mathscr{P}\}$ is quantificationally inconsistent. Hence there is no interpretation on which $\sim \mathscr{P}$ is true. So $\mathscr{P}$ is true on every interpretation; that is, $\mathscr{P}$ is quantificationally true.

d. Assume that $\Gamma \cup \{\sim \mathscr{P}\}$ has a closed truth-tree. Then, by Exercise 1, $\Gamma \cup \{\sim \mathscr{P}\}$ is quantificationally inconsistent. Hence there is no interpretation on which every member of Γ is true and $\sim \mathscr{P}$ is also true. That is, there is no interpretation on which every member of Γ is true and $\mathscr{P}$ is false. But then $\Gamma \vDash \mathscr{P}$.

3.a. $\mathscr{P}$ is obtained from $\sim \sim \mathscr{P}$ by $\sim \sim$D. It is straightforward that $\{\sim \sim \mathscr{P}\} \vDash \mathscr{P}$.

d. $\mathscr{P}$ or $\sim \mathscr{Q}$ is obtained from $\sim (\mathscr{P} \supset \mathscr{Q})$ by $\sim \supset$D. On any interpretation on which $\sim (\mathscr{P} \supset \mathscr{Q})$ is true, $\mathscr{P} \supset \mathscr{Q}$ is false—hence $\mathscr{P}$ is true and $\mathscr{Q}$ is false. But, if $\mathscr{Q}$ is false, then $\sim \mathscr{Q}$ is true. Thus $\{\sim (\mathscr{P} \supset \mathscr{Q})\} \vDash \mathscr{P}$, and $\{\sim (\mathscr{P} \supset \mathscr{Q})\} \vDash \sim \mathscr{Q}$.

e. $\mathscr{P}(a/x)$ is obtained from $(\forall x)\mathscr{P}$ by $\forall$D. It follows, from 11.1.4, that $\{(\forall x)\mathscr{P}\} \vDash \mathscr{P}(a/x)$.

4.a. $\sim \mathscr{P}$ and $\sim \mathscr{Q}$ are obtained from $\sim (\mathscr{P} \,\&\, \mathscr{Q})$ by $\sim$ &D. On any interpretation on which $\sim (\mathscr{P} \,\&\, \mathscr{Q})$ is true, $\mathscr{P} \,\&\, \mathscr{Q}$ is false. But then either $\mathscr{P}$ is false, or $\mathscr{Q}$ is false. Hence on such an interpretation either $\sim \mathscr{P}$ is true, or $\sim \mathscr{Q}$ is true.

5. The path is extended to form two paths to level $k + 1$ as a result of applying one of the branching rules $\equiv$D or $\sim \equiv$D to a sentence $\mathscr{P}$ on Γ_k. We consider four cases.

a. Sentences $\mathscr{P}$ and $\sim \mathscr{P}$ are entered at level $k + 1$ as the result of applying $\equiv$D to a sentence $\mathscr{P} \equiv \mathscr{Q}$ on Γ_k. On any interpretation on which $\mathscr{P} \equiv \mathscr{Q}$ is true, so is either $\mathscr{P}$ or $\sim \mathscr{P}$. Therefore either $\mathscr{P}$ and all the sentences on Γ_k are true on $\mathbf{I}_{\Gamma k}$, which is a path variant of $\mathbf{I}$ for the new path containing $\mathscr{P}$, or $\sim \mathscr{P}$ and all the sentences on Γ_k are true on $\mathbf{I}_{\Gamma k}$, which is a path variant of $\mathbf{I}$ for the new path containing $\sim \mathscr{P}$.

b. Sentence $\mathscr{Q}$ (or $\sim \mathscr{Q}$) is entered at level $k + 1$ as the result of applying $\equiv$D to a sentence $\mathscr{P} \equiv \mathscr{Q}$ on Γ_k. Then $\mathscr{P}$ (or $\sim \mathscr{P}$) occurs on Γ_k at level k (application of $\equiv$D involves making entries at two levels, and $\mathscr{Q}$ and $\sim \mathscr{Q}$ are entries made on the second of these levels). Since $\{\mathscr{P} \equiv \mathscr{Q}, \mathscr{P}\}$ quantificationally entails $\mathscr{Q}$ (and $\{\mathscr{P} \equiv \mathscr{Q}, \sim \mathscr{P}\}$ quantificationally entails $\sim \mathscr{Q}$), it follows that $\mathscr{Q}$ and all the sentences on Γ_k ($\sim \mathscr{Q}$ and all the sentences on Γ_k) are all true on $\mathbf{I}_{\Gamma k}$, which is a path variant of $\mathbf{I}$ for the new path containing $\mathscr{Q}$ ($\sim \mathscr{Q}$).

c. Sentences $\mathscr{P}$ and $\sim \mathscr{P}$ are entered at level $k + 1$ as the result of applying $\sim \equiv$D to a sentence $\sim (\mathscr{P} \equiv \mathscr{Q})$ on Γ_k. This case is similar to (a).

d. Sentence $\mathscr{Q}$ (or $\sim \mathscr{Q}$) is entered at level $k + 1$ as the result of applying $\sim \equiv$D to a sentence $\sim (\mathscr{P} \equiv \mathscr{Q})$ on Γ_k. This case is similar to (b).

6. Yes. Dropping a rule would not make the method unsound, for, with the remaining rules, it would still follow that if a branch on a tree for a set Γ closes, then Γ is quantificationally inconsistent. That is, the remaining rules would still be consistency-preserving.

7. In proving that the tree method for *SL* is sound, there are obvious adjustments that must be made in the proof of Metatheorem 11.3. First, not all the tree rules for *PL* are tree rules for *SL*. In proving Lemma 11.4, then, we take only the tree rules for *SL* into consideration. And in the case of *SL* we would be proving that certain sets are truth-functionally consistent or inconsistent, rather than quantificationally consistent or inconsistent. The basic semantic concept for *SL* is that of a truth-value assignment, rather than an interpretation. With these stipulations, the proof of Metatheorem 11.3 can be converted straightforwardly into a proof of the parallel metatheorem for *SL*.

Section 11.5E

1.a. Assume that a sentence $\mathcal{P}$ is quantificationally false. Then $\{\mathcal{P}\}$ is quantificationally inconsistent. It follows from Metatheorem 11.5 that every systematic tree for $\{\mathcal{P}\}$ closes.

b. Assume that a sentence $\mathcal{P}$ is quantificationally true. Then $\sim \mathcal{P}$ is quantificationally false, and $\{\sim \mathcal{P}\}$ is quantificationally inconsistent. It follows from Metatheorem 11.5 that every systematic tree for $\{\sim \mathcal{P}\}$ closes.

d. Assume that $\Gamma \vDash \mathcal{P}$. Then on every interpretation on which every member of Γ is true, $\mathcal{P}$ is true, and $\sim \mathcal{P}$ is therefore false. So $\Gamma \cup \{\sim \mathcal{P}\}$ is quantificationally inconsistent. It follows from Metatheorem 11.5 that every systematic tree for $\Gamma \cup \{\sim \mathcal{P}\}$ closes.

2.a. The lengths are 6, 2, and 6, respectively.

b. Assume that the length of a sentence $\sim (\mathcal{Q} \,\&\, \mathcal{R})$ is k. Then since $\sim (\mathcal{Q} \,\&\, \mathcal{R})$ contains an occurrence of the tilde and an occurrence of the ampersand that neither $\mathcal{Q}$ nor $\mathcal{R}$ contains, the length of $\mathcal{Q}$ is $k - 2$ or less and the length of $\mathcal{R}$ is $k - 2$ or less. Hence the length of $\sim \mathcal{Q}$ is $k - 1$ or less, and the length of $\sim \mathcal{R}$ is $k - 1$ or less.

d. Assume that the length of a sentence $\sim (\forall x)\mathcal{Q}$ is k. Then the length of the formula $\mathcal{Q}$ is $k - 2$. Hence the length of $\mathcal{Q}(a/x)$ is $k - 2$, since $\mathcal{Q}(a/x)$ differs from $\mathcal{Q}$ only in containing a wherever $\mathcal{Q}$ contains x and neither constants nor variables are counted in computing the length of a formula. Hence the length of $\sim \mathcal{Q}(a/x)$ is $k - 1$.

3.a. $\mathcal{P}$ is of the form $\mathcal{Q} \vee \mathcal{R}$. Assume that $\mathcal{P} \in \Gamma$. Then, by e, either $\mathcal{Q} \in \Gamma$, or $\mathcal{R} \in \Gamma$. If $\mathcal{Q} \in \Gamma$, then $\mathbf{I}(\mathcal{Q}) = \mathbf{T}$, by the inductive hypothesis. If $\mathcal{R} \in \Gamma$, then $\mathbf{I}(\mathcal{R}) = \mathbf{T}$, by the inductive hypothesis. Either way, it follows that $\mathbf{I}(\mathcal{Q} \vee \mathcal{R}) = \mathbf{T}$.

c. $\mathcal{P}$ is of the form $\mathcal{Q} \supset \mathcal{R}$. Assume that $\mathcal{P} \in \Gamma$. Then, by g, either $\sim \mathcal{Q} \in \Gamma$ or $\mathcal{R} \in \Gamma$. By the inductive hypothesis, then, either $\mathbf{I}(\sim \mathcal{Q}) = \mathbf{T}$ or $\mathbf{I}(\mathcal{R}) = \mathbf{T}$. So either $\mathbf{I}(\mathcal{Q}) = \mathbf{F}$ or $\mathbf{I}(\mathcal{R}) = \mathbf{T}$. Consequently, $\mathbf{I}(\mathcal{Q} \supset \mathcal{R}) = \mathbf{T}$.

f. $\mathcal{P}$ is of the form $\sim (\mathcal{Q} \equiv \mathcal{R})$. Assume that $\mathcal{P} \in \Gamma$. Then, by j, either both $\mathcal{Q} \in \Gamma$ and $\sim \mathcal{R} \in \Gamma$, or both $\sim \mathcal{Q} \in \Gamma$ and $\mathcal{R} \in \Gamma$. In the former case, $\mathbf{I}(\mathcal{Q}) = \mathbf{T}$ and

$\mathbf{I}(\sim \mathcal{R}) = \mathbf{T}$, by the inductive hypothesis; so $\mathbf{I}(\mathcal{Q}) = \mathbf{T}$ and $\mathbf{I}(\mathcal{R}) = \mathbf{F}$. In the latter case, $\mathbf{I}(\sim \mathcal{Q}) = \mathbf{T}$ and $\mathbf{I}(\mathcal{R}) = \mathbf{T}$, by the inductive hypothesis; hence $\mathbf{I}(\mathcal{Q}) = \mathbf{F}$ and $\mathbf{I}(\mathcal{R}) = \mathbf{T}$. Either way, it follows that $\mathbf{I}(\mathcal{Q} \equiv \mathcal{R}) = \mathbf{F}$, and so $\mathbf{I}(\sim (\mathcal{Q} \equiv \mathcal{R})) = \mathbf{T}$.

g. $\mathcal{P}$ is of the form $(\exists x)\mathcal{Q}$. Assume that $\mathcal{P} \in \Gamma$. Then, by m, there is some constant a such that $\mathcal{Q}(a/x) \in \Gamma$. By the inductive hypothesis, $\mathbf{I}(\mathcal{Q}(a/x)) = \mathbf{T}$. By 11.1.5, $\{\mathcal{Q}(a/x)\} \vDash (\exists x)\mathcal{Q}$. So $\mathbf{I}((\exists x)\mathcal{Q}) = \mathbf{T}$ as well.

5. Clauses 7 and 9. First consider clause 7. Suppose that $\mathcal{Q} \supset \mathcal{R}$ has k occurrences of logical operators. Then $\mathcal{Q}$ certainly has fewer than k occurrences of logical operators, and so does $\mathcal{R}$. But, in the proof for case 7, once we assume that $\mathcal{Q} \supset \mathcal{R} \in \Gamma$, we know that $\sim \mathcal{Q}$ or $\mathcal{R}$ is a member of Γ by property g of Hintikka sets. The problem is that we cannot apply the inductive hypothesis to $\sim \mathcal{Q}$ since $\sim \mathcal{Q}$ might contain k occurrences of logical operators. In the sentence '(Am & Bm) $\supset$ Bm', for instance, this happens. The entire sentence has two occurrences of logical operators, but so does the negation of the antecedent '$\sim$ (Am & Bm)'. However, it can easily be shown that the *length* of $\sim \mathcal{Q}$ is less than the *length* of $\mathcal{Q} \supset \mathcal{R}$.

Similarly, in the case of clause 9 we know that if $\mathcal{Q} \equiv \mathcal{R} \in \Gamma$, then either both $\mathcal{Q} \in \Gamma$ and $\mathcal{R} \in \Gamma$ or both $\sim \mathcal{Q} \in \Gamma$ and $\sim \mathcal{R} \in \Gamma$. But then we are not guaranteed that either $\sim \mathcal{Q}$ or $\sim \mathcal{R}$ has fewer occurrences of logical operators than does $\mathcal{Q} \equiv \mathcal{R}$. For instance, '$\sim$ Am' and '$\sim$ Bm' each contain one occurrence of a logical operator, and so does 'Am $\equiv$ Bm'.

6. If $\exists$D were not included, then we could not be assured that the set of sentences on each nonclosed branch of a systematic tree has property m of Hintikka sets. And in the inductive proof that every Hintikka set is quantificationally consistent we made use of this property in steps (12) and (13).

7. Yes, it would. For let us trace those places in our proof of Metatheorem 11.5 where we appealed to the rule $\sim \forall$D. We used it to establish that the set of sentences on a nonclosed branch of a systematic tree has property l of Hintikka sets, and we appealed to property l in step (12) of our inductive proof of Lemma 11.7. So let us first replace property l by the following:

> l*. If $\sim (\forall x)\mathcal{P} \in \Gamma$, then, for some constant a that occurs in some sentence in Γ, $\sim \mathcal{P}(a/x) \in \Gamma$.

It is then easily established that every nonclosed branch of a systematic tree has properties a to k, l*, and m to n. In our inductive proof of Lemma 11.7, change step (12) to the following:

12*. $\mathcal{P}$ is of the form $\sim (\forall x)\mathcal{Q}$. Assume that $\mathcal{P} \in \Gamma$. Then, by l*, there is some constant a such that $\sim \mathcal{Q}(a/x) \in \Gamma$. By the inductive hypothesis, $\mathbf{I}(\sim \mathcal{Q}(a/x)) = \mathbf{T}$, and so $\mathbf{I}(\mathcal{Q}(a/x)) = \mathbf{F}$. Since $\{(\forall x)\mathcal{Q}\} \vDash \mathcal{Q}(a/x)$, by 11.1.4, it follows that $\mathbf{I}((\forall x)\mathcal{Q}) = \mathbf{F}$ and $\mathbf{I}(\sim (\forall x)\mathcal{Q}) = \mathbf{T}$.

8. Certain adjustments are obvious if we are to convert the proof of Metatheorem 11.5 into a proof that the tree method for *SL* is complete for sentential logic. The tree method for *SL* contains only some of the rules of the tree method for *PL;* hence we have fewer rules to work with. We replace talk of quantificational concepts (consistency and the like) with talk of truth-functional concepts, hence talk of interpretations with talk of truth-value assignments.

A Hintikka set of *SL* will have only properties a to j of Hintikka sets for *PL*. And trees for *SL* are *all* finite, so we have only finite open branches to consider in this case. (Thus Lemma 11.6 would not be used in the proof for *SL*.) Finally, the construction of the characteristic truth-value assignment for a Hintikka set of *SL* requires only clause 2 of the construction of the characteristic interpretation for a Hintikka set of *PL*.

9. We must first show that a set Γ^* that is both maximally consistent in *PD* and $\exists$-complete has the 14 properties of Hintikka sets. We list those properties here. (And we refer to the 7 properties a to g of sets that are both maximally consistent in *PD* and $\exists$-complete as 'M(a)', 'M(b)', . . . , 'M(g)'.)

a. For any atomic sentence $\mathcal{P}$, not both $\mathcal{P}$ and $\sim \mathcal{P}$ are members of Γ^*.

Proof: This follows immediately from property M(a) of Γ^*.

b. If $\sim\sim \mathcal{P}$ is a member of Γ^*, then $\mathcal{P}$ is a member of Γ^*.

Proof: If $\sim\sim \mathcal{P} \in \Gamma^*$, then $\sim \mathcal{P} \notin \Gamma^*$, by M(a), and $\mathcal{P} \in \Gamma^*$, by M(a).

c. If $\mathcal{P} \,\&\, \mathcal{Q} \in \Gamma^*$, then $\mathcal{P} \in \Gamma^*$ and $\mathcal{Q} \in \Gamma^*$.

Proof: This follows from property M(b) of Γ^*.

d. If $\sim (\mathcal{P} \,\&\, \mathcal{Q}) \in \Gamma^*$, then either $\sim \mathcal{P} \in \Gamma^*$ or $\sim \mathcal{Q} \in \Gamma^*$.

Proof: If $\sim (\mathcal{P} \,\&\, \mathcal{Q}) \in \Gamma^*$, then $\mathcal{P} \,\&\, \mathcal{Q} \notin \Gamma^*$, by M(a). By M(b), either $\mathcal{P} \notin \Gamma^*$ or $\mathcal{Q} \notin \Gamma^*$. By M(a), either $\sim \mathcal{P} \in \Gamma^*$ or $\sim \mathcal{Q} \in \Gamma^*$.

e to j are established similarly.

k. If $(\forall x)\mathcal{P} \in \Gamma$, then at least one substitution instance of $(\forall x)\mathcal{P}$ is a member of Γ and for every constant a that occurs in some sentence of Γ, $\mathcal{P}(a/x) \in \Gamma$.

Proof: This follows from property M(f) of Γ^*.

l. If $\sim (\forall x)\mathcal{P} \in \Gamma^*$, then $(\exists x) \sim \mathcal{P} \in \Gamma^*$.

Proof: If $\sim (\forall x)\mathcal{P} \in \Gamma^*$, then $(\forall x)\mathcal{P} \notin \Gamma^*$, by M(a). Then, for some constant a, $\mathcal{P}(a/x) \notin \Gamma^*$, by M(f). Then $\sim \mathcal{P}(a/x) \in \Gamma^*$, by M(a). So $(\exists x) \sim \mathcal{P} \in \Gamma^*$, by M(g).

m. If $(\exists x)\mathcal{P} \in \Gamma^*$, then, for at least one constant a, $\mathcal{P}(a/x) \in \Gamma^*$.

Proof: This follows from property M(g) of Γ^*.

n. If $\sim (\exists x)\mathscr{P} \in \Gamma^*$, then $(\forall x) \sim \mathscr{P} \in \Gamma^*$.

Proof: If $\sim (\exists x)\mathscr{P} \in \Gamma^*$, then $(\exists x)\mathscr{P} \notin \Gamma^*$, by M(a). Then, for every constant a, $\mathscr{P}(a/x) \notin \Gamma^*$, by M(g). So, for every constant a, $\sim \mathscr{P}(a/x) \in \Gamma^*$, by M(a). And $(\forall x) \sim \mathscr{P} \in \Gamma^*$, by M(f).

Second, we show that every Hintikka set is ∃-complete follows from property m of Hintikka sets.

Third, we show that some Hintikka sets are *not* maximally consistent in *PD*. Here is an example of such a set:

{(∀x)Fx, (∃y)Fy, Fa}

It is easily verified that this set is a Hintikka set. And the set is of course consistent in *PD*. But this set is *not* such that the addition to the set of any sentence that is not already a member will create an inconsistent set. For instance, the sentence 'Fb' may be added, and the resulting set is also consistent in *PD:*

{(∀x)Fx, (∃y)Fy, Fa, Fb}

Hence the set is not maximally consistent in *PD*.